International Federation of Library Associations and Institutions
Fédération Internationale des Associations de Bibliothécaires et des Bibliothèques
Internationaler Verband der bibliothekarischen Vereine und Institutionen
Международная Федерация Библиотечных Ассоциаций и Учреждений
Federación Internacional de Asociaciones de Bibliotecarios y Bibliotecas

IFLA Universal Bibliographic Control
and International MARC Programme
Deutsche Bibliothek, Frankfurt am Main

UBCIM Publications – New Series Vol 25

Subject Retrieval in a Networked Environment

Proceedings of the IFLA Satellite Meeting held in Dublin, OH, 14-16 August 2001 and sponsored by the IFLA Classification and Indexing Section, the IFLA Information Technology Section and OCLC

Edited by
I.C. McIlwaine

K · G · Saur München 2003

UBCIM Publications
New Series

Edited by Marie-France Plassard

Bibliographic information published by Die Deutsche Bibliothek
Die Deutsche Bibliothek lists this publication in the Deutsche Nationalbibliografie; detailed bibliographic data is available in the internet at http://dnb.ddb.de.

∞

Printed on acid-free paper / Gedruckt auf säurefreiem Papier

K. G. Saur Verlag GmbH, München 2003

Printed in Germany

Printed and Bound by Strauss Offsetdruck GmbH, Mörlenbach

ISBN 3-598-11634-9

Contents

Introduction

The IFLA Classification and Indexing Section together with the Information Technology Section, and with sponsorship from OCLC, hosted this conference from August 14th to 16th 2001. The support, both in terms of financial backing, and even more in human resources provided by OCLC was the deciding factor in making the event so successful and IFLA is indebted to the organization, and especially to Joan Mitchell, for both the administrative and the technical backup that was given.

The conference got off to a flying start with a most memorable and thought-provoking keynote address from Cliff Lynch. This set the tone for the succeeding two and a half days. Many of the points which he highlighted recurred in the papers presented and contained in this volume. It was salutary to be reminded of the past rôle of librarians in the business of organizing knowledge and to hear him warn against "throwing out the baby with the bath-water". He emphasized the part that librarians have always played in creating standards for subject retrieval. These past endeavours have much to contribute to the networked environment and should not be disregarded by computer scientists and others in the attempt to improve retrieval systems in the networked environment. Conferences such as this one which bring together the efforts of both disciplines must surely be the most profitable way forward to the solution of today's problems.

Eric Jul, in his summing up at the end of the conference, returned to the points that were raised at the outset and attempted to pull together some of the themes that had been explored. He identified the problems that had been addressed and the proposed solutions which in many cases go part of the way in the attempt to cope with today's challenges but which still have some ground to cover before all the difficulties are resolved. The aim is to provide information seekers with what they want when they want it, in a format they can use and at an affordable price. This sounds simple when put into words, it is far from simple when it comes to actions. The challenge is not a light one, especially given the rising user expectations and the acceleration of the pace of change. Knowledge itself is constantly changing and new fields are emerging daily.

It has been suggested that today we live in a "knowledge economy" or an "information economy" and that future historians may refer to the period around 2000 as the "age of information" (Burke, 2000).[1] We are not, however, indulging in anything new. We are following in very well trodden footsteps, and the organization of information has been practised by governments for more that two and a half millennia. The principal difference that faces us today is the speed with which information is amassed and the quantities of it, together with constant economic pressures. All these conflicting aims were only too apparent in the discussions which ranged over two and a half days that August in Dublin OH.

Librarians, however, have great strengths on which they can draw, as Cliff Lynch was quick to point out at the outset of the proceedings, not least in their classification schemes and approach to subject analysis, which is a feature that shines through the present collection of papers. They also have the most widely adopted metadata standard formats, in addition to widely distributed institutions for organized and efficient access to knowledge resources. The long and outstanding history of professional training, and the resultant methodologies, values and ethics that are evidence of true professionalism, together with the tradition for co-operation, all make librarians eminently suited to cope with today's challenges. The ways in which they are attempting to do this can be deduced from the varied research projects and experiments discussed in the following pages.

In order to face the future with confidence, information professionals have to realize that the need for information is universal, but that the types of information required are infinite. It is a fundamental human characteristic to have an enquiring mind. This has always been the case, but we have to adapt our responses to this need to ways that can cope with our current challenge. Here, we need to guard against responding too slowly – caution is valuable, but there are times when speed is even more important. It is also important to bear in mind the need to achieve a successful outcome without exorbitant expense. The situation today is highly complex both for those who are creating knowledge (or information) and for those concerned with knowledge organization and knowledge management.

But, above all, it is the user of that knowledge whose needs must be paramount in the minds of professionals. It is essential that there is quick action, and it is those who have always been in the forefront of organizing knowledge and responding to requests for information who must take the lead and face the challenges of the future. This conference was conceived with the specific purpose of exploring ways in which that can be achieved. It is highly necessary to demonstrate the value of what we have to offer to our users, who will be our sternest critics. We have to respond rapidly to the new users of information, who are working in an unfamiliar environment. We have to find flexible approaches and we have constantly to bear in mind the economics of what we are attempting.

The papers presented at this conference demonstrate clearly our present predicament. We are still at the stage of trial and error. The diversity of context, both in term of the representation of all sectors of the information community, academic and commercial, public service and private organizations and the geographic spread over at least fourteen different countries and three continents demonstrates just how universal these concerns are. We were presented with many discrete projects and approaches to solutions. The use of the thesaurus remains the most favoured solution, and we were shown many projects involving mapping, attempts to cope with multilingual solutions and with pleas for better and more frequently revised standards to assist in the task. Classification schemes, too, are attempting to adapt themselves and redefine their parameters to handle a situation which is no longer primarily concerned with books on shelves, though that traditional usage must not be overlooked, which adds to the complexity. At the present time, there is a vital need for participation and the sharing of ideas, both through formal written media and informal fora. Communication and collaboration have to be the way towards resolving our dilemma. The way forward must lie with international interchange of information, and what better forum that IFLA to promote this. We need to exchange ideas about our activities and talk about experiments with new methods and the redesign of the old tried and tested ones, to cope with the present situation. The combination of our traditional systems with innovative approaches proposed by those working in allied fields, such as Computer Science, will advance the cause of information exchange in the networked world. Open standards and hybrid approaches must be the way forward to reaching solutions.

All these, and many other ideas were discussed at the conference, where there was ample opportunity for the interchange of ideas, both in the formal setting of the presentation of papers and in the intervals and social events provided, which all made for the encouragement of informal discussions and the amicable debate and argument which provides a fruitful environment for communication and interchange. Additionally, there were receptions each evening, hosted by OCLC and the Forest Press, and the added delight of entertainment from the OCLC string quartet. All who attended the conference expressed their gratitude for the organization, and once again, in conclusion, a special vote of thanks is owed to OCLC for its splendid organization and to Joan Mitchell and her staff for ensuring that everything proceeded so smoothly. It was a very memorable occasion.

These papers will provide a permanent record of the time spent at Dublin OH. In editing, the minimum of alteration has taken place. Some adjustments of settings have had to be made to conform with the required printed format, and this has necessitated the editing of a few tables and reproductions from web pages. The spelling has been standardized to British English, in line with IFLA policy for its publications, and a skeleton index has been appended.

I.C. McIlwaine
Norfolk
September 2002

[1] Burke, P. *A social history of knowledge*. Cambridge: Polity, 2000, p. 1.

Session 1

RETRIEVAL IN A MULTILINGUAL ENVIRONMENT

MACS: subject access across languages and networks

Elisabeth Freyre and Max Naudi

Abstract: This paper explains how MACS meets the challenge of multilingualism created by the new network environment. Based on the equality of languages and making use of work already carried out by the partners, the MACS project sets up equivalences between subject heading languages. It enables in this way, with a monolingual subject search, to retrieve all the pertinent documents held in catalogues in different languages.
This process is very different from traditional translation; it frees the search language from the language of the catalogue and creates a multilingual dictionary of subject heading languages that has a promising future for various applications. The federative approach of networked cooperation has enabled the MACS team to set up a flexible and pragmatic solution to the problem of multilingual searching. The service aims to be fully operational in 2002, and may currently be tested on the Web.

Users accessing bibliographic databases within an international framework are faced with the issue of multilingualism: while a monolingual Subject Heading Language is used in each database, subject access to all of them requires the mastery of several languages. The multilingual access proposed within the MACS Project was designed to spare library users the need for this knowledge of many languages. Contrary to common practice used for classifications, it is not based on a translation of one particular scheme (and therefore bias). Instead, the MACS approach respects languages and indexing languages, considering they reflect different cultures, and in addition enhances indexing work already done.

After first describing the problem faced by libraries in a new multilingual environment, this paper will briefly present MACS and its underlying principles. This will be followed by a description of the new solution proposed and how the partners envisage the way it should be managed in order to develop a fully operational multilingual subject access system.

1. Subject Heading Languages in a multilingual environment

Multilingual access has become a major challenge and will continue to be so for a long time, both for libraries as well as for those who work in the field of providing access to document content.

1.1 Monolingual Subject Heading Languages

Faced with the multiplicity and linguistic diversity of documents, information specialists have created tools over the years to describe their contents and to organize searches by subject. Due to their flexibility, their ability to respond swiftly to change, their sophisticated semantic structure as well as the syntactical models developed to refine indexing, Subject Heading Languages (SHLs) have shown themselves to be particularly effective at following the permanent evolution of knowledge. SHLs allow precise and relevant access via one single language to all documents whatever their original language. However, they only offer this access in the majority language of the documents to be indexed, generally the national language of the institution. They are based on a "natural" language and thus reflect that language's linguistic and cultural specificities, the language of the documents and the language of indexing being disconnected. Therefore, an effective service is provided as long as the environment remains national or, to be more precise, monolingual.

1.2 The new multilingual environment

However, this environment is becoming more and more complicated. On the one hand, because it is sometimes both national and multilingual such as in Switzerland where four national languages coexist and, on the other hand, especially because national barriers have been broken by the advent of networks and international telecommunications, particularly the Internet. Subject searching, within today's easily accessible international framework, comes up against the multiplicity of languages: to obtain relevant retrieval, users must know the various languages of the catalogues, and even the rules of various SHLs used. Therefore we can say that today's environment is universally multilingual.

1.3 The current situation of subject retrieval

As far as libraries are concerned, the challenge of multilingualism is becoming more and more crucial. Each library catalogue may be accessed from all over the world (www.bnf.fr, www.snl.ch), and many databases can be retrieved using a single search. For instance, the Karlsruher Virtueller Katalog (KVK[1]), a service launched by the Karlruhe University Library allows simultaneous subject searching within more than twenty library catalogues and union catalogues from not only German-speaking countries but also many others, thus allowing over 60 million records of documents to be accessed.

However, within a local catalogue or in the KVK, users are limited by the language they do their search in. As a result, the answer to their request is poor and irrelevant. In fact, a multi-database subject retrieval has no chance of being successful unless the subject search key fortunately happens to be the same in several languages :

> thus the subject search under "*Commedia dell'arte*" in the KVK provides answers in almost every bibliographic database, whereas the search under "*Amateur theater*" gives no answer in the German and French databases since their documents are not indexed in English.

2. The European project MACS (Multilingual Access to Subjects)

To find an efficient and consistent solution to the problem of multilingual subject access to bibliographic databases, four national libraries launched the *MACS Project*, on behalf of the Conference of European National Librarians. The four libraries are the Swiss National Library (SNL), coordinator of the project, the Bibliothèque nationale de France (BnF), the British Library (BL) and the Deutsche Bibliothek (DDB).

2.1 The aim of the project

This project aims to provide multilingual subject access to library catalogues. MACS enables users to search simultaneously with a single query in the language of their choice (English, French or German) for all relevant documents indexed by the project's partner libraries in their own language. This multilingual search is made possible thanks to the equivalence links established between the three Subject Heading Languages used in these libraries: SWD/RSWK[2] for German, RAMEAU[3] for French and LCSH[4] for English. Concepts (subject headings) from these three SHLs are mapped thanks to an intellectual work (identification of exact or partial, simple or complex equivalences) which is neither a translation, nor the creation of a new thesaurus.

2.2 The milestones of the project

The MACS project began in 1997 with a feasibility study that tried to take into account the partners' existing tools since they had of course already invested considerable time and effort in the creation and maintenance of indexing languages. These SHLs already offered subject access to millions of documents and could not be simply abandoned for a totally new one.

The study concluded[5] that it is possible to link different SHLs and proposed that a prototype should be developed to confirm the technical and operational feasibility of this approach, and to demonstrate how to use the links to search across different databases using the Z39.50 protocol. This prototype should be a Web application based on existing standards (MARC, Z39.50, etc.) and independent of the partners' systems. The prototype was to develop the mechanism for managing equivalences between headings, including multiple links, when a subject heading is equivalent to two headings in another language ("*Jumping*" = "*Hochsprung*" OR "*Sprung*") or when it is equivalent to a combination of two headings ("*Child actors*" = "*Kind*" AND "*Schauspieler*"). The prototype also had to provide a trilingual interface (German, English and French), be flexible and not too expensive to scale up towards a fully operational system incorporating new catalogues and new languages.

This prototype, developed by Index Data (Denmark) and Tilburg University Library (Netherlands), contains a small subset of data from the indexing languages and the libraries' databases so that link management and searching can be explored in order to test the performance of the MACS system. Thus, 2001 is a transitional year allowing the partners to collect the findings and the results of the prototype and above all to identify the organizational structure required to enable efficient cooperation using the MACS system. This should be operational in 2002 and then be able to welcome new partners.

Further information about the different steps of the project is available in the paper presented by Patrice Landry during the workshop "Crosswalks" of the Section on Classification and Indexing in Jerusalem[6].

2.3 The principles

The basic principles defined during the feasibility study remain and will remain valid throughout this cooperation:

Equality of languages and Subject Heading Languages, maintaining autonomy of each SHL. No language, no SHL is used as a pivot and each SHL is managed in its own database.

Establishment of equivalences between the SHLs involved. Neither searches nor subject headings are ever translated either automatically or manually.

Equivalence links conceived as concept clusters. The MACS system only contains mappings considered as conceptual clusters, identified by a numeric identifier only and nameless.

Consistency of results. The goal is pragmatic: to allow users to retrieve consistent and complete sets of bibliographic records in the different catalogues. The results of subject search thus validate "*in fine*" the established links, as they allow them to be checked for accuracy.

3. Subject retrieval with MACS

Searching with MACS prototype allows one to appreciate the benefits of this approach, based on the independence of the search language versus the indexing language.

3.1 The prototype on the Web

The prototype was intended to demonstrate the validity of the approach by simulating how the multilingual system should work with two Web accessible interfaces. The Search Interface allows users to choose one or more subject headings in a preferred source language for searching in target catalogues. Using the Z39.50 protocol, the query is then simultaneously sent to the local catalogues using the equivalence links established in the other interface of the prototype, the Link Management Interface.

By comparing the results with those retrieved without MACS support, MACS results are very convincing. It is now possible for any interested party directly to test and experiment with this multilingual subject access using the Guest access to the prototype, opened in June 2001. Over 100 people have already signed up to access the system at :
http://infolab.kub.nl/prj/macs.

3.2 What MACS offers

The way the prototype functions shows the benefit of the MACS approach which allows two major goals to be reached: the multilingual extension of a subject search to other catalogues using other languages, and the multilingual subject searching in each catalogue.

- With MACS, each partner library can first offer its national or linguistic community relevant access to foreign databases and catalogues. Library users search in their own language to retrieve documents indexed in the other languages:

  so, British Library users searching under "*Amateur theater*" retrieve the relevant documents in DDB as well as in the BnF, and these documents may be in English.

- MACS also allows each national library partner to offer the international community relevant access to its own catalogue which foreign users can search in their own language and not in the indexing language, which is the language of the catalogue. This multilingual access is possible in a multilingual environment (e.g. a French-speaking user of the SNL catalogue) as well as in a monolingual one :

  thus, to retrieve documents about "*Theâtre de rue*" in the BnF catalogue, the English-speaking user can search under "*Street theater*", and the German-speaking one with "*Strassentheater*". Both will retrieve relevant documents, some of which will be in their own language.

In addition, even if it is not an expressly sought goal, MACS can also simplify and improve subject cataloguing work by allowing indexers, thanks to established equivalences, to re-use indexing done by the other partners.

As well as being useful for the subject cataloguing of foreign documents, the project is turning out to be encouraging for the subject heading languages themselves, as it promotes convergence, in particular on the terminological level.

3.3 Languages and MACS

Subject searching is today necessarily carried out via the language of the catalogue in which the search takes place. Usually, all the documents are indexed in this language with one SHL. But, if users do not speak this language they cannot find the document they are looking for, even if this document is in their own language. However, the solution should not be applied at the indexing level. Multilingual indexing is too expensive and would not be a good solution anyway: the language of the catalogue, which is perfectly mastered, linguistically and culturally, by cataloguers must remain unique in order to achieve the best results.

In order to keep the advantages of monolingual indexing without retaining the language barriers that result from the monolingual approach, MACS aims at *disconnecting the language of the search from the language of the catalogue*. By allowing users to search in the language of their choice, MACS can restore the linguistic proximity between the document and the user that has disappeared in the cataloguing process: a French-speaking user can retrieve a document in French in the SNL catalogue, even though the document has been indexed in German (SWD). There is a clear distinction between the language of document, the language of catalogue (SHL) and the language of the search (user):

> thus this complete separation allows, for example, to access under English *"Shadow shows"* to a document in French which was indexed in German at the Swiss National Library.

This independence of languages is obtained thanks to equivalences established between SHLs. One might say that MACS plays the role of a *multilingual dictionary*, not of languages, but *of Subject Heading Languages*. So, contrary to the established practice of translation which enables "international" classification schemes to be extended to other languages, MACS is not a dictionary of words or even concepts but a bridge between systems that are themselves designed to organise and name concepts, in fact a dictionary of ontologies. This is a promising path for the construction of "multilingual thesauri" from existing indexing systems.

Besides allowing multilingual subject access, MACS (being a "dictionary of languages") could be used, at an advanced stage of cooperation, as a more economic and efficient tool in the indexing process. Faced with documents written in a language they do not master, cataloguers will be able to base their subject cataloguing on the work already carried out by foreign colleagues in their own catalogues. Or even simply to "translate" with MACS the indexing given in the language of the document, so that original subject indexing would be done only once.

4. MACS link management

In order to move to a live system, the MACS partners now have to define an organizational model for the flexible and federative management of links between the different SHLs, to consider the automation of certain procedures, and to work with national networks to speed up and share the labour-intensive work to do.

4.1 Organization of the network

The Link management interface of the prototype provides a system for creating and maintaining link equivalences. During a series of tests, the partners were able to try out this new tool and to learn more about the framework and constraints of network cooperation. They are now in a better position to define the organization of the future operational system. The solutions provided by the prototype are already very satisfactory. The "professional" interface is user-friendly and reliable (with a system of authorizations), and incorporates communication and discussion facilities. Currently, it allows the management of links among partners. However, at present any operation in any link requires the agreement of all the partners. This procedure is heavy and time-consuming and would make the extension of MACS to new partners very difficult.

A reliable, but more flexible *organizational model* is therefore being designed, based on a federated management approach which clearly specifies the share of responsibilities among partners. Its broad outline reflects the underlying principles of the project:
- Autonomy of each SHL (Link management system outside the local systems).
- Limited responsibility of each partner in link-establishment (he is the only one authorized to fully manage the equivalence between the MACS link and his own subject headings).
- Unlimited capacity of proposal concerning other parts of the link (to be confirmed by the responsible partner, with information provided by the system about new or modified links).
- Total right to comment on the work done by the others (checking of equivalences through an "Annotations" function, intended to regulate possible conflicts).

4.2 Work automation

Even with an effective model of cooperation, MACS can only manage and not create links. The subject specialists must establish the equivalences, and their intellectual work must be moreover introduced into the system. However, in order to build a multilingual system with a significant number of links, the prototype content must be multiplied by 20 or even by 50. It is therefore necessary to provide technical solutions without a loss of quality and without changing the principles. These solutions should allow the partners to reach their goal in a fast and economic way, thanks to the re-use of work already carried out and to the automation of certain tasks.

The subject heading mapping method was developed in detail in the feasibility study: in a selected subject field, three monolingual lists of subject headings were drawn up and mutually compared. The links were analysed, first on the terminological level (subject heading), then on the semantic level (authority record), and finally on the syntactic one (application). This reliable, but very time-consuming, work has shown that the existing equivalences between RAMEAU and LCSH, which had been systematically established by the BnF in its own authority records, were of great interest. Their accuracy was such that they could be used as a basis for scaling-up MACS.

So, the partners decided to use this work. The appropriate fields from the RAMEAU records (clearly identified in UNIMARC format) will be loaded into the system in order to feed it automatically with a substantial set of RAMEAU/LCSH links. New specifications will be developed to make the downloadings possible as well as the automation of updates, from local systems, of subject headings already existing in MACS.

4.3 Involvement of national networks

But this loading of about 70,000 bilingual RAMEAU/LCSH equivalences must moreover be done in phases. It is crucial to carry out work *subject field by subject field* to allow its correct development: confirmation of English equivalences (BL), creation of German equivalences (SWD, by DDB and SNL), and a final checking of all the links established in each field.The partners therefore decided to add a suitable *classification field* to the MACS Link management interface. In fact, such information is already available in RAMEAU records, which are classified in broad subject domains based on the Dewey Decimal Classification, notably thanks to an automatic mapping between call numbers and subject indexing in documents held in the open access BnF collections. Without assuming that this will be the final word on the future MACS classification, downloading of headings will be done from RAMEAU subject field after subject field. It will start with two fields selected by common agreement: mathematics and psychology.

This use of a classification will supply homogeneous groups of headings by subject, allowing partners the effective distribution of work not only amongst themselves, but also across the *national subject-headings networks*. This is because the teams managing the SHLs are organized according to the different fields of knowledge and, both in Germany and in France, these teams are in contact with all the libraries using the SHL, thus creating more or less structured networks of excellence. Within RAMEAU, the network is managed through a Web application, the "Fichier national des propositions" (FNPR, national proposals file), that allows users (about 100 active libraries today), to collaborate fully in the evolution of the SHL. We plan to involve the subject knowledge and linguistic skills of these users to distribute the work in cooperation within the RAMEAU network, especially for link checking, which will be shared out by subject fields under the management of the RAMEAU office.

Conclusion

As we have seen, it is by using networks themselves, at both an international and national level, that MACS is trying to provide an original solution to the challenge of subject access in the networked age. By virtue of its multilingual and multicultural nature, this challenge could only be addressed through international cooperation.

This work is not of course without its difficulties and requires long discussions; for example, to reach a consensus about an appropriate classification and the depth of its notations. However, we have to underline the great value of this continuous process of cooperation. Thanks to our experience of working together, thanks to the practical experience we have gained, we can now foresee how the prototype must evolve to move to a live system.

This operational system is planned for 2002, after the finalization of our organizational model and the preparation of complementary specifications needed for scaling-up to a system that retains current principles and stability. Two significant problems, however, remain to be solved. First a direct access via Z39.50 to the partners' catalogues needs to be set up since the end goal of MACS is to give the user better access to the richness held in the different databases. The first results should be available at the end of 2001, with access via MACS to DDB catalogue.

Then the system needs to be extended since the basic concept of MACS means that it can theoretically be applied to large numbers of SHLs. It is hoped that by mid-2002 a new partner will thus join, bringing a new language and a new SHL, and allowing the partners to test the extensibility of the "concept clusters" and the solidity of the organizational model.

Once this stage has been successfully carried out, MACS should go on towards "Version 2", comprising the direct access to the "local" authority lists in order to improve searching (using *"See"* and *"See also"* references) and the updating of the organization in order to integrate the partners' daily work. At this point the MACS system will show if it can fully provide a reliable and efficient solution to the challenge of multilingual access to documents. It should also serve to underline the value of SHLs as search tools compared to traditional classification systems whose updates are so difficult to implement.

If MACS succeeds as we hope, we shall see that this very precise and concrete cooperative project is far from insignificant. It should bring real changes to the way we see subject searching, therefore in our catalogues, and to our daily practice of indexing work, as we improve our SHLs thanks to comparisons and the use of the MACS "dictionary" to assist indexers.

References

---

[1] Karlsruher Virtueller Katalog <http://www.ubka.uni-karlsruhe.de/kvk.html>

[2] SWD/RSWK: Schlagwortnormdatei/Regeln für der Schlagwortkatalog

[3] RAMEAU: Répertoire d'Autorité-Matière Encyclopédique et Alphabétique Unifié: http://rameau/bnf.fr

[4] LCSH: Library of Congress Subject Headings

[5] CoBRA+ working group on multilingual subject access, Final report (1999): http://portico.bl.uk/gabriel/cobra/finrap3.html

[6] Landry, P. (2000). The MACS project : multilingual access to subjects (LCSH, RAMEAU, SWD). In *66th IFLA Council and General Conference August 13-18, 2000, 165-181(WS)-E, 7 p.* <http://www.ifla.org/IV/ifla66/papers/165-181e.pdf>

MACS Project is at: http://infolab.kub.nl/prj/macs

Information languages and multilingual subject access

Gerhard J.A. Riesthuis

Abstract: In this paper the possibilities for a multilingual thesaurus in which not all descriptors in a given language have equivalent descriptors in all other languages and in which the hierarchical structure can have variations in the different languages and a small model of such a thesaurus is given. It is argued that the searching possibilities that more recent programs for bibliographic databases offer make such non-identical thesauri possible.

1. Introduction

Multilingual and crosslingual access to information is receiving more and more attention. Maybe the most important reason for this development is the Internet. There are estimations that about half of its users are people with a mother tongue other than English and that this proportion is growing.

Crosslingual access in this context means the possibility to get free text access to information using another (natural) language than the language of the information itself. This type of access is important for users with a good passive knowledge of a language but with only a small active vocabulary of the same language, e.g. a Englishman who can read Russian, but has difficulties in formulating adequate search request in that language. Crosslingual access can also be valuable for monolingual users who can automatically or manually have translations of foreign language documents. The search requests will be translated or converted into the language of the information.

Multilingual access assumes that the instruments used for access, the controlled information languages, are available in more than one language. An classic example is the Englishman who uses his English edition of the Universal Decimal Classification to search the catalogue of a library in China, although the classification of the library is done using a Chinese edition. In this case the searching and the classifying results in a notation that is the same irrespective which language edition was used for indexing. Another possibility is the use of a multilingual thesaurus or subject headings list, such the trilingual edition of the Library of Congress Subject Headings built at the Royal Library in Brussels (Belgium) or the Macrothesaurus of the OECD. Here, words are the access points – in one language into which each search request will be converted, or, alternatively, into all the languages involved. Multilingual information languages and guidelines on how to build them are the subject of this paper. Particular attention will be paid to multilingual thesauri.

2. Problems

The problems with multilingual access to information are well know (Hudon, 1997). Therefore I shall just sum them up and give some examples. The problems are:

- stretching a language to make it fit a foreign conceptual structure;
- transferring a conceptual structure from one culture to another whether it fits or not;

- translating literally terms from a source language into meaningless expressions in a target language.

A well known example is the English word *siblings*. This word means both 'children of a couple' and 'one's own brothers and sisters'. An equivalent term in French that has both meanings does not exist. In the *Population Multilingual Thesaurus* the following construction is used:

SIBLINGS
USE: SIBSHIP

SIBSHIP / FRATRIE
SN: CHILDREN OF THE SAME COUPLE

Whether this is very helpful for an English-speaking end user, who has no easy access to the printed thesaurus is doubtful. The English *sibship* is a artificial term. The French term *fratrie* means 'the whole of brothers and sisters of a (nuclear) family', i.e. one of the meanings of *siblings*. Frâncu, 2000 suggests another possibility:

English	French	Romanian
Siblings	--	--
UF Brothers and sisters	*Frères et soeurs*	*Frați și surori*

Her solution has the advantage that the use of artificial terms is avoided, but the disadvantage that it is ambiguous. Which meaning is meant here? Probably both, but why no reference to the French *fratrie*? A Romanian term does not exist.

Multilingual information languages

Each language version of a multilingual information language should be usable independent of the others, but at the same time should be connected with them. It should be possible to use a Dutch edition of the *Universal Decimal Classification* without to be obliged to have access to an edition in any other language. The same applies for multilingual thesauri: for each language the thesaurus should present a fully developed conceptual and semantic structure. At the same time, however, the results in searching should in principle be the same irrespective which language version is used.

There are three ways to approach multilingual information languages:

- Translation in one or more new languages of an existing classification or thesaurus. This is often the most simple way and for classifications the normal case. Both the *Dewey Decimal Classification (DDC)* and the *Universal Decimal Classification (UDC)* are nowadays developed in English and translated into other languages – often with small adaptations in classes, like geographical places and history. An example of a thesaurus that is translated in two other languages, English and Russian, is the *Schlagwortlist für die Sozialwissenschaften* of the *Informationszentrum Sozialwissenschaften* in Bonn (Germany). The main problem with translations is that the source information language is culturally biased in almost cases and this bias is reflecte in translations.

- Merging of existing monolingual information languages, especially thesauri or subject headings lists. The result can be a 'new' multilingual information language or concordances between the information languages involved. This approach, in most cases, gives severe practical problems. The structure of the information languages involved can differ considerably as to extent and depth of coverage. A good example is the so-called MACS project which tries out a concordance between the Library of Congress Subjects Headings, the French RAMEAU system and the German Schlagwortdatei (SWD) (Landry, 2000). Another example where a classification and several word systems were involved is discussed by Anders (1986).
- Development of versions in distinct linguistic versions from scratch. In this case the adjustment of the different versions is relatively easy, source and target languages can change places.

4. Multilingual information languages and conformity

In the existing international standard for multilingual thesauri (ISO 5964-1985) the languages of a multilingual thesaurus have equal status when each descriptor has one and only one equivalent descriptor in a target language and is related to the same descriptors. It is not necessary that each non-descriptor has an equivalent, as the *siblings* example shows. This requirement forces the creation of artificial terms (coined terms in the terminology of ISO 5964) in the case where the target language has no equivalence and it eliminates one equivalence in instances where one term in the source language has two equivalences in the target language. Also false hierarchical hierarchies can be generated when a term belongs to one hierarchy in one language, but to a different one in the other language.

The alternative is to build a multilingual thesaurus where the descriptors do not always have equivalents in all languages and where also the referential structure can be different for different language versions. Based on the terminology used by Hudon (1997) the term *non-identical thesaurus* will be used for this type thesaurus and *identical thesaurus* for one made according to ISO 5964-1985.

5. Example of a non-identical thesaurus

A complete example of a non-identical thesaurus would take far more space than is available in this paper. To give an idea I prepared a small model. In Aitchison (1990) we find the following hierarchy. 'Media' have many narrower terms, but 'Representational media' and 'Documents' both have only one narrower term.

```
Media
  NT Representational media
    NT Documents
       NT Records
```

'Representational media' has a scope note: ' Media for which the presence of both communicator and receiver at the same time is not required'. A Dutch equivalent for this term does not exist. It is not, however, necessary to create a coined term. The following hierarchy will work in Dutch:

Media
  NT Documenten

Documenten are always representational in sense of the scope note, and when *documenten* is defined as 'A combination of a medium and the information recorded on it' all representational media are *documenten* in Dutch.

Really problematic is an equivalent term for *records*.

Records 7KR.DE
SN Record: (a) A set of related data. (b) or information treated as a unit within a file. Records: Documents (manuscripts, printed matter, photographs, motion pictures, sound recordings, magnetic tapes, etc.) created or recieved in the conduct of some transaction of which they themselves formed a part, thus becoming evidence of that transaction. They may arise in the affairs of an organization, a business or an individual
BT Documents 7KR.D
RT Forms (blank) 8MR
*BT Primary materials 8D
*NT Archive records PVR
*NT Bibliographic Records LFO
*NT Current records P3S.C
*NT Educational records TDH
*NT Machine readable records FW7
*NT Medical records SA5.R
*NT Noncurrent records P3S.U
*NT Official records P3O
*NT Personnel records QW7
*NT Semicurrent records P3S.S
*NT Vital records P3Q
*RT Files NF
*RT Office record systems QUP.0
*RT Records managment P3

The meaning of this descriptor in Aitchson (1990) is clear from the scope note and the narrower term. It is clear that *records* has two meanings in English. In Dutch we use *records* for the first meaning. *Bibliografische records* and *Machineleesbare records* are narrower terms. To find a Dutch term for the second meaning is not simple. *Document* might be a candidate, but it is already in the upward hierarchy with a broader meaning, which is also more common. *Archiefstukken* could be another candidate, but not all NTs are included here. Some of the NTs could be taken together under the BT *Verslagen*.

Still not all NTs of the English descriptor are given in the Dutch version.

English	***Dutch***
Media	Media
Representational media	
Documents	Documenten
Records	
	Records
Bibliographic records	Bibliografische records
Machine readable records	Machineleesbare records
	Archiefstukken
Current records	Levende archiefstukken
Noncurrent records	Dode archiefstukken
Personnel records	Personeelsstukken
	Verslagen
Medical records	Medische verslagen
Educational records	Onderwijsrapporten
Vital records	Bevolkingsregisterdocumenten

Vital records in Dutch is on the same level as *Verslagen* etc. and a possible descriptor is *Bevolkingsregisterdocumenten*.

In this way each narrower term of the English *Records* can have a place in the Dutch version of this thesaurus. It is not uncommon for each descriptor in either version to have an equivalent in the other version. The English descriptor *Records* has no Dutch equivalent, and the Dutch descriptor *Records* has no English equivalent and so on, although there is a *partial equivalence*: in Dutch the word *record* has a narrower meaning than the English word; the Dutch records are a type of the English term records.

The model also deals with *single-to-multiple equivalence* and *non-equivalence*. A few remarks now about *loan terms* and *inexact equivalence*. Loan terms are terms from a source language that are adopted in a target language when they refer to concepts that are unknown to the users of that language. Many of them can be considered as a sort of name, e.g. the name of a city, a currency or a type of school. A Hungarian-Romanian thesaurus will adopt the term *Lei* for the Romanian currency in the Hungarian version and *Forint* for the Hungarian currency in the Romanian version. There is nothing wrong here, more problematic is the use of loan terms for abstract concepts. In such cases often inexact equivalent terms are used between the languages and it is better to treat them as exact equivalences for indexing, the more so as they are often given as equivalences in translation dictionaries. Examples are the German *Gemütlichkeit* and the English *cosiness*, or *Wissenschaft* and *Science*.

6. Searching and non-identical thesauri

The use of non-identical thesauri is only advisable if the searching possibilities of the bibliographic systems in which they are used cooperate. The next table shows how a identical thesaurus could look if ISO 5964 is followed. Note that the descriptors with + signs are just one compound descriptor, not a combination of descriptors combined with Boolean ands.

English	***Dutch***
Media	Media
Representational media	Representational media
Documents	Documenten
Records (in general)	Records + Archiefstukken + Verslagen + Bevolkings-Registerdocumenten
Records (computerfiles)	Records
Bibliographic records	Bibliografische records
Machine readable records	Machineleesbare records
Archival records	Archiefstukken
Current records	Levende archiefstukken
Noncurrent records	Dode archiefstukken
Personnel records	Personeelsstukken
Medical records + Educational records	Verslagen
Medical records	Medische verslagen
Educational records	Onderwijsrapporten
Vital records	Bevolkingsregisterdocumenten

Let us assume that the thesaurus is used for an English and a Dutch bibliographic database, each indexed by the thesaurus versions of the its language. A document dealing with *records* in the English sense of the term will have the descriptor *Records* in the English database, and in the Dutch database the descriptor *Records + Archiefstukken + Verslagen + Bevolkingsregister-documenten*. Searching with English is no problem for the English database, nor for the Dutch one – in searching the English descriptor is replaced by the Dutch one. With Dutch it is a problem: who can think of the Dutch descriptor without studying the thesaurus?

With a non-identical thesaurus indexing with the English version is the same, and with the Dutch version, in theory, one would expect the combination *Records; Archiefstukken; Verslagen*; *Bevolkingsregisterdocumnten*. In practice, often only a few of these will be given, e.g. *Archiefstukken; Verslagen*. At first sight, searching with the English descriptor *Records* will not result in the retrieval of the Dutch document. A search system with a little intelligence can, however, search with different Boolean and/or combinations of the four descriptors and also find this document. This search procedure can be combined with relevance ranking.

7. The Guidelines and non-identical thesauri

To adapt the *Guidelines for multilingual thesauri* to the idea of identical and non-identical thesauri a number of changes are necessary. In the first place the differences between the two types has to be discussed and the definitions adjusted. Especially the notion of *equal status* has to be redefined. No longer it can be said that the languages of a multilingual thesaurus have equal status when each preferred term i.e. descriptor, is matched by an equivalent preferred term in all other languages. It can be argued that just when this is the case, one

language is more equal than the others: mostly one of the languages functions de facto as target language and is dominant.
The rules for establishing equivalent terms in different languages has to be revised completely. They will not be the same for identical and non-identical multilingual thesauri with the biggest changes for the single-to-multiple term equivalence and the non-equivalence. Many new examples have to be added, and existing ones revised.

8. Conclusion

The search possibilities available in modern programs for bibliographic databases and OPACs have increased enormously. The rules for cataloguing and subject indexing have not kept pace with this development. The basis for them was laid down in the nineteen-seventies – also for ISO 5964-1985 – when only very few people could foresee the changes the computer would bring in information storage and retrieval. Another development that has to be taken into account is that the end-user – for whom we work even if we often tend to forget it – is more and more a user at a distance behind a computer screen, maybe even at the end of the world, with in many cases, another mother tongue than the language of the catalogue. We can not expect users to know cataloguing rules, all the complexities of building a complex notation in DDC or UDC, or to study a multilingual thesaurus in detail before searching. We have to make the tools used for cataloguing and indexing more intuitive for our users.
In this paper I have restricted myself to multilingual thesauri. The developments mentioned make it possible and advisable to build what Hudon (1997) would call a multilingual thesaurus with 'true equality for all languages'. In such a thesaurus single-to-multiple equivalence, descriptors without equivalence ('orphans') and variations in the hierarchical structure are allowed. The goal is a system where an end user can use term from a language familiar to him and have results.

References

Aitchson, Jean. (1990). Communication and information thesaurus : final draft prepared for Unesco and FID. Letchworth : The author, 1990.

Anders, Monika. (1986). Probleme der Erarbeitung des mehrsprachigen Thesaurus Staat und Recht des ISGI. *Informatik,* 33(2), 54-57, 80; (3) 94-98

Frâncu, Victoria. (2000). Harmonizing a universal classification system with an interdisciplinary multilingual thesaurus: advantages and limitations. In *Dynamism and stability in knowledge organization: Proceedings of the Sixth International ISKO Conference, 10-13 July 2000, Toronto, Canada.* Würzburg: Ergon Verlag. pp.200-205

Hudon, Michèle. (1997). Multilingual thesaurus construction - integrating the views of different cultures in one gateway to knowledge and concepts. *Information Services & Use,* 17 (3/4), 111-123. Also pub. in *Knowledge Organization,* 24(1997)2: 84-91.

Landry, Patrice. (2000). The MACS project : multilingual access to subjects (LCSH, RAMEAU, SWD). In *66th IFLA Council and General Conference August 13-18, 2000, 165-181(WS)-E, 7 p.* Internet: www.ifla.org/IV/ifla66/papers/165-181.pdf

Session 2

RETRIEVAL ACROSS MULTIPLE VOCABULARIES (1)

Integrating LCSH and MeSH in Information Systems

Tony Olson

Abstract: The Library of Congress Subject Headings system, and the National Library of Medicine's Medical Subject Headings thesaurus have been mapped. The mapping data have been entered into 7XX fields of USMARC authority records. The data continue to be updated as subject headings are added, deleted, or changed in information languages. It is planned to distribute the mapping data in both MARC and non-MARC formats to libraries, vendors, bibliographic utilities and other developers of information systems.

1. The LCSH/MeSH Mapping Project

The problems that are created when two or more information languages reside in the same system have been widely studied. Most of the solutions to these problems involve the integration or harmonization of the languages (Maniez, 1997). One method for integrating multiple information languages in library catalogues and other databases is to map terms in each language to corresponding terms in the other languages (Mandel, 1987). This is the approach taken by the Northwestern University libraries in a project to map the Library of Congress Subject Heading (LCSH) system to the National Library of Medicine's Medical Subject Headings (MeSH) thesaurus. The mapping project was begun in 1990 and continues at the present time. The project was divided into two phases: (1) a retrospective phase that mapped LCSH as it existed on April 14, 1990 and the 1989 MeSH; and (2) an ongoing phase during which the mapping data have been updated to take into account additions, deletions and changes to the two information languages.

During the "retrospective" phase of the project, 9,823 MeSH headings were mapped to 9,427 LCSH headings, and 9,824 LCSH headings were mapped to 8,799 MeSH headings. This was accomplished by using machine methods to generate 310,507 heading pairs (consisting of one MeSH heading and one LCSH heading) that represented potential correspondences between LCSH and MeSH. Subject editors then reviewed each heading pair to determine if there was an actual correspondence, in which case the headings were mapped. The mapping data were then entered into 7XX linking entry fields of USMARC LCSH and MeSH authority records in the Northwestern online catalogue (Figure 1). For a full description of this phase of the project, which was completed in 1991, see (Olson & Strawn, 1997).

008/11 a *[code indicating LCSH]*	008/11 c *[code indicating MeSH]*
150: : ǂa Breast ǂx Cancer	150: : ǂa Breast Neoplasms
750: 2: ǂa Breast Neoplasms	750: 0: ǂa Breast ǂx Cancer
	750: 0: ǂa Breast ǂx Tumors

Figure 1
Examples of LCSH and MeSH authority records with linking entry fields.

Since 1991, staff at the Northwestern University libraries have continued to update and maintain the mapping data. This is done by reviewing the weekly LCSH updates, and the annual MeSH updates that are added to Northwestern's online catalogue. New, deleted, or changed headings are checked to see if there are corresponding MeSH or LCSH headings, and if necessary the mapping data is changed.

2. Mapping Guidelines

During both phases of the project, several guidelines were (and continue to be) used to determine when an LCSH and a MeSH heading are equivalent and should be mapped. These are summarized below.

(1) Only topical headings are mapped.

(2) One-to-one mapping is preferred, although there are instances when exceptions have to be made (Figure 2).

(a) LCSH: Drug allergy
MeSH: Drug Hypersensitivity

(b) LCSH: Allergy
MeSH: Allergy and Immunology
Hypersensitivity

(c) LCSH: Obesity + Diabetes
MeSH: Obesity in Diabetes

Figure 2
Examples of main heading correspondences: (a) One-to-one mapping; (b) LCSH heading corresponds to two MeSH headings; (c) The two LCSH headings used together in the same bibliographic record correspond to the MeSH heading.

(3) Main heading correspondences are mapped. Also main headings that correspond to main heading/subheading strings are mapped. However, correspondences between main heading/subheading strings are not mapped (Figure 3).

(a) LCSH: Liver--Regeneration
MeSH: Liver Regeneration

(b) LCSH: Breast--Cancer--Treatment
MeSH: Breast Neoplasms--therapy

Figure 3
Examples of correspondences between main heading/subheading strings. (a) The headings are mapped because only one is a main heading/subheading string. (b) The headings are not mapped because both are main heading/subheading strings.

(4) Generally, mapped headings have to be co-extensive, which implies that the existing syndetic structures of LCSH and MeSH will be relied on to direct a user from a known heading to a broader or narrower heading (Figure 4). (It should be noted that the hierarchical structure of MeSH is implicit in MeSH authority records through category numbers in 072 fields. In order to make this structure explicit in the online catalogue, a computer program was designed to translate the coding in 072 fields into broader and narrower reference tracings that were then added to MeSH authority records.)

Autonomic Ganglia *[LCSH]*

Ganglia, Autonomic *[MeSH]*
NT: Ganglia, Sympathetic

Figure 4
In this example the MeSH heading, Ganglia, Sympathetic has no LCSH equivalent, nor is it mapped to the broader LCSH heading. Instead the later is mapped to its corresponding MeSH heading, from which the user will be directed by a narrower term reference to Ganglia, Sympathetic.

(5) New main headings in either LCSH or MeSH will *not* be established in order to create a mapping, but main heading/subheading strings will be established when needed. Of course, if the subject editors think that either a new LCSH or MeSH main heading should be established, this is communicated to the appropriate agency through the normal channels (such as SACO for LCSH).

It is interesting to note the similarities between these guidelines and the methodology used by the CoBRA+ Working Group on Multilingual Subject Access in their study on establishing links between multilingual thesauri. Specifically: the preference for one-to-one linking, with exceptions; and the linking of main headings to main heading/subheading strings (MacEwan, 2000).

3. Distribution of the Mapping Data

Except for the ongoing maintenance of the mapping data, the LCSH/MeSH mapping project has been completed. The next step is to distribute the mapping data to libraries, vendors, bibliographic utilities, and developers of other information systems or languages (such as metathesauri, classification systems, etc.). As stated above, the mapping data resides in authority records in the Northwestern libraries online catalogue. In 1997 a file of these enhanced records was copied from the catalogue and this file was made available for distribution via FTP. Several organizations, including the National Library of Medicine and OCLC, subsequently acquired the files. Unfortunately, updated files of the enhanced records have not been distributed since 1997, because Northwestern switched library management systems in 1998. Northwestern's new system does not yet have the capability for extracting authority records containing 7XX fields. It is hoped that this situation will be rectified soon, and that the distribution of the updated files with the enhanced authority records can begin again. When this happens, the plan is to make the files available in at least two different formats: (1) two files (LCSH and MeSH) of records in the USMARC authority format; and (2) two files in a tab delimited ASCII format for non-MARC applications.

4. Applications of the Mapping Data

One of the first and more obvious applications would be in online library catalogues where the mapping data could be used to link equivalent LCSH and MeSH headings. This would be accomplished by *see also* (or "Equivalent Heading") references that are generated from the 7XX fields in authority records. However, depending upon the type of correspondence, the references might be suppressed. Correspondences between LCSH and MeSH can be divided into three broad types.

(1) After normalization, an LCSH heading is identical to a MeSH heading (for example, CENTRAL NERVOUS SYSTEM). Approximately 50% of the correspondences are of this type. In these cases duplicate entries will be generated if both headings are used in the same bibliographic record. Depending upon the system architecture, the duplicate entries can be suppressed, along with the *see also* references from authority 7XX fields that link the two headings.

(2) An established heading in one language is identical (after normalization) to a cross reference in the other language. For example, the normalized LCSH heading, CLINICAL PHARMACOLOGY, is identical to a MeSH cross reference directing a user to PHARMACOLOGY CLINICAL. Approximately 10% of the correspondences are of this type. The resolution of these conflicts would depend upon the system architecture, along with the option to suppress or display the *see also* references from the linking entry fields.

(3) Correspondences (approximately 40%) that do not fall into categories 1 or 2. For example, the MeSH heading, History of Medicine, 17th Cent., is equivalent to the LCSH heading, Medicine--History--17th century. In this case the 7XX linking entry fields could be used to generate *see also* references between the two equivalent headings. As another example the MeSH heading, Obesity in Diabetes, is equivalent to the LCSH headings, Obesity and Diabetes, used together in the same record. In this later case a note could be generated linking the equivalent headings. At present, most library management systems (with one possible exception) have not developed the capability of displaying or otherwise using the mapping data in LCSH and MeSH authority records. However, the implementation of this functionality should not be too difficult. The display or suppression of references from 7XX fields should be just an extension of existing functionality in which references are displayed from 4XX and 5XX fields in authority records. It is hoped that most of the major systems will add this functionality soon.

Although the most obvious uses of the LCSH/MeSH mapping data in its current form would be in online library catalogues, there is a number of other potential uses for the data.

(1) The mapping data would benefit cataloguers who are attempting to assign MeSH headings in a record that contains only LCSH headings, or vice versa. By displaying the appropriate MeSH or LCSH authority record, a cataloguer could easily find an equivalent heading (if it exists) in the other information language.

(2) In a similar manner the data could be used in the construction of smaller more specialized thesauri or subject headings lists that incorporate both LCSH and MeSH.

(3) The data could be incorporated into a higher level integrated vocabulary or metathesaurus such as the one in the National Library of Medicine's Unified Medical Language System.

(4) The data could also be used as an aid in the development of tools for the automatic harmonization of indexing languages. Such tools might include concordance tables, intermediate switching languages or reference languages.

5. Summary

The integration of multiple information languages in library catalogues and other databases can be difficult, time consuming, and expensive. However, in the case of LCSH and MeSH most of the integration has been accomplished by the mapping of the two languages. The mapping data continue to be updated and maintained. The data should soon be available for distribution to libraries, vendors, bibliographic utilities and other system developers.

References

MacEwan, A.(2000). Crossing language barriers in Europe: linking LCSH to other subject heading languages, *Cataloging & classification quarterly*, 29, 199-207.

Mandel, C. (1987). *Multiple thesauri in online library bibliographic systems*. Washington, DC: Library of Congress, Cataloging Distribution Service.

Maniez, J. (1997). Database merging and the compatibility of indexing languages. *Knowledge organization*, 24, 213-224.

Olson, T. & Strawn, G. (1997). Mapping the LCSH and MeSH systems. *Information technology and libraries*, 16, 5-19.

Renardus: Cross-browsing European subject gateways via a common classification system (DDC)

Traugott Koch,[1] Heike Neuroth and Michael Day

Abstract: This paper presents the approach and first results of the classification mapping process in the EU project Renardus. The outcome in Renardus is a cross-browsing feature based on the Dewey Decimal Classification (DDC) and improved subject searching across distributed and heterogeneous European subject gateways. The paper presents the project's initial experiences and decisions, e.g. an investigation of the use of classification systems by Renardus partners' gateways, general mapping approaches and issues, the definition of mapping relationships and some information on technical solutions and the mapping tool. There is also a demonstration of the use of the mapping information in Renardus and the presentation of several features that have been implemented to aid end-user navigation in a large and deep browsing structure like the DDC. Classification mapping for cross-browsing is a labour intensive and complex effort which at the moment raises many open questions and leaves many more future potential work tasks than completed useful solutions.

1. The EU project Renardus

Renardus[2] is a project funded by the European Commission as part of the Information Society Technologies (IST) programme, part of the European Union's 5th Framework Programme. Partners in Renardus include national libraries, research centres and subject gateway services from Denmark, Finland, Germany, The Netherlands, Sweden and the UK, co-ordinated by the National Library of the Netherlands. The project aims to develop a Web-based service[3] to enable searching and browsing across a range of distributed European-based information services designed for the academic and research communities - and in particular those services known as subject gateways. These gateways are services that provide access to Internet resources. They tend to be selective with regard to the resources they give access to, and are usually based on the manual creation of descriptive metadata. Services typically provide users with both search and browse facilities, and often offer hierarchical browse structures based on subject classification schemes (Koch & Day, 1997).

Predecessor projects like the EU project DESIRE[4] have already developed solutions for the description of individual resources and for automatic classification at the level of an individual subject gateway using established classification systems. Renardus intends to develop a service that can cross-search and cross-browse a number of distributed subject gateways through the use of a common metadata profile and by the mapping all locally-used classification schemes to a common scheme.

A thorough review of existing data models (Becker, *et al.*, 2000) was used as the basis for the agreement of a minimum set of Dublin Core-based metadata elements that could be utilised as a common data model. A comprehensive mapping effort from the individual gateways' metadata element sets and content encoding schemes to the common profile has taken place. This provides the infrastructure for interoperability between all participating databases and thus is the necessary prerequisite for cross-searching.

Renardus

Enhanced subject access is considered to be one of the key services offered by subject gateways, and an important part of the Renardus service is its attempt to provide some kind of subject browsing across all participating gateways. The project has been, therefore, investigating ways that would enable users to browse a single subject hierarchy covering the content of all partner gateways. However, different gateway services use a wide range of classification schemes to provide browsing access to Internet resources. These include well-known universal schemes, as well as a number of more subject specialised or locally produced systems. In order to accomplish consistent browse access to the content of Renardus partner gateways, all of the different classification systems in use need, therefore, to be mapped to a common classification system. The cross-browsing service in Renardus aims to mediate between the different classification systems in use by using the Dewey Decimal Classification (DDC) as a common switching language and browsing structure. An initial detailed description of the mapping effort and some preliminary guidelines are available from the project (Koch, Neuroth & Day, 2001a; 2001b).

The advantages of using classification systems to support subject access and topical navigation in large systems, e.g. interoperability, multilingual access, options to broaden or narrow searches, etc., are described elsewhere (e.g., Koch & Day, 1997). The Renardus service aims to give access to resources from all subjects, published world-wide and in many languages, and it is intended to be offered to an international multidisciplinary community of users. Taking these requirements into consideration, it appeared that utilising an existing universal classification system would be the most suitable tool upon which to build the common browsing structure in Renardus. Closer investigation demonstrated that DDC had important advantages, when compared with other schemes, for use in an application like the cross-browsing facility in Renardus. The main advantages lie in its online availability (e.g., WebDewey is a useful tool for the Renardus mapping process) and that its size and structure means that it is suitable for the task in hand. Other advantages include the scheme's global use, the large number of digital resources that have been classified with it and the speed and frequency of updates, especially with regard to the content of digital resources. Also advantageous are the research and methodological development efforts continually being undertaken by OCLC (Koch, Neuroth & Day, 2001a). The enhanced DDC also contains intellectually and statistically mapped vocabularies like the Library of Congress Subject Headings (LCSH) which are very useful for the Renardus mapping work.

The basis for the use of the DDC within the project is a research agreement with the scheme's owner, OCLC Forest Press. The licence allows Renardus to use the full DDC classification system to construct and offer the Renardus cross-browsing pages. Co-operation with regard to methodological issues will also take place.

The classification and browsing solutions currently adopted by participating gateways are very heterogeneous. In order to prepare the mapping effort, it was necessary to conduct a thorough review of the schemes in use by partner gateways.[5] An analysis showed, for example, that many gateways use special subject schemes with a deep structure. For example, one gateway has 800 thematic classes structured in five levels that will have to be mapped. Other gateways' subject structures are not so extensive, with one or two levels of hierarchy and between 18 and 60 classes that will require mapping.

2. Mapping approach and issues

A few practical principles are required to maintain consistency in the mappings and to ensure that the resulting Renardus browsing pages are balanced. Mapping relationships are expressed between a pair of classes and not between a DDC class and individual resources. The mapping is carried out in one direction only, from the DDC to the local classification, i.e. the gateway's local browsing system. In order to help establish a balanced Renardus service at all times, it is suggested that gateways should finish mapping the top level of a local browse hierarchy completely, before moving progressively down through it. The ultimate goal is, naturally, to map all local classes to the DDC. The priority, however, is to map the most frequently used classes in the local gateway.

Many other issues will need to be discussed and solutions devised, possibly resulting in the periodic revision of the mapping guidelines. These issues may include specifics of how the DDC should be used to create a browse structure and how the mappings should be displayed in the Renardus browse interface. Other issues might include how deep the mapping should be on both sides (DDC and the local systems), how to treat local classes that contain both generalities and specialities, the exclusion of non-topical classes (e.g. auxiliary tables), the average number of allowed mappings, etc. Some of the subject areas that may provide the main focus of a gateway may be located deep within the DDC hierarchy. It is also not clear how the project should solve the conflict between the compact disciplinary structures that are often used in specialized subject classifications and the "shattering" of the same discipline within universal systems; for example, engineering is expressed in 800 classes within the specialised Ei classification system, but dispersed in about 2,300 categories in the DDC. Another problematic issue is the influence of the degree of subject overlap between the Renardus participants on the mapping practice. Similarly, Renardus has already discovered inconsistencies resulting from gateways' use of more than one classification scheme; for example, a subset of resources in one gateway might be classified using the DDC, while all resources are also classified with a different system; the one that would normally serve as the basis for the complete class-level mapping in Renardus. A permanent and very important issue is how to find the best trade-off between consistency, accuracy and usability in the Renardus cross-browsing service.

3. Mapping relationships

Many other mapping projects, (e.g. those involved in conversions between two classification systems for use in OPACS or union catalogues), limit themselves to the establishment of simple connections between pairs of classes. They are often unspecific concerning defining the character and degree of the indicated equivalence. However, the structures and levels of detail, the vocabularies, languages and cultural contexts of the locally applied classification systems used by Renardus gateways and the DDC are very different. The project, therefore, assumes that a simple equivalence between the content of two classes will be rare. The same judgement has been made by other mapping projects, including CARMEN.[6]

In the Renardus subject browsing pages, users need to be advised that certain links from a DDC class point to a class in a local gateway containing broader or narrower areas of content, or showing major or minor overlaps with the DDC class. This is especially true, as there will quite often be several mapping links to different classes found within a number of different gateways. One link might be fully equivalent, another might show just a minor overlap. The need for a more detailed specification of the degree of equivalence is even greater when the mapping between the local class and the DDC classes is used in the Renardus advanced search feature. The result list could be ranked according to the degree of relationship between the individual resource's local class and the DDC class used for searching.

Renardus has defined five distinct mapping relationships. The local class is deemed to be either fully equivalent, a narrower or broader equivalent, or has a major or minor overlap when compared with the DDC class. These relationships are influenced by the possible relationships between sets in set theory and can be illustrated via Venn diagrams. This approach allows formal treatment and certain calculations on the relationships between the classes. "Fully equivalent" means that the subject content of the local page that one is linked to, is generally the same as the subject indicated on the Renardus browsing page. "Narrower equivalent" indicates that the subject content of the local page is a true subset of the browsing page, whereas "Broader equivalent" reflects the opposite scenario; the local page contains all of the subject content of the Renardus browsing page. Finally, "Major overlap" exists when the content of the local page represents a large part of the browsing page plus other related subjects. Conversely "Minor overlap" indicates some equivalence to part of the browsing page but that it may also include other related subjects.[7] Renardus maps in one direction only, from the DDC to the local classification(s). The three types of equivalence require that one of the two classes is a true subset of the other, i.e. that it cannot also be mapped to another part of the classification scheme. Full equivalence is the intermediate situation where both classes are basically 100% equivalent. The two overlapping relationships require that parts of both classes clearly do not belong to the subject content of the other class. Thus certain logical rules apply which would permit a formal quality control of the mapping process.

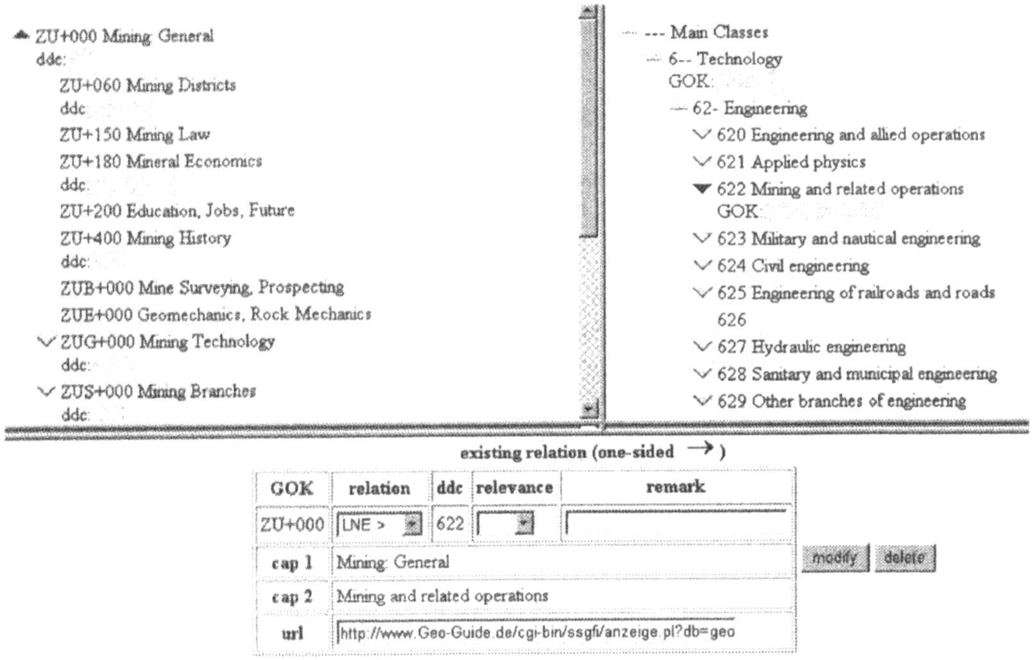

Fig. 1: The Renardus mapping tool

4. Technical solutions and tools

The main sources that are used for the classification mapping effort are the local classification systems and the enhanced DDC as presented in OCLC's CORC WebDewey. To support the practical effort, Renardus has adapted a mapping tool developed by the German CARMEN project. The Renardus mapping tool is Web-based and requires the open-source database software mySQL, an Apache Web server, JavaScript, and PHP scripts at the server side. The classification systems and mapping information are stored on different servers, partly for legal reasons. Each gateway participating in the mapping effort needs to provide a machine-readable version of the classification scheme (or schemes) that they use for use by the mapping tool. The user interface (Fig.1) consists of three main windows: one for the local target classification, another for displaying and navigating the source classification (DDC). The third window receives and displays the mapping information, including relationships and notes. Mapping relationships are displayed as links in both classification windows. The tool has been adapted to create and store the mapping information in a mySQL database in a syntax specified by Renardus. This information is imported by Perl scripts into the main Renardus system in order to create the mapping links on the subject browsing pages and is also used by each gateway's local normalisation scripts in order to generate a DDC mapping for each resource in the local gateway's Renardus database.

The enhanced DDC is delivered by OCLC in several XML encoded data files with an XML DTD, tag/attribute information and additional information about hierarchy. They contain 25,500 main schedule entries (notations) and 35,700 different records. Using these files, an initial complete hierarchical set of web pages is generated allowing a user to navigate through the DDC structure. Completely empty branches in the lower part of the DDC hierarchy, however, can be removed from the display, assuming they are not required to assist as transitional steps during the browsing.

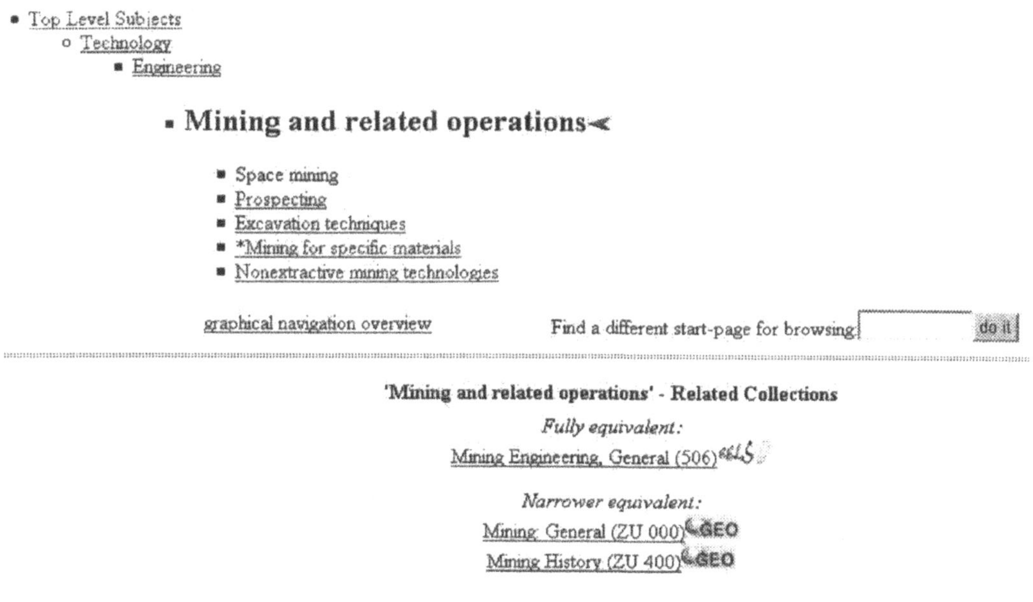

Fig. 2: Renardus DDC browsing page for mining and related operations

5. The resulting cross-browsing feature in Renardus

The DDC mapping information is used in two different ways by the Renardus prototype, firstly to create the cross-browse service, but secondly to provide information for the advanced search feature. The aim of the cross-browse part of the Renardus is to allow users to navigate through the subject hierarchies of the DDC classification and to "jump" from a chosen class to related (i.e. mapped) classes and directories in the local subject gateways. This type of navigation can be called "browse and jump." The Renardus system specifies the different equivalences and degrees of overlap in the user interface. This approach allows the user to visualise the resources in the context of their local browsing structures and to continue browsing there (Fig. 2). The upper part of every page displays the available categories in the actual section of the hierarchy, with links to all levels above and one level below for users to follow. The lower half of the browsing pages shows one or more links to related resource collections. The local classification caption, the local classification code and the icon of the gateway that the user would "jump" to when clicking on the link, are also displayed. The related collections are presented in a ranked order according to the recorded mapping relationship: fully equivalent classes are displayed first and minor overlapping classes last, thus to encourage the user to explore first the collections that are closest in coverage to the chosen DDC class.

Clearly, very large browsing structures, like that represented by the full DDC, need to provide additional assistance to guide users and features that supply an overview of options. Project investigations did not find any "tried-and-tested" solutions that Renardus could immediately apply. Therefore, the following preliminary navigation support features have been implemented for practical evaluation and criticism:

a) *Initial search for start page*. On all browsing pages (apart from the top level) a search box is offered to "Find a different start-page for browsing". Normally several valid alternative browsing pages are displayed. This feature offers a short cut for users who know significant terms from a valid category elsewhere in the Renardus DDC structure. This may also be an option if users want to try their luck at finding a relevant entry for browsing, or if they have difficulty finding exactly where their main area of interest is hidden within the hierarchy. From the alternative list, users can go to a selected browsing page or graphically explore the hierarchical environment of this subject for further navigation.

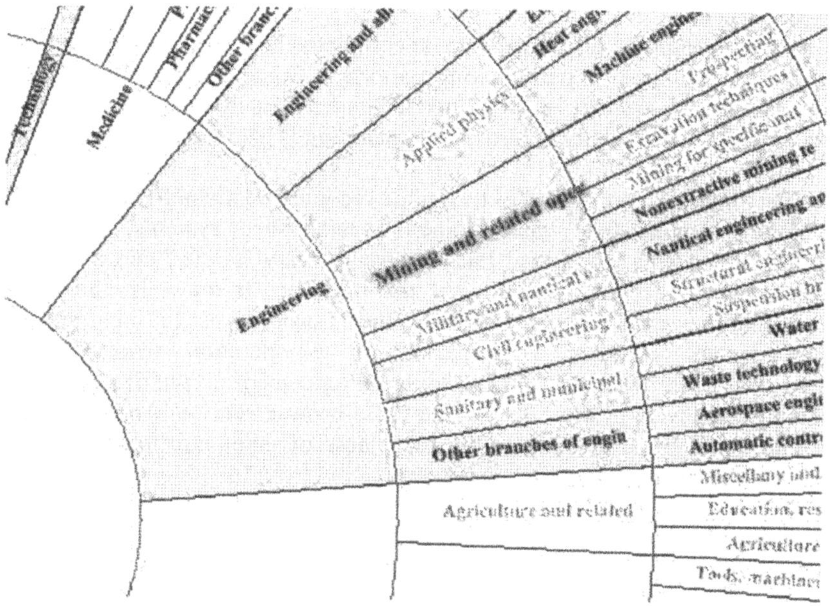

Fig. 3: Graphical navigation overview

b) Graphical navigation overview. A "Graphical navigation overview" (Fig. 3) is available on every browse page. It provides a visual overview of all the available categories that surround a chosen subject term, normally at one level above and two levels below within the hierarchy. Colours are used to help display the selected class within its context and all other classes that contain mappings. This feature is intended to increase the speed of users' navigation of the browse structure and to provide an immediate subject overview. Clicking on categories within the graphical display shows the relevant Renardus browsing page for this subject. An experimental text-based version of the browsing overview is also available.
c) Merge. Renardus also offers a short cut to viewing individual resource descriptions from all related collections with the feature: "Merge the resource-descriptions from all related collections listed here." The main disadvantage with this "virtual browsing" is that users may lose some context and potential additional information if they do not explore the local gateway's browse structure. However, users may save time and will be shown an integrated list of resources from all related collections listed on the page, presented in the usual Renardus results display. The same kind of search can be carried out on the "advanced search" page by selecting the "DDC Classification" element for the search.

The DDC mapping information is also used in the Renardus advanced search feature. While the general subject element allows searching on all local subject information (e.g. uncontrolled keywords, controlled keywords from thesauri and subject headings, classification captions and notations, etc.) the "DDC classification" element enables searches to be made of the mapped DDC classes. A search normally opens an index scan window that allows the user to select from subject entries retrieved by the search. Layout and user interface solutions still need to be optimised based on user evaluation and usability research.

6. Future work
The remaining mapping effort needs to be completed by Fall 2001, with the goal being to map all of the local classes of participating gateways. Some loosely related gateways still have concerns about the amount of effort needed and the intellectual property rights involved. A more comprehensive quality control of the mapping is also required.

The project investigators intend to formulate recommendations for subject access in gateways and broker systems (e.g., the choice of established systems, the granularity of the classification systems, continued local browsing features, etc.) and will give advice on the consistency, accuracy and usability of the mapping. It may also be possible to identify captions that may need to be adapted to reflect European usage, including experiments with Internet-adapted "end-user vocabularies" in co-operation with OCLC Forest Press. Furthermore, Renardus hopes to get additional agreement on the use of multilingual captions for the highest levels of the DDC in the cross-browse service. Another area of possible co-operation would be to investigate the usefulness of automatic mapping (and classification) experiments to support the mapping process.

The mapping methodologies and practical solutions developed by Renardus might need to be further refined. It would also be useful to explore the usability of the browsing service with real users. User interfaces for browsing in large distributed digital services are not as yet well developed. Co-operative development and standardization efforts are needed in order to prepare vocabularies for distributed usage over the Internet with suitable encoding, identification and appropriate search protocols. In the longer term, the owners of established classification systems may need to become convinced of the need to provide mappings themselves and to maintain them as part of their vocabulary services, thus making the mapping task more sustainable.

The Renardus classification mapping effort is a large-scale experiment and, as yet, cannot build very much on theory or the practical experiences of others. It may raise more questions and problems than provide solutions and answers. One has to hope that the effort can be continued, embedded in broad international co-operation, as a combined development and research effort that can influence future solutions.

Notes
1. Part of the preparatory effort of T. Koch was supported by a Visiting Scientist scholarship at the Maastricht McLuhan Institute, European Centre for Digital Culture, Knowledge Organisation and Learning Technology, The Netherlands in August-September 2000.
2. The Renardus project Web-site can be found at: http://www.renardus.org/
3. A beta version of the Renardus broker pilot can be viewed at: http://renardus.lub.lu.se/
4. DESIRE II (http://www.desire.org): automatic classification efforts: http://www.lub.lu.se/desire/DESIRE36a-overview.html
5. Renardus project overview of classification systems in use - follow the link: "Overview Classification Systems": http://renardus.sub.uni-goettingen.de/wp7/d7.4/
6. CARMEN (Content Analysis, Retrieval and MetaData: Effective Networking) project: AP12: http://www.bibliothek.uni-regensburg.de/projects/carmen12/
7. See the illustration at: http://renardus.sub.uni-goettingen.de/conferences/elag2001/mapping_language.gif

References

Becker, H. J., *et al.* (2000). *Evaluation of existing data models*, Renardus D6.1. http://www.renardus.org/deliverables/

Koch, T. and Day, M. (1997). *The role of classification schemes in Internet resource description and discovery*, DESIRE D3.2 (3). http://www.ukoln.ac.uk/metadata/desire/classification/

Koch, T., Neuroth, H. and Day, M. (2001a). *DDC mapping report*, Renardus D7.4. http://renardus.sub.uni-goettingen.de/wp7/d7.4/

Koch, T., Neuroth, H. and Day, M. (2001b). *DDC mapping guidelines*, Renardus D7.4 (internal deliverable).

Session 3

RETRIEVAL ACROSS MULTIPLE VOCABULARIES (2)

Putting the World Back Together: Mapping Multiple Vocabularies into a Single Thesaurus

Patricia S. Kuhr

Abstract: This paper describes an ongoing project in which the subject headings contained in twelve controlled vocabularies covering multiple disciplines from the humanities to the sciences and including law and education among others are being collapsed into a single vocabulary and reference structure. The design of the database, algorithms created to programmatically link like-concepts, and daily maintenance are detailed. The problems and pitfalls of dealing with multiple vocabularies are noted, as well as the difficulties in relying purely on computer generated algorithms. The application of this megathesaurus to bibliographic records and methodology of retrieval is explained.

The dictionary[1] defines "Renaissance man" as "the typical educated, cultured man... who, because the knowledge of the world was generally limited, was able to know everything there was to know about a great variety of different subjects". We have come a long way since the Renaissance and become progressively more specialized. While philosophers could also be physicians and astronomers in ancient Greece, by the early 19th century a physician's knowledge was concentrated on matters medical, and an astronomer's on matters celestial, but neither on the metaphysical. By the late 20th century, general practitioners were no longer the majority of medical doctors. Now there were paediatricians, surgeons, gynaecologists and gerontologists, each with a special knowledge of only one area of medicine.

Along a similar path, the first periodical index of note, the *Nineteenth Century Readers' Guide* (1890) closely followed by *Readers Guide to Periodical Literature* (1902) indexed magazines across a wide spectrum, and both were intended for a general audience. And although this spectrum and audience remain today, the addition of specialized indexes throughout the history of the H.W.Wilson Company, reflected the growing trend of specialization. Eventually, there were 12 periodical indexes covering all categories of the Dewey Decimal Classification system.

Following the principles of good indexing, each product that the company developed considered the nature of the material, the number of periodicals indexed (size of the collection), the complexity of the subject matter, and above all, the user, in the development of subjects with which to access the material indexed. The biologist who uses *Biological and Agricultural Index* to locate material on the "Tympanic membrane" is not the student looking in *Readers' Guide for Young People* for "Eardrum" for his homework. Both search with the expectation of finding what they are looking for under the subject headings that they use.

But like all other things affected by the introduction and growing use of computers and the Internet, technology has played a rôle in how the library world responded (or did not respond) to the patron. Previously, a reference librarian would direct the patron to whichever index was likely to satisfy the topic of the patron's search. But patrons increasingly rely on the computer, and not the librarian, to guide their search.

Putting the world back together

In the mid-eighties, when the Wilson company began distributing its indexes in MARC format on computer tapes for local mounting, we discovered that tapes were being mounted, not as individual databases, but as one "Wilson" periodical database. Much to our chagrin, the years we had spent developing unique products for unique audiences was now threatened by the complaint that the subject headings aren't the same across the indexes!

At this juncture, unlike our own online system (Wilsonline) or our CD-Rom products, OPACS were incapable of displaying cross references, a problem which still exists today in many systems, (and for which we, as librarians, are to blame). How were we to get the user from the controlled vocabulary in one index to the controlled vocabulary of another? How could we make one search result in multiple retrievals?

Fortunately, the single database concept has pretty much disappeared, but the issue of multi-file searching, and multiple vocabularies remains. The latest generation of library patron has become used to "easy and instantaneous" solutions eschewing thorough and/or accurate searching techniques. (But this is another issue). How were we to respond to "easy and instantaneous." We investigated and discarded a number of schemes before we settled on a "megathesaurus" format and "automatic switching". We began by creating a department to develop the project, headed by an Editor of Subject Authorities. Next we created a database containing the controlled vocabulary of each periodical index. Initially we began with 11 indexes, but have since added *Sears' List of Subject Headings* and *Readers' Guide for Young People*, and soon are to add *Biography Index*. The initial load contained 580,000 authority records. After loading the initial set, those records containing the same term were programmatically merged. This reduced the original set to 380,000 records. It has since grown to over 900,000.

A single record contains the subject term(s), a tag identifying each of the indexes which "owns" the term, the broader and related terms, and the indexes which "owns" that reference, along with any notes or messages written by the editor for indexing purposes. In addition, fields were created for a megathesaurus term, broader and related megathesaurus terms, scope notes, messages to the index editors from the Subject Authority Editor, Library of Congress term and a top term.[2] We maintain a proprietary database at Wilson with tagged fields, and since these records contain information not found in a MARC format, I have displayed them neither in Wilson or MARC, but rather in plain English text. A typical record from this first stage would look like this:

Authority main term:
Index main term: Astrophysics: AST BAI GSI HUM
Index broader term: Space sciences: AST RDG
Index broader term: Astronomy: BAI EDI HUM RDG
Index broader term: Stars: BAI EDI HUM
Index broader term: Physics: BAI HUM RDG
Index broader term: Cosmic physics: EDI HUM
Index related term:
Authority broader term:
Authority related term:
Messages:
Scope note:
Library of Congress: Astrophysics: 85009032
Top term:

Figure 1. Sample authority record

The next step was to create some algorithms which would help us identify other matches. We began with singular/plural forms. After creating a list of terms that matched except for a trailing s, or a y/ies combination, we discovered that there were indeed terms that had different meanings in the singular/plural form, e.g., Film/Films. In *Library Literature*, "Films" meant movies, but in *Applied Science*, the singular form "Film" meant a surface coating. Since the percentage of these anomalies was small, we wrote a programming rule stating that all singulars and plurals would merge, except if both records contained an Authority main term. Authority terms were added to all the records with anomalies and then all the other records were merged programmatically. In the example above, the record for "Films" was later merged with "Motion pictures," creating the following:

Authority main term:
Index main term: Films: LIB
Index main term: Motion pictures: ART AST BPI EDI GSI HUM RDG RGC SRS

Figure 2: Sample authority record with 2 terms

Since the English language is full of exceptions to every rule, all other variants of singular/plural, e.g., Goose/Geese, needed to be searched and dealt with manually.
Following this, we created a list of terms that were inverted and matched an uninverted form, e.g., "Insurance, Health" and "Health insurance." Once identified, we discovered that there were no exceptions (the only algorithm with no exceptions) and these were merged programmatically. In addition, every time a new subject record is added to the authority file, this algorithm is in place to continue to merge these terms without human intervention, whenever it finds a match.

Our next attempt at programmatic merges was to look at heading/subdivision combinations that were reversed, e.g., "Economic policy--France" and "France--Economic policy." While this reversal fits the scheme of like-concepts, "Bibliography--Germany" and "Germany—

Bibliography" did not. At the time we began this project, form subdivisions were just beginning to be considered. Today, if we were to establish a subfield $v, which we have yet to do, you could write an algorithm for merging terms when both terms are $a...$s terms, but not merging if one term is an $a...$s and one an $a...$v term.

A third variation of reversals that added to our problem was a geographic/geographic relationship, e.g., "United States--Foreign relations--Italy" and "Italy--Foreign relations--United States." While these are indeed like-concepts, the fact is, that we use both headings on the same bibliographic record. When one is used, the second is automatically applied as well, making retrieval on either combination instantaneous rather than resorting to a *see* reference as was our previous print-oriented methodology.[3]

Clearly an algorithm could not be designed for the programmatic merger of all reversals, but we did devise a computer process which we refer to as our dotted term list. After trying several combinations, we constructed a single term by alphabetizing all words in a subject string, stripping all subdivision delimiters and spaces, and preceded each newly created string with a dot (or period/full stop) to alphabetize the terms outside the normal list in our inverted index (or browse display). The term "United States--Foreign relations--Great Britain" looks like this: .britainforeigngreatrelationsstatesunited
Every new subject heading added to the file is constructed in this manner and on a daily basis, an update process checks all new terms and prints a report containing all records with more than one occurrence of a dotted term. These are inspected manually and, if they fit the criteria of like-concept, they are merged.

Our next algorithm explored the possibility of two terms having a certain number of matching characters at the beginning of the string. This could only be done with single segment terms, e.g., "Agriculture laws" and "Agricultural laws" or "Agricultural laws and regulations." Anything with subdivisions would create too many false drops. Once a list was identified, a unique record (not an authority record) was devised which contains both terms, and every time one of the two terms with a subdivision is established, the computer looks for the other term with the same subdivision. Once "Agriculture laws" and "Agricultural laws" were identified, "Agriculture laws--India" would programmatically merge with "Agricultural laws--India."

Since we first created this synonym matching, we have extended this to include same first term, variant subdivisions. This led us to an unique problem in subject matching. Like the Library of Congress, all of the periodical indexes, with one exception, utilized the concept of free-floating subdivisions. This concept generally avoids the need to create a subject authority record for subdivisions which are used regularly. Free-floating subdivisions cause two problems. One is misapplication: either adding a wrong subdivision, adding a subdivision to a subject heading which should not be subdivided in that manner, or creating the wrong sequence of multiple subdivisions. The other is that no record exists to merge. If both *Readers' Guide* and *Business Periodicals Index* use the subdivision --Bibliography under a term, but only *Business* creates an authority record, we cannot create a match. While this is not much of a problem when the main heading is the same, it becomes a problem when the main heading varies, e.g., "Hotels and motels--Bibliography" and "Hotels, motels, etc.--Bibliography." Without a match, the automatic switching mechanism utilized on bibliographic records (to be described later) cannot take place. So before continuing with our project we had to create records for every subject heading in the bibliographic files that did not have an authority record, and turn off validation for free floating subdivisions. In *Readers' Guide* alone, three free-floating subdivisions created 19,000 new authority records.

Another process we tried was to match all terms used as *see* references in one index with a matching subject heading in another index. The searching was accomplished programmatically, but the inspection of terms was a human project. This was probably how we found "Bombina bombina" and "Firebellied toad".

But computers, being the exacting tools that they are, still cannot do what the human mind can and programmatic mergers of terms like "Astrochemistry" and "Cosmochemistry" or "Nociceptors" and "Pain receptors" are a long way down the road. They are still subject to a *search and merge* methodology.

One thing we have learned from our study of subject headings is how inventive the human mind truly is. To wit, how many ways would you think one could refer to those sounds made by creatures that fly that we call birds? How about seven? Needless to say, after merging the seven records, we exercised some authority and requested that all indexes use the same term. But variety, if nothing else, has taught us that, like our editors, our users employ similar variations in searching our indexes, and the need for *see* references is greater than we (or any other authority list) have managed to provide.

After like-concepts are identified and merged, the Library of Congress authority records are searched for a match and added to the record. At this point a megathesaurus term and structure can be added to the authority record. We have developed several rules to guide us, e.g., all inverted terms will be created in natural language format. This rule applies even if every index is using the same inverted term. Initially, headings and structure are not created term by term, but rather cluster by cluster; for example, all the headings for foods were worked on at the same time. This allows us to create a more unified and consistent hierarchical structure. Guidelines can be generated for both the Authority Department and individual indexes in the hope that newly created headings will begin to be uniform across the databases. On average, all the indexes have about 1000 new subject records added a week. The megathesaurus file updates daily to keep pace with new headings, revised headings and deletions. Additionally, the Library of Congress tapes are loaded weekly, and all new and revised records are run against the megathesaurus file to find matches.

The purpose of all this intellectual activity, of course, is to apply this information to the retrieval process. In the bibliographic records the subject field was expanded to include additional subelements, the most important of which is the megathesaurus term. Every bibliographic article released into a database validates against its own authority file. The computer then checks the megathesaurus file. If the record containing the index term also contains an authority main term (see figure 3), that authority main term is mapped to the appropriate subelement in the bibliographic record. Additionally, every weekend all terms added to the megathesaurus during that week are extracted, a match is found in the bibliographic records of each index and terms are mapped to retrospective records.

Authority main term: Agriculture--Laws and regulations
Index main term: Agriculture--Laws and regulations: AST SSI
Index main term: Agricultural laws and legislation: BAI
Index main term: Agricultural laws and regulations: BPI HUM
Index main term: Agricultural administration: RDG

Figure 3. Record with authority main term

The presence of the authority main term (or megathesaurus term) on the bibliographic record allows three things to happen: 1) When searched individually either electronically or in print, the subject term that the user is accustomed to seeing in that index will still be the subject retrieved; 2) If a user searches multiple indexes simultaneously, the soon to be released search engine used for electronic retrieval, will retrieve records from all indexes with different terms which have been linked together by the megathesaurus term; or 3) If the user is searching the combined indexes in the multi-file *OMNI Index*, all the records retrieved will have the megathesaurus term displayed regardless of the original index term.

We believe that this concept allows for the unique individuality of each index's material, language, and audience, while answering a need for ease of retrieval for the contemporary patron, or, for those "Renaissance men" among us who prefer the "sum of the parts."

References

[1] *Random House dictionary of the English language: The unabridged edition*, 1966.
[2] A top term refers to a broad category under which the subject heading would belong, e.g., Science or Ethnic groups.
[3] Initially we discovered that the indexes used only one form, but they varied on rules for selection (some always established the term in alphabetical order; some with United States always first, if it were one of the two countries, etc.) and cross reference structure (some with a *see* reference from the reverse, some with *see also* references from the secondary country--Foreign relations). To create uniformity, all indexes were instructed to establish and use both headings on each bibliographic record.

Access methods in a database of e-journals

Friedrich Geisselmann

Introduction
The paper[1] is based on the database "E-journals Library" ("Elektronische Zeitschriftenbibliothek" - EZB). http://www.bibliothek.uni-regensburg.de/ezeit/. This database was developed by the University Library of Regensburg to offer a user-friendly interface independent of publishers' websites (like ScienceDirect). The main criterion for the service is real usage, not descriptive cataloging. The system is a web-based service, a dedicated system, outside the traditional catalogue.
What are the functions of such a dedicated system? If we want to bring users to our digital libraries we should ask what they want from such a library and which service we should offer.

1. Content: as much as possible and highly relevant content.
2. Tools to search and browse for the content wanted. Browsing in a digital library is comparable to browsing in a reading room.
3. The digital library should have a clear profile of content.

If these criteria coincide, the usage can be high. In the case of EZB it will be 4,000,000 users this year.[2] The service is growing steadily, corresponding to the increasing supply of electronic journals and the increasing acceptance of digital publications.
When I compare such a dedicated system with a reading room, I want to say: "There are different functions necessary compared to a collection of printed books. The EZB is not merely a catalogue; it has the functions of a virtual reading room, which are quite different from an OPAC.

Another question is: what is necessary to present electronic journals? This material is different from monographs, which are normally highly specialized.
The purpose of this paper is to show the different methods of access which are offered to the user and which methods are used most.

1. Description of the service
The database is a cooperative service. In 1997 the University Library of Regensburg started, as one of the first German libraries, to deal with the opportunities and problems of electronic journals. At that time, the supply of electronic journals was still quite small, amounting to a number of some hundred titles in the field of science and research. However, one could expect a quick growth in this sector, as more and more universities and academic institutions started to issue journals via their web servers and an increasing number of publishers started to offer electronic editions of their print journals on the Internet.

At the moment (August 2001) there are 151 libraries cooperating. The service is customized to the needs of the cooperating libraries. The individual libraries administer their access rights themselves.

Methods of access in a database of e-journals

The database contains 9,634 full text scientific journals: free titles, licensed e-journals and those not licensed. The licensing policy is different for each library.

All participating institutions collect bibliographical data and catalogue them into a central database located in Regensburg. The EZB does not store any contents of electronic journals. The recorded journals have to be scientific or academic and their articles have to be available as full texts on the internet. We do not file journals on the popular science level or journals offering only tables of contents or abstracts. This rather narrow selection of academic/scientific full text journals can be considered as a quality characteristic of the EZB, because it guarantees a high degree of transparency of EZB content for the user.

It is the most comprehensive and successful database of e-journals in Europe. Some statistics regarding to content:

- electronic only 978 titles; parallel editions 8,656 titles
- print only - parallel editions: Compared with the subscriptions of the University Library of Regensburg - overall highly relevant titles - two thirds of the titles in science and medicine are published in parallel editions (Slide 5)

Print journals / electronic journals

Print journals subscribed by the University Library of Regensburg / existing parallel journals (03-01-2001)

Subject	**in Regensburg subscribed print journals**	**print only**	**parallel electronic editions**	**titles in the EZB**
Biology	272	86	186	1156
Medicine	817	234	583	2279
Physics	143	42	101	642

5

- Statistics according to subject (Slide 6)

EZB title content (06-29-2001)

Subject	Nr. of titles	Subject	Nr. of titles
Medicine	2543	History	222
Technology	1744	Geography	184
Biology	1211	Philosophy	176
Chemistry, Pharmaceutics	888	Ethnology	127
Economics	848	General Science	106
Physics	667	English, American Studies	103
Computer Science	573	Theology, Religious Studies	94
Mathematics	523	Sports Science	71
Psychology	485	Art History	41
Sociology	467	Archaeology	41
Education Science	373	Musicology	38
Political Science	362	Classical studies	34
Agriculture, Forestry etc.	312	Romance Studies	27
Law	303	German Studies	26
Geology, Paleontology	282	Slavonic Studies	6
Linguistics, Literary Studies	234		

6

As might be expected, most titles are offered in the fields of medicine, technology and science. In the fields of social sciences and arts, the number of e-journals is still considerably lower. But nevertheless some other subjects, such as economics with 714 titles and psychology with 454 titles, have a surprising number.In other subjects, however, there is still quite low activity in the domain of electronic publications.

Some words about the interface:
Access is possible either by searching or by browsing. Each library can determine its own method of access.

Information about the access to journals: A traffic light symbol shows the accessibility of each title so that users always know which titles really offer full text access to them.

- A green light marks free e-journals.
- A yellow light denotes titles which are licensed at the respective member library; full texts can be accessed by the institutional users. An additional "Readme" page shows further information concerning access and use.
- A red light stands for journals without a subscription. In these cases, full text access is not possible. Usually, a table of contents and sometimes even abstracts are freely available.

The distribution of yellow and red lights depends on the institution, as each member library has different journals on subscription.

The specific view to be shown is determined in various ways. For example, a library may pass a parameter within a link to the EZB which enables viewing its own collection. Furthermore, it is possible to make a selection according to the IP-address of the requesting client. Additionally, each user can always choose for himself which institution's view he wants to have displayed.
Besides the choice of the participating institution one can also choose to have only free and licensed titles shown for the browse and search functions.

Some statistics about the usage (Slide 8). It is steadily growing. This shows that the service is accepted though it would not be necessary for the user to use this service. Our users could store bookmarks as well - but the growing numbers show that users know the value of a high quality service.

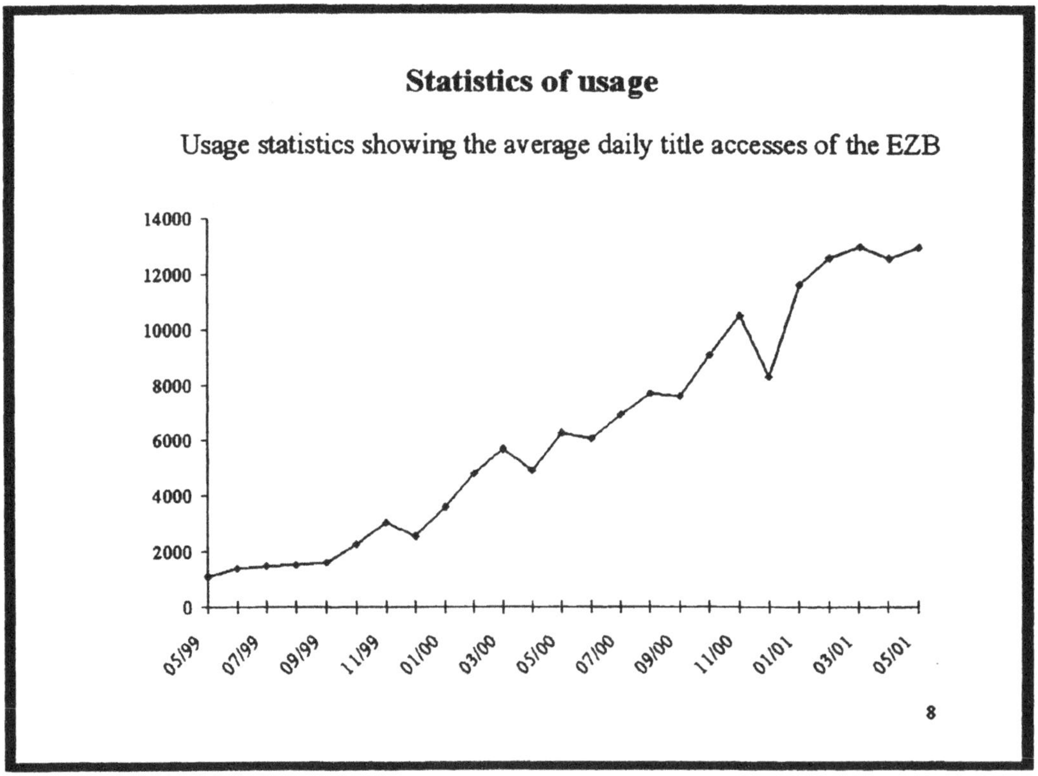

Slide 9 shows the usage at the University Library of Regensburg. There will be about 200,000 users in 2001. This has to be compared with 2,300,000 users in our reading rooms and 475,000 books used outside our library.

Statistics of usage

Usage statistics showing the average daily title accesses on the EZB pages of the University Library of Regensburg

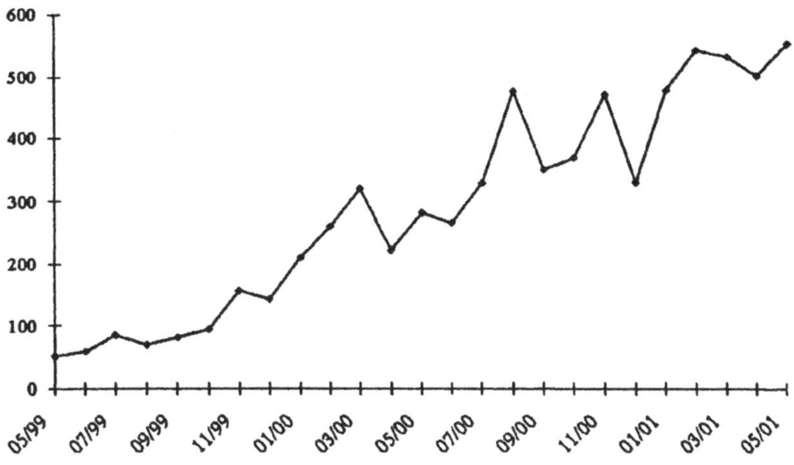

9

One of the reasons for the success is the quality of content: The EZB offers an exhaustive collection as well as a selection of high quality material - which is quite different from search engines.

2. Methods of access

The EZB contains material for all subject areas. The methods of access are created for the user who has general interests. Problems arise with specific needs of some libraries. We can classify journals into more than one discipline.

The main method of access is browsing in lists arranged according a broad classification which follows RVK (Regensburger Verbundklassifikation). At present, we only classify to the first level. In each class alphabetical lists of journals are offered.

Browsing functions: The titles entered in the EZB can be displayed as an alphabetical list of all titles or in subject lists (titles of one discipline). A list of all subjects gives primary information on all e-journals. This overview shows how many titles are available for each subject. The respective subject lists show the journal titles in alphabetical order.

A click on the journal title leads directly to the journal homepage, and if it is on subscription, one can access the full text articles. A little information symbol "i" leads to the bibliographic data of each title. The licensed titles have an additional "readme" link, where the user can find library specific access information.

Search functions: Besides the browsing possibilities, one can also search for particular journal titles. The EZB offers search possibilities for title keywords, publisher and ISSN. In addition, the user may create a combined alphabetical list of journals belonging to various selected subjects. The search can be restricted to free and/or licensed titles only and the user can search for new entries by means of a date search.

There are some questions regarding classification:
The classification depends on the number of titles; we reclassify big classes. How can we show the relations between different parts of a discipline? In medicine we will reclassify and show the results in two levels.

- Should we classify according to the full range of the classification?
- Should we use DDC?

The EZB is connected to library catalogues and bibliographic databases and is thereby integrated into the service spectrum of libraries in different ways. This connection permits the user to search for electronic journals just as for traditional library media, and also to access them from OPACs and from databases.

Some German libraries, e.g. our library, file electronic journals in their OPACs and make them accessible by means of the EZB. This connection between the catalogue and the EZB is accomplished by indicating in the catalogue entry the journal's EZB URL instead of the publisher's homepage. Thus, this internet address does not link directly to the journal homepage but to a so-called "frontdoor" page in the EZB. This frontdoor shows which EZB member libraries offer full text access to the title and contains a link to the actual journal. This way of connecting EZB and library catalogues avoids double input, because URL and licence changes have to be made in the EZB only and not additionally in the catalogue. The specific user and access information is maintained in the EZB. It is to the users' advantage that they can search simultaneously for electronic and printed media and always receive currently valid access information. For example, they can search for a journal title in the OPAC of the University Library of Regensburg and retrieve entries for the print and the electronic edition, if both exist. The entry for the electronic edition shows an internet address which leads to the EZB frontdoor. This frontdoor makes clear whether the University of Regensburg has access rights to the full text articles of the respective title. If it is marked by a yellow light, the user can jump directly to the journal and open articles. This frontdoor concept derives from cooperation between the EZB and the Zeitschriftendatenbank ZDB (Union Catalogue of Serials), the national catalogue for serials in Germany. The electronic journals are cataloged in the ZDB.

We have also achieved a connection between the EZB and bibliographic databases. While browsing the result list of a database search, e.g. the Silverplatter databases, it is possible to switch to the EZB and access full text articles if they are available. In practice, this means that buttons with the inscription "Full Text via EZB?" are displayed next to the articles in the result list. A click on such a button starts a search for the specific journal in the EZB, guided via the ISSN of the title. The result is a EZB page which shows whether the title is electronically available. In case of appropriate access rights, the user can download the requested article.

3. Statistics of usage

The main access of users is for browsing. If we count the users of all libraries, 43% browse the overview of all subjects and then a specific subject list, 26% browse an alphabetical list of all journals, 31% search with specific criteria for a specific journal. This means 69% browse, while 31% search.

Yet the relations depend on what the library offers as its main feature of access. The library can offer one standard feature on its homepage, e.g. the University Library of Regensburg offers browsing, the University Library of Karlsruhe offers searching, or it can offer all three options as, e.g. the University Library of Düsseldorf. As a result,

- at Regensburg only 14% of the users use searching. The total usage at this university is high.
- at Düsseldorf 42% of the users use searching, browsing is divided between alphabetical and subject lists, the total usage at this university is high.
- at Karlsruhe 85% of the users search, 15% browse; the total usage is very low[3].

These data show that browsing is an essential element of the virtual reading room of a digital library. Another interesting result is that access to the journals from the catalogue is seldom used This applies to access from other databases as well This is a real surprise as most librarians think there is a great demand for interoperability between databases and full text. Furthermore it is interesting that licensed journals are used most. Nevertheless, freely accessible journals also play an important role. It is astonishing at first sight that journals which are not licensed are used as well. This does not prove that users are wrong; it makes sense, as at least table of contents and often abstracts can be used.

Concluding remarks

The paper deals with existing functionalities. Nevertheless the service will be improved. New methods of access will be developed as soon as retrieval of journal articles is possible. The success of this digital library leads to the question: Is a dedicated system for a special type of material useful? The answer is definitely yes. The EZB offers special features a library catalogue cannot offer. This applies especially to searching for journal articles and the management of rights.

Nevertheless we have to discuss the relations between a dedicated system and the library catalogue. In our opinion, the catalogue should offer search functions for all types of material; a dedicated system can offer additional functions. Comparable special materials are:

- Teaching materials,
- Databases,
- Maps.

---

[1] I thank Ms. Evelinde Hutzler for her contributions to this paper.

[2] This number means access of users to journals not access of users to the database. Access for administrative purposes is not included.

[3] Karlsruhe is a big university with a lot of science and informatics. The usage should normally be higher than at Regensburg or Düsseldorf.

Mundane Standards, Everyday Technologies, Equitable Access

Hope A. Olson and Dennis B. Ward

Abstract: The problem of access to marginalized knowledge using general subject access standards is well-established, but few successful solutions have been developed. This paper surveys four different approaches to ameliorating bias: revision of general standards, adaptation of general standards, specialized standards for particular knowledge domains and specialized standards for particular situations. It then examines their technological alternatives and institutional barriers to solutions. The analysis of standards, technologies and barriers is addressed through Ursula Franklin's interpretation of the *real world of technology*.

1. The Problem of Access to Marginalized Knowledge

Bias in access to knowledge and information for and about marginalized groups is well-documented. The literature of librarianship is replete with critiques of subject heading lists and classification schemes for their poor representation of gender, race, ethnicity, nationality, religion, ability, sexuality and age (Olson & Schlegl 2001), but few solutions are offered. In contrast, many specialized libraries and information centres, and subject communities, have developed their own standards. Such specialized standards have long existed for particular disciplines and areas of study and continue to be developed. These standards have typically been in conventional disciplines, but may also be useful in marginalized areas.

If we are looking at subject access in a networked environment we need to make decisions about standards in light of technological implications. Therefore, it is important to think about the nature of technology and how it relates to representation of marginalized knowledge.

2. Control, Compliance and Technology

Physicist Ursula Franklin offers an interpretation of technology that is useful for considering the values we employ in making judgments such as those about subject access for marginalized knowledge. Franklin defines technology as a system. "It entails far more than its individual material components. Technology involves organization, procedures, symbols, new words, equations, and, most of all, a mindset" (1990, 12). This broad definition expands our focus beyond hardware and software to include the work and the people of technology as well. In library and information work it means that technology includes subject access standards and our application of them.

Franklin makes a useful distinction between holistic and prescriptive technologies. Holistic technologies are characterized by workers being in control of the process from beginning to end, as artisans control the integrated technologies of their crafts. In prescriptive technologies "the making or doing of something is broken down into clearly identifiable steps" (1990, 20). The result is that each worker performs only one step and workers do not control the process. Franklin recognizes the efficiencies of such Fordist technologies. That they have made possible certain enhancements to our quality of life is indisputable. However, they also have a negative side. "Prescriptive technologies constitute a major social invention. In political terms, prescriptive technologies are *designs for compliance*" (1990, 28).

Because technologies, in Franklin's view, include organization and procedures as well as material and digital elements, designs for compliance of prescriptive technologies result in "a workforce ... acculturated into a milieu in which external control and internal compliance are seen as normal and necessary" (1990, 23). In this milieu, workers become more and more accustomed to the notion that we comply with one way of doing things and that way is controlled externally. Decision-making is taken out of workers' hands: "prescriptive technologies eliminate the occasions for decision-making and judgement in general and especially for the making of *principled* decisions" (1990, 25) such as those regarding the margins of society.

Franklin's ontological framework of levels of reality - vernacular, extended, constructed and projected - is helpful in determining how we can take back some of the control while maintaining a reasonable level of efficiency. *Vernacular reality* is "that nitty-gritty stuff, the direct action and immediate experience," the "bread and butter, soup, work, clothing and shelter, the reality of everyday life" (1990, 36). *Extended reality* is what comes from the immediate experience of others. *Constructed* or *reconstructed reality* is the archetypal reality presented by discourses within our society through devices such as advertising and propaganda. *Projected reality* is the vernacular reality of the future. Vernacular, extended and projected realities are tangible and reflect our everyday existence: our *mundane reality*. Constructed reality is no less real, but it is more closely related to instruments of compliance and control. In constructed reality we need to ask who is doing the constructing and why.

If we want to make library and information services part of everyone's everyday lives we need to consider our technological decisions and the reality in which they are made.

3. General *vs* Special Subject Access Standards—Content

Four categories of subject access options face individual libraries as they decide how best to serve users seeking marginalized knowledge—that knowledge or information of particular use to, and often produced by, groups who stand at the margins of society:

1) revision of existing general standards
2) locally applicable adaptations of general standards
3) specialized standards for a particular knowledge domain
4) specialized standards for a particular situation

It is important to remember that these options are not mutually exclusive.

3.1 Revision of Existing General Standards

Revision of existing general subject access standards, the first option, is a constant process that is externally controlled by the institutions such as national libraries and editorial bodies responsible for these standards. For example, last year the *Library of Congress Subject Headings* (LCSH) changed 600 headings having the dated adjectival form "Afro-American" to the more accepted "African American" and changed "Man" to "Human beings" in 1997. Revision also includes adding new concepts. Also in LCSH, the heading "Gifted men" was added in May 2001. Previously there had been headings for "Gifted persons" and "Gifted women" as though women being gifted was an exception and men being gifted was the norm. The process of revision is slow, but the efforts made are nevertheless laudable and the results positive as far as they go. General subject access standards tend to reflect a mix of constructed and extended realities depending on the level of reciprocity between the institution responsible for the standard and various people's vernacular realities. For example, the use of literary warrant for updating a standard gives some control to the realities of published literature, but it still may not reflect anyone's mundane experience. Hence, standards tend to be closer to a constructed reality that carries some mainstream view.

Further, the structure of a general subject standard will construct it in a particular mould. Our usual hierarchical structure, whether in classification or in the syndetic structure of thesauri and subject heading lists, subsumes some concepts under others. It gives primacy to some facets, usually disciplines, and organizes knowledge on that basis. These facets are more likely to be part of a constructed reality than an extended or vernacular one. For example, disciplines bear little relation to the everyday life of anyone not associated with education. Even then, they constrict the growing array of interdisciplinary studies.

General subject access standards are typical of cataloguing as a prescriptive technology. The task of creating and revising standards is done by one institution and its application is performed by workers in other institutions. These two closely related processes are distanced from each other in terms of institutional, individual and geographic differences. Compliance with the standard is at a distance from control over the standard.

3.2 Locally Applicable Adaptations of General Standards

A fundamental problem with the revision of mainstream schemes is that it can never meet all possible concerns of bias. Bias is to at least some degree contextual—its amelioration requires some sort of local alternative. For example, LCSH is the responsibility of the Library of Congress, the national library of the United States. It is not inappropriate that it have a bias toward greater accommodation of US topics. The National Library of Canada has developed the *Canadian Subject Headings* as a supplement to LCSH. If even the differences between Canada and the US, small in comparison to many other social and cultural differences, require two different approaches, a universal solution to bias in subject access is almost certainly unattainable.

The second option for addressing bias, adaptation of general standards, results in the sharing of control. Few such adaptations exist for use by marginalized groups. Some regional examples exist such as expansions of the *Dewey Decimal Classification* (DDC) and the *Library of Congress Classification* (LCC) for Arab countries (Soltani 1995) and for India, Malaysia, New Zealand and Australia (Gupta n.d. and Beall 1991). However, expansions and supplements do not seem to have been used to provide access for marginalized users except at Hennepin County Library in Minnesota. There, Sanford Berman adapted LCSH for a public library with particular sympathy for marginalized populations.

Expansions and adaptations bring the standard much closer to extended reality. They are more likely to reflect the lived experience of a marginalized community. They do, however, require compatibility with the structure of a general standard. So while the content may reflect an extended reality, it will be housed in a structure grounded in constructed reality.

Another approach to local adaptation is to use options built into a subject access standard. DDC includes options for emphasis of particular literatures. The Universal Decimal Classification

(UDC) includes a more encompassing and radical option in allowing for change in the standard citation order of facets. This option allows major restructuring so that discipline, language, format, geography or any other facet can be the primary organizing factor of the classification in any particular instance. Such options allow more local control and less compliance with external authority than the conventional application of such standards.

In a recent study, we developed an expansion of DDC to address bias in access to women's studies and feminist information. We incorporated three types of changes: revision of existing numbers, addition of greater specificity, and introduction of more options for local application. We discovered that expansion would not effectively address bias without revision. DDC as it is organized by disciplines reflects the constructed reality of the academy. It has been revised over the years to be more open to the extended realities of different communities. However, further revision is required: feminist theory is classed with women as a social group when it deals mainly with philosophical issues such as epistemology, sexual practices are found only as deviant instances to be controlled, and the ethics of reproductive technologies are grouped with professional medical ethics or with prostitution, obscenity and pornography.

Greater specificity was needed for accommodating information likely to be found in a general collection and even more so for a specialized collections. For example, DDC has only one number for feminism, which also includes everything about the social role and status of women. Local options such as changing the citation order for social groups (so a work on older, middle class, African American women could be classed under any one of those aspects according to local usefulness) were required to allow different emphases for the reflection of vernacular reality.

3.3 Specialized Standards for a Particular Knowledge Domain

The third option is to apply a specialized standard developed for a particular knowledge domain and used across several institutions. Specialized standards exist in abundance, even for marginalized domains. The field of women's studies and information for women is a good example. *A Women's Thesaurus* (Capek 1987), the *Women in Development Thesaurus* developed in Indonesia in cooperation with UNICEF (Nasrul 1991), the Boston Women's Health Book Collective's *Women and Health Thesaurus* used by members of the international Women and Health Documentation Center Network, the bilingual *Canadian Feminist Thesaurus/Le Thésaurus féministe du Canada* (1990), the classification scheme developed by the Akshara Resource Centre for Women in Mumbai, India and used throughout Asia and the Pacific, and the *European Women's Thesaurus* (1998) are examples of specialized standards used across institutions. These standards are controlled within a particular community.

Specialized standards commonly employ terminology that reflects the usage of the audience in a particular knowledge domain. They also include topics of importance to the knowledge domain. Their boundaries are intended to be roughly coextensive with the domain's, thus reflecting its extended reality. The development of *A Women's Thesaurus* is particularly interesting. While following established standards for thesaurus construction, it did so in the context of a large collectivity of feminist librarians and scholars. The editor, four advisory editors, and a thesaurus task force with sixteen members coordinated the work of eleven subject groups. Thirty-five specialized vocabularies were used as a basis for the thesaurus—an extended reality.

3.4 Specialized Standards for a Particular Situation

Many subject access standards are developed for a single purpose and used in only one agency exhibiting local control—a part of the vernacular reality of an institution. An example is the classification scheme and subject heading list developed for and by Chiripaq, the Cultural Centre for the Indigenous People of Peru in Lima and Ayacucho, to satisfy the unique subject demands of women's issues combined with the concerns of indigenous people in Peru. The creation of standards for particular situations is most likely to reflect a vernacular reality, presuming that it is created by those who will use it. As noted previously, some of these standards become more widely used and thereby convert one situation's vernacular reality into the extended realities of others.

A compromise is the use of specialized standards within a domain for adaptation to a particular situation. For example, *New Books on Women & Feminism* published by the University of Wisconsin Women's Studies Librarian's Office uses a list of terms they have used previously. If no suitable term is on the list, they consult *A Women's Thesaurus* or the *Women's Resources International* database. By maintaining a list of terms used, control is maintained locally. By using terms from other sources, labour is saved and the extended reality of the wider women's studies community is included. This hybridized solution is a *de facto* local specialized standard. To bring the advantages of a specialized standard to our feminist expansion of DDC, we used the concepts in *A Women's Thesaurus* to identify problems areas in DDC. Linking most of the descriptors to DDC numbers we evaluated the goodness of each link. We were then able to focus on the areas such as ethics, health, customs, and social groups showing the greatest need for revision and expansion (Olson & Ward 1997 and 1998). Testing the result showed its ability to accommodate successfully concepts in *The Canadian Feminist Thesaurus* and in current print and electronic publications. Once it is disseminated and used in local collections we will be able to assess whether or not the local options make it capable of representing vernacular realities.

4. Information Technology Issues

Computers are the dominant means for implementing subject access under the general standards described above, and the development of World Wide Web interfaces has provided a convenient method of access to libraries following those standards, at least for anyone who is on the Internet. Information technology also has great promise for facilitating the use of specialized access standards and modifications of general standards the better to serve marginalized groups. The main advantage lies in the ability of the Internet to provide economies of scale to groups that are globally very populous even though they may be minorities locally. A second aspect of the research described above, in which a feminist thesaurus is linked to DDC, provides enhanced access through existing Web catalogue interfaces (Ward & Olson 1998). The machine that provides the DDC linkages could be located anywhere on the Internet, and the resulting DDC numbers could usually be inserted into the Web catalogue of a local library. In principle, a single central server could provide a service like this to any Internet user in the world for any particular knowledge domain.

The construction of new and modified standards can benefit from similar economies of scale. The development of the system described above was carried out in one location, but all the work was done using Web-interfaced databases that could accept input from anywhere on the Internet. Thus source" software. The feminist system was implemented using Linux, Apache, PHP and MySQL. All of these products were free, and most of them depend on voluntary development effort from computer programmers around the world. Proprietary software tools were also available, but the free tools generally worked just as well or better, and could be used on old, slow computers making them more widely useable.

The open source model is one likely to be very beneficial for development of new or modified subject access standards. Like the computing community, the library world has many practitioners who are both highly skilled and committed to their profession. One could envision cooperative efforts to build access tools for marginalized groups, and perhaps even more general standards. These standards would be controlled by communities and not by institutions focussed on designs for compliance.

UNESCO's CDS/ISIS system is a successful example of freely available software. It has versions for various technological resources from DOS to Windows, is multilingual and is controlled by a diffuse community. Over 20,000 copies have been registered worldwide (UNESCO CII - WebWorld 2001). The feminist system described above is a different kind of example, designed for a Web environment and building on already existing catalogues. It was completed, worked satisfactorily, but was never made available to the community because of copyright objections. An open source approach would avoid such institutional barriers to access.

5. Institutional Issues

The process of subject cataloguing is to a greater or lesser degree a prescriptive technology in most of our libraries. One record from our local catalogue told this story: the standards for classification and for subject headings originated with the Library of Congress. Some of the subject headings from the National Library of Canada's *Canadian Subject Headings*. The record is coded in MARC (before harmonization, so it is the US MARC employed by the system vendor). It was created at the University of British Columbia, perhaps as a Cataloguing-in-Publication record, and the coding indicates that it was revised by the National Library of Canada and at our university. The interface through which I found the record was created by a major vendor and allowed some local adaptation. The catalogue reflects the policies of a consortium. Further, authority records for the subject headings have been downloaded and originated with the National Library of Canada and the Library of Congress. More recent records in the catalogue will be in harmonized MARC and will have been edited by OCLC's outsourcing service.

An example of a holistic technology is the cataloguing done at Chiripaq, the Cultural Centre for the Indigenous People of Peru. Chiripaq has a small budget and staff and yet they were still able to develop subject access standards in-house and apply them on a MICROISIS system. The university library and the local information centre are very different institutions with very different demands. The use of prescriptive cataloguing technology for large libraries has produced an enormous body of high quality catalogue records available to individual libraries through a variety of avenues. It has probably enhanced some local economies by creating flourishing businesses at the same time that it has provided lower cost cataloguing to libraries all over the world. However, it has also acculturated us to compliance.

Our compliance in subject access means that we presume that we must follow general standards without significant variation to achieve the goals of quality with economy. It is an instance of what Franklin calls the *production model* in which things are:

> made under conditions that are, at least in principle, entirely controllable. If in practice such control is not complete or completely successful, then there is an assumption, implicit in the model itself, that improvements in knowledge, design, and organization can occur so that all essential parameters will become controllable. . . .
>
> Production models are perceived and constructed without links into a larger context. This allows the use of a particular model in a variety of situations. At the same time such an approach discounts and disregards all effects arising from the impact of the production activity on its surroundings. (1990, 27)

For subject access, this means that we have accepted the central control of general standards, trying to perfect their application, without recognizing that they are not perfectable and not necessarily suited to our local vernacular realities and without recognizing that there are other viable options. Enforcement of prescriptive technologies is at an institutional level. The discourses that operate around it are largely economic: the economies of scale justify the use of prescriptive technologies and the restrictions on their use via copyright, licensing and contractual limitations control that use. They foster the replication of a constructed reality rather than a concern with our nitty-gritty everyday vernacular reality.

6. Projected Reality

How can we bring control back to a local level? The focus needs to be on *projected reality*: the vernacular reality of the future. In anticipating it we need to look at the vernacular and extended realities of the present—the mundane reality of everyday information. Can we revise or adapt our prescriptive technologies or do we need to move to a more holistic approach? Certainly we seem to need a better balance between the two if we are to address the needs of those on the margins of our societies. The homogenization of culture feared by critics of globalization is a genuine concern in applying subject access standards.

Ursula Franklin suggests *redemptive technologies* that "use existing technical knowledge in a changed structure and for a changed task" (1990, 128). Our effort to use *A Women's Thesaurus* to search library catalogues via DDC is one example. Freer and farther reaching alternatives would follow from the open source approach described above. Following Franklin's definition of technology as including organizations, procedures and people - as being a mindset - the model of open source software may well be applicable to subject access standards and their applications as well. Sharing is a long tradition in cataloguing, going back at least to the 13th century union catalogue of British monastic libraries, the *Registrum Librorum Angliae*. If we are to maintain our values as a profession we need to take seriously the need for equitable access to marginalized knowledge.

Acknowledgement

The authors thank Anna E. Altmann of the School of Library & Information Studies, University of Alberta for her assistance.

References

Beall, J. (1991). International aspects of DDC 20. In *Dewey: An international perspective*, ed. R.P. Holley. New York: K.G. Saur. Pp.64-80.

Canadian Women's Indexing Group. (1990). *The Canadian feminist thesaurus/le Thésaurus féministe du Canada*. Toronto: OISE Press.

Capek, Mary Ellen, ed. (1987). *A women's thesaurus: An index of language used to describe and locate information by and about women*. New York: Harper & Row.

European Women's Thesaurus. (1998). International Information Centre and Archives for the Women's Movement (IIAV).

Franklin, Ursula. (1990). *The real world of technology*. Montreal: CBC Enterprises.

Gupta, V.K. Dewey Decimal Classification System bibliography. Available at: http://www.oclc.org/dewey/about/bibliography/index.htm (Accessed 19 June 2001)

Nasrul, Zurniaty, *et al.* (1991). *Women in Development Thesaurus*. Jakarta : Clearinghouse for Information on Women in Development, Centre for Scientific Documentation and Information, Indonesian Institute of Sciences in cooperation with Unicef.

Olson, Hope A. & Ward, D.B.. (1997). Feminist locales in Dewey's landscape: Mapping a marginalized knowledge domain. In *Knowledge organization for information retrieval: Proceedings of the sixth International Study Conference on Classification Research*. The Hague: International Federation for Information and Documentation. Pp. 129-133.

Olson, Hope A. & Ward, D.B. (1998). Charting a journey across knowledge domains: Feminism in the Dewey Decimal Classification. In *Structures and Relations in Knowledge Organization: Proceedings of the Fifth International ISKO, August 25-29 1998, Lille, France*, ed. Widad Mustafa el Hadi et al. Würzburg: Ergon Verlag. Pp.237-244.

Olson, Hope A. & Schlegl, R. (in press 2001). Critiques of subject access bias: a meta-analysis. *Cataloging & classification quarterly*, 32(2).

Soltani, Poori. (1995). Translation and Expansion of Classification Systems in the Arab Countries and Iran. In *61st IFLA General Conference - Conference Proceedings - August 20-25, 1995*: http://www.ifla.org/IV/ifla61/61-solp.htm

UNESCO CII - WebWorld. (2001). *The UNESCO micro CDS/ISIS Software*. Available at: http://www.unesco.org/webworld/isis/isis.htm (Accessed 19 June 2001)

Ward, D.B. & Olson, Hope A. (1998). A shelf browsing search system for marginalized user groups. In *Information Access in the Global Information Economy: Proceedings of the 61st Annual Meeting of the American Society for Information Science, October 25–29, 1998, Pittsburgh, Pennsylvania*. Medford, NJ: Information Today. Pp. 342–347.

Session 4

CROSS-SECTORAL RETRIEVAL

HILT: Subject Retrieval in a Distributed Environment

Dennis Nicholson and Susannah Wake

Abstract: The HILT High Level Thesaurus Project aims to study and report on the problem of cross-searching and browsing by subject across a range of communities, services, and service or resource types in the UK given the wide range of subject schemes and associated practices in place in the communities in question (Libraries, Museums, Archives, and Internet Services) and taking the international context into consideration. The paper reports on progress to date, focusing particularly on the inter-community consensus reached at a recent Stakeholder Workshop.

1. HILT and its Aims

The HILT High Level Thesaurus Project[1] is a one year project funded jointly by RSLP[2] and JISC[3] in the UK. A wide range of partners and stakeholders are involved in the project. Full lists can be found at http://hilt.cdlr.strath.ac.uk/AboutHILT/partners.html (project partners in archives, museums, libraries and internet services) and at
http://hilt.cdlr.strath.ac.uk/AboutHILT/stakeholders.html (project stakeholders).
HILT aims to study and report on the problem of cross-searching and browsing by subject across a range of communities, services, and service or resource types in the UK given the wide range of subject schemes and associated practices in place, looking at Libraries, Museums, Archives, Higher Education, Further Education, Public Libraries, electronic services, distributed catalogues based on Z39.50, the Distributed National Electronic Resource (DNER), the Resource Discovery Network (RDN), bibliographic databases, numeric data, and so on – in essence, everything.

2. Approach

The project is charged with:

- Researching the problem through literature and stakeholders surveys, analysis, focus group and workshop discussion and so on
- Analysing and documenting its exact nature in detail
- Determining whether it can be solved and, if so, how it can best be solved
- Attempting to reach a consensus on the issue across the various communities, services and initiatives identified by the project as stakeholder
- Ensuring that any proposed solution is compatible with international terminological activity
- Ensuring that any solution proposed is affordable, sustainable, useful to users and staff alike, implementable, acceptable to stakeholders and funding bodies, takes things like user terminologies and staff, user training into account, is future proofed, has multi-lingual capability, and many other things

The approach agreed with the funding bodies prior to the project start was that we should first of all research the problem by:

- Surveying and reviewing the literature and expert opinion
- Identifying key communities, services and initiatives
- Establishing their perspectives on the problem and on the requirements of their users
- Determining the schemes in use in the communities
- Determining what other schemes were available as possible solutions

- Identifying relevant organizational, inter-organizational, 'political' and other issues (e.g. legacy metadata retro-conversion cost

We were then to identify and agree on a solution through

- Analysing and organising the data
- Charting and discussing the results
- Producing an interim report
- Discussing it in depth at a workshop
- Aiming to reach a consensus in the community through the workshop and an Interim Report

3. Progress to Date

At time of writing, the position as regards project progress is as follows:

- The main literature survey is complete and there is a searchable database with abstracts at http://ocelot.cdlr.strath.ac.uk/ISC105/
- The survey of stakeholders complete and there is a report on the web-site at http://hilt.cdlr.strath.ac.uk/Reports/SurveyResults.html
- Various discussions have been held at project meetings, a focus group, and elsewhere (The report of the HILT Focus Group can be found at
- http://hilt.cdlr.strath.ac.uk/Reports/Focus2602.html)
- A survey on machine solutions and interfaces is well underway
- The stakeholder workshop has just been held and a consensus reached on the preferred way forward in respect of HILT recommendations (The report of the workshop and its conclusions will be mounted on the web-site at http://hilt.cdlr.strath.ac.uk/Dissemination/workshop.html in due course. It may not be there until late July. However, further information on the outcome is provided later in this article)

The results of the workshop will inform compilation of the Interim Report. This will be widely circulated for comment in late July and will mark the final stage in the formal consultative process. Feedback will be sought on the interim conclusions from project stakeholders, other participants, key UK and international bodies and funding bodies. The results will feed into the draft Final report, which will then be evaluated by a thesaurus expert with experience of the various communities before becoming the Final Report. The project will end in September or early October 2001.

4. Current Position: The HILT Stakeholder Workshop

A description of the activities and outcomes of the HILT Stakeholder Workshop, together with helpful references and data from earlier activities as appropriate, is the best way of outlining the current position in the project. A more chronologically based perspective is relatively easy to piece it together from elements of the web-site reports section at
http://hilt.cdlr.strath.ac.uk/Reports/index.html.

The workshop was held in Glasgow on the 19th June. The project had aimed for and succeeded in attracting a balanced and representative set of 50 delegates from archives, libraries, museums, online information services. As is clear from the associated delegates list mounted at http://hilt.cdlr.strath.ac.uk/Dissemination/Workshop%20documents/Delegates%20E-mails.doc, many organizations were represented – most of the stakeholders in fact.

5. Workshop Structure

The day was split into two distinct sessions. The morning session consisted of a number presentations given by stakeholders partners and consultants on the different perspectives of the various communities to the issues HILT is addressing, together with sessions on mapping terminologies, thesaurus interface issues and, with the future in mind, the vision of the semantic web. The slide sets are on the web site at http://hilt.cdlr.strath.ac.uk//Dissemination/WorkshopPresentations.html The afternoon session comprised a breakout session followed by reporting and discussion at a plenary session. The aim of the workshop was to attempt to reach consensus on a range of possible solutions proposed by HILT and devised in conjunction with the project's Management and Steering Groups. The key to this process was the breakout and plenary discussion sessions held in the afternoon.

There were four breakout groups, balanced to ensure a fair representation of each community and each was given the same task - the task of reaching a consensus on a number of issues outlined in a preparatory document entitled HILT Workshop Breakout Sessions: Discussion Issues (and notes) available at: http://hilt.cdlr.strath.ac.uk//Dissemination/Workshopdocuments/BrkoutfullFINAL.rtf.rtf.
This gave the participants sufficient data to enable them to hold an informed discussion of the problem and possible solutions. Since it was a relatively long document, participants had been asked to read it prior to attendance at the meeting and most – possibly all – appeared to have done so.

6. Workshop Option Sets

Attendees were first reminded of the nature of the problem faced by HILT as follows:
The HILT stakeholder survey charted a range of variant practices in respect of the subject description of resources across online services offered by the UK library, archive, museum, and electronic information communities. Although there is no hard empirical evidence one way or another, there is a strong likelihood that this is disadvantaging users, undermining the value of cross-searching and browsing facilities, and wasting public money by 'hiding' relevant resources. As a consequence it could be argued that the situation is worsening and becoming more expensive to remedy, with every resource catalogued utilising these variant schemes and practices.
Details of these variant practices had been provided in the Stakeholder Survey, available to participants on the web-site. Some of the detail is provided below in Appendix A.1.

They were then presented with the option sets describing possible responses to the problem situation faced by HILT listed in Appendix B below and asked to attempt to reach a consensus on:

- Which option set offered the best basis of a preferred response to the situation faced by HILT
- Which option within that option set HILT should recommend as the preferred response
- Which options from other option sets should be considered in addition to this
- Which option set they would choose as a 'second best' alternative to their preferred set

Cases for and against each of these options were provided in the HILT Workshop Breakout Sessions background document noted above and instructions on how best to structure the breakout session were also given. All four breakout groups reached the same – or very similar – conclusions. These are summarized below.

7. Workshop Conclusions

There was clear consensus that the best way forward for HILT was the pilot mapping service listed in Appendix A.2 as option 5.2, combined with a terminologies task force or agency enabling community involvement and control at a practical level. The service envisaged - probably based on an existing commercial approach such as Wordmap or Semio - would map key schemes like LCSH, UNESCO, DDC, UDC, AAT and (perhaps) user and regional terminologies and local adaptations of standard schemes, perhaps using one of them such as DDC as the central spine of the approach. Users would be able to input the term or terms that describe their problem using the terminology that is most meaningful to them, specify their query more closely if necessary by specifying a context (e.g. lotus, the flower, or lotus, the software, or lotus, the position), then obtain a list of equivalent or near-equivalent terms with which to then cross-search or cross-browse the various services. For an example of this type of service see http://www.wordmap.com/ and try typing in 'lotus' then choosing the last context option (starts science > biology). You will see the additional terms. The software will let you control the nature of the search sent using the Boolean operator OR, so synonym A OR synonym B OR synonym C would be one search possibility. Work would be required to interface such a system to many services - in Z39.50 services in particular - but CAIRNS[4] work interfacing web-based Z39.50 clients with an sql-compliant collection descriptions database suggests that this is quite feasible.

The Workshop indicated that the proposed pilot service should:

- Have a strong user focus
- Aim to determine reliable data on costs
- Include costs against benefits at various service and mapping levels as a key deliverable
- Look to involve major international players in funding and management
- Look at how best to integrate semantic web and artificial intelligence developments
- Aim for a quick implementation (NOF projects a concern)
- Involve a broad range of target services
- Use existing machine-readable mappings wherever possible
- Be closely linked to a cross-sectoral and cross-domain task force at a practical level
- Use contexts, relationhips, clustering, etc.
- Look at user terminologies as against DDC as the central spine to which other schemes were to be mapped
- Define things like 'mapping', 'task force', 'terminologies agency' more closely

A pilot mapping service was preferred because a mapping service was the viewed as the best - and possibly the only - basis of a consensus between the stakeholder communities and also solved a greater part of the problem more quickly than any other option, and because a pilot would allow us to put it in place quickly but also allow us to collect more information on costs against benefits and a range of other issues (e.g. costs, user needs, user terminology as 'spine' or DDC, how best to incorporate semantic web and artificial intelligence developments, design, and so on) before making a long-term commitment.

It was also clear from discussion in the plenary session at the end that:

- Everyone agreed there was a problem
- No one thought that it was acceptable to do nothing (OS 1)

- No one had any enthusiasm for the adoption of one or other existing schemes as an option, or even a fall back option (OS 4). Even DDC, regarded by HILT as the most likely scheme on which there might be a consensus was not seen as a way forward in this respect (although it was seen as a key part of a mapping service)

Next Steps

As indicated above, the HILT Interim Report will be widely distributed towards the end of July and represents the last stage in the formal consultative process. Given the degree of consensus achieved in the Stakeholder Workshop, there is reason to hope that a recommendation to proceed to follow up research based on a pilot terminologies mapping service will meet with general approval. If it does, a meeting of potential UK and international funders will be scheduled for late August or early September with a view to turning consensus into practical progress on an issue of vital importance to the coherent development of the global information landscape.

Appendix A.1: Stakeholder Survey: Schemes in Use

Table 1 presents the range of thesauri, classification and subject headings schemes used by the various stakeholders. (The numbers in brackets indicate numbers of respondents reporting use of a scheme.)

Stakeholder Community	Classification Scheme	Subject Heading Scheme	Thesauri
Archives (7)	In house (2)	In house (2) LCSH (1)	UNESCO (5) BET (2)
Libraries (11)	DDC (5) LC (4) In house (1)	LCSH (8) MeSH (1)	In house (2) UNESCO (1)
Museums (5)	UDC (2) DDC (1) SHIC (1)	LCSH (2) MeSH (1)	AAT (2) mda: British Museums Materials Thesaurus (2) In house (2) ROOT Thesaurus (1)
Special Collections (2)		LCSH (2)	UNESCO (1)
Online Information Services (15)	DDC (5) In house (4) LC (1) UDC (1)	LCSH (6) In house (4)	AAT (2) HASSET (2) In house (2) mda Thesauri (1) UNESCO (1)
Government agencies and initiative (2)	Subject Categorization Guide for Defense Science and Technology (1) In house (1)		UNESCO (1) In house (1)

Table 1: HILT stakeholders controlled vocabularies

In most of the communities there are one or two dominant schemes or combination of schemes. In Archives for example, this is the UNESCO Thesaurus, whilst in Libraries and Online Information Services and Hubs DDC combined with LCSH is prominent. LCSH is also used in Museums and Heritage, however this community has invested considerable resources in building controlled vocabularies specifically for objects in certain subject areas. It should also be noted that there are a number of stakeholders in all communities that have created "in house" schemes.
The problem of cross-searching is further intensified due to the fact that many stakeholders do not use their particular preferred approach consistently across all of their resources. There are two main reasons for this. Firstly, when a particular scheme is updated retro-conversion of records cannot take place due to lack of resources and the size of collections. Secondly, stakeholders have created and added new terms where no term from the chosen approach is felt to be suitable.

Appendix A.2: Stakeholder Workshop Breakout Sessions Option Sets
[Note: These option sets were drawn from the HILT Hypothesis Grid - see Appendix A.1 in the document at http://hilt.cdlr.strath.ac.uk/Reports/HILThyp5.rtf]

[OS1] Do nothing:
1. Artificial Intelligence will solve it in time
2. Big business - Microsoft or similar - will solve it
3. Its not really that important
4. No solution is necessary
5. The problem cannot be solved

[OS2] Set up a human process intended to lead to a solution in time:
Set up a Terminologies Agency, perhaps based on National Libraries/mda/NCA
1. Set up an inter-domain, inter-sectoral Task Force to move the communities towards a solution
2. Set up a Terminologies Agency and a Task Force

[OS3] Adopt a base-level, gradual approach, with an eye on future developments:
Adopt a single scheme such as DDC and apply to all collection level descriptions in the UK
1. Gradually create inter-service and inter-community terminology 'cross-walks' eventually building up to a partial but adequately broad solution
2. Aim to solve the problem for electronic services only, perhaps via the semantic web vision
3. Provide more flexible retrieval facilities for users
4. One or more of these four together (please specify)

[OS4] Adopt a single scheme:
1. Adopt: LCSH/UNESCO/DDC/UDC/AAT/Another scheme (say which)/A New Scheme in addition to the existing scheme used by any given service [Please specify which scheme]
2. Adopt: LCSH/UNESCO/DDC/UDC/AAT/Another scheme (say which)/A New Scheme instead of the existing scheme used by any given service [Please specify which scheme]

3. Adopt a single scheme: without retroconversion of legacy metadata/with retroconversion funded by the host organisation/with retroconversion funded centrally [Specify which]

[OS5] Mapping service alternatives:

1. Set up a mapping service, ideally with international participation and support, and gradually build towards a complete mapping of LCSH, UNESCO, UDC, and AAT to a DDC backbone. Include local adaptations and extensions from major services such as the National Libraries. Use the international service with the mapping of UK adaptations and extensions as a model for other countries. Determine and implement the best international funding and maintenance model
2. Set up a 2 year mapping service pilot to measure costs against benefits of both a full scale service and all of the various alternative responses detailed on this page.

---

[1] http://hilt.cdlr.strath.ac.uk/

[2] http://www.rslp.ac.uk/

[3] http://www.jisc.ac.uk/

[4] http://cairns.lib.gla.ac.uk/ and http://cairns.lib.strath.ac.uk/

The Colorado Digitization Project: Subject Access Issues

William A. Garrison

Abstract: The Colorado Digitization Project (CDP), begun in the fall of 1998, is a collaborative initiative that involves Colorado's archives, historical societies, libraries, and museums. The project is creating a union catalogue of metadata records and is investigating the use of Dewey Decimal Classification numbers through WebDewey to allow linkage of general subject terms and highly specialized subject terms within a subject browse feature of the union catalogue.

1. Project Overview and Union Catalogue

The Colorado Digitization Project (CDP) is a collaborative initiative that involves Colorado's archives, historical societies, libraries, and museums. The CDP's goal is to create a virtual digital collection of resources that provide the people of Colorado access to the rich historical, scientific and cultural resources of the state. Project participants are able to contribute content that has been reformatted into digital format as well as the born digital. The virtual collection will include such resources as letters, diaries, government documents, manuscripts, music scores, digital versions of exhibits, artifacts, oral histories and maps.

One of the key objectives of the CDP is to increase access to digital collections. The first effort undertaken was to identify the approaches used among the existing project participants to provide access to their collections. Even at the early stages of the project, it became clear that the institutions used different approaches and that there was no dominant standard or approach. The CDP reviewed current and emerging standards, including Encoded Archival Description (EAD), MARC, Government Information Locator Service (GILS), Dublin Core (DC), Visual Resources Association (VRA), etc., for common elements. As web searching would not provide the desired access, and a single centralized metadata and image system would not be politically or financially feasible, the CDP recommended the development of a union catalogue of metadata to provide a desired level of access, hoping that future developments in web searching would negate the long term need for the union catalogue. Based on an analysis of the metadata standards, the CDP adopted the Dublin Core/XML metadata standard for the union catalogue.

There is a wide range of issues for the union catalogue. Subject terminology and subject retrieval are the primary topic of this paper. The mix of cultural heritage institutions resulted in many specialized institutions, for example the Florissant Fossil Beds National Monument and its collection of 6,000 unique fossils, or the Crow Canyon Archaeological Center and its large collection of archaeological materials or the Boulder History Museum and its more than 4,000 costumes and accessories. The first two institutions use taxonomies from their specialized fields and the third uses Chenhall (Blackaby and Greeno, 1988). At the same time, some of the smaller more general collections contain these same types of resources or subjects but use a more generalized subject heading list such as the *Library of Congress Subject Headings* or may use only uncontrolled vocabulary for subject access. The CDP union catalogue will provide access to this entire range of terms without an authority control system. As a result, unless the user knows both the general and specialized taxonomy, retrieval will be limited to term input. To address this situation the project is investigating the use of WebDewey with Dewey Decimal

Classification numbers to allow the linkage of general terms and highly specialized terms within a subject browse and possibly a subject keyword search.

2. Colorado Term and Name Lists

While no authority control exists as part of the CDP union catalogue, a couple of areas of authority control are being addressed. In order to assure some level of consistency in terminology, the CDP has developed a list of Colorado terms that a user can search on the web. This list is terms for Colorado geographic names and Library of Congress subject headings with the word *Colorado* or the abbreviation, *Colo.* appearing in the subject string. The list can be searched by specific term or through browse functions. The Colorado Subject Term list may be found at http://babu.coalliance.org:10101. The term list was generated from subject headings in the Prospector database, a union catalogue reflecting the collections and holdings of sixteen major public and academic research libraries in Colorado and Wyoming (http://prospector.coalliance.org), and may be searched directly at the address above or may be searched while creating or modifying records on the CDP input site. Institutions that are creating metadata records can search this list for LC subject headings to use if another subject list or thesaurus is not being used. The CDP has begun exploring the idea of turning this list into a real thesaurus and/or a full authority file. The latter would be approached through a statewide NACO/SACO project creating name headings and subject headings through the Program for Cooperative Cataloging.

The CDP has also begun to experiment with creating a list of Colorado authors (both personal and corporate). This list of names is also being generated from the Prospector database and is much more difficult to create than the subject term list. It is hoped that this name list will be available in the near future. Currently, the user has the option to search the Prospector catalogue to retrieve names.

Both the subject term list and the names list are being created to help gain consistency in terminology used in the union catalogue, though it is recognized that some project participants will not use these lists.

3. The Union Catalogue and Dublin Core

The CDP union catalogue is using OCLC SiteSearch. Project participants may ftp or send files of records to the CDP to have them loaded into the database or may create records in a metadata input system developed and programmed by the CDP. Records created in the input system are marked for transfer to the CDP database. Participants contributing records in MARC or another format provide the CDP with a profile so that the fields coming into the CDP database can be mapped to the CDP Dublin Core record format. The Dublin Core (DC) elements as implemented can be found at http://coloradodigital.coalliance.org/glines.html. It should be noted that the CDP has departed slightly from the DC elements as currently defined by the W3C at http://dublincore.org/documents/dces/. The mandatory elements, the core set of metadata, that must be supplied are Title, Creator, Subject, Description, Identifier, Date and Format.

The CDP does not store the actual digital images. Links to the images are provided in the union catalogue, but the images reside on the server used by the project participant. Some participants may create metadata records for each image residing locally or may create metadata only for a "collection" that consists of many images; for example, one site has digital images of the Moffat Tunnel, but there is only one metadata record and access point for the images of the tunnel. There are four images of the East Portal of the Moffat Tunnel and four images of the West Portal of the Moffat Tunnel, but only one metadata record exists for the main site where the images of the tunnel reside and from which links are provided. The user can view 8 images of the Moffat Tunnel but retrieves only one record. The CDP union catalogue is not publicly available as of the writing of this paper. It is hoped that it will be accessible in the near future.

4. Dewey Decimal Classification

The CDP wants to map the subject terms in the union database to Dewey Decimal Classification numbers. Currently, project participants, if they input Dewey numbers into the metadata, must use a printed version of Dewey and manually key the Dewey number or must search WebDewey to obtain a classification number and then type or copy/paste the numbers into the metadata record. A model such as that developed for use in the Cooperative Online Resource Catalogue (CORC) seems desirable to follow (Hickey and Vizine-Goetz, 1999). Automatic classification needs to be further developed before it can be implemented in a project like the CDP, and the OCLC SiteSearch software needs to be further developed to incorporate the features of CORC, such as automatic classification. The classification process as described by Hickey and Vizine-Goetz where the Dewey schedules may be displayed with scope notes, related topics, and references to the DDC manual is a tremendous tool for the classifier. The ability to index and search DDC numbers in a catalogue may be beneficial as well (Drabenstott, 1985). This use of the actual classification schedules with notes and references to the manual will most likely not work for the person searching the CDP database. A display of terms with context seems to be the most useful.
Figure 1 represents a model of what the retrieval might be in the CDP catalogue for a user entering the subject search term "gold".

Figure 1

Search Term: Gold

Results and context	**No. of hits**
Gold mines and mining	3
Gold prospecting/prospectors	4
Gold tableware	1
Gold coins	2

Possible Retrieval Display in the Union Catalogue

When the term "gold" is entered, the system retrieves the following Dewey Decimal Classification numbers, 622.3422 (Gold mines and mining), 622.1841 (Gold prospecting), 739.2283 (Gold tableware), and 737.43 (Gold coins). These numbers would have matched or been mapped to terms in the metadata records. The end user does not see the DDC numbers retrieved but views the terms/context in order to select records that match the users needs. Using this model, the user retrieves records for digital objects by subject regardless of subject thesaurus or taxonomy used.

Another major issue that needs to be addressed is the display terms that appear to the user. The terms appearing in Figure 1 do not necessarily match the terms as used in the Dewey schedules. For example, "Gold mines and mining" appears as 622.3422 in the schedules with the caption text "*Gold". Simply displaying "*Gold" to the end user is not going to be meaningful as the context is not clear without the hierarchy. So a method needs to be developed to try to get the display term to include hierarchical context as it would appear in the Dewey schedule as in Figure 2.

Figure 2

600	Technology	
620	Engineering	
622	Mining and related operations	
622.3	*Mining for specific materials	
622.34	*Metals	
622.342-622.349	Nonferrous metals	
	622.342	*Precious metals
	622.3422	*Gold

Entry from WebDewey with Hierarchy

There is a problem with DDC numbers that may be quite specific for a taxonomy used by an institution such as the Florissant Fossil Beds National Monument and its digital images of fossils. The DDC numbers for fossil invertebrates that occur in class number 569 provide an example of a detailed breakdown with taxonomic names in the schedules.

Figure 3

569	Fossil Mammalia
569.3-569.9	Eutheria
569.7	Carnivores
569.74	Feloidea--paleozoology
569.75	Felidae--paleozoology
569.76	Canoidea--paleozoology
569.77	Canidae--paleozoology
569.78	Ursidae--paleozoology
569.79	Pinnipedia--paleozoology

Entry from WebDewey with Hierarchy and Taxonomic Terms

It is highly doubtful that anyone without a detailed knowledge of the above taxonomic terms would understand the retrieval if these were the terms displayed. If an end user were looking for digital images of fossils of dogs, the terms from the DDC schedule above would not help. In the search for fossils of dogs, the end user would also not be helped by the DDC Relative Index as there is no entry under dogs with aspect fossils. From this example, it becomes clear that there will need to be additional terms mapped either through a means such as the LCSH mapping that has been done in WebDewey.

There will be considerable work to be done in mapping the subject terms in the CDP database to the DDC numbers as well as effort put into term retrieval and display. The end user must be able to retrieve using both specific terminology and taxonomy as well as general terminology. From the above, it is necessary to let the taxonomist retrieve digital images if he/she searches for "canidae" and to let the general user retrieve digital images if he/she is searching for "dogs fossils".

In determining the level of specificity that is required in using DDC numbers for retrieval, it might be that the use of the DDC Table 2 geographic area -788 for Colorado becomes meaningless for some subject areas in a database that consists of digital resources located only in Colorado. All of the digital images for gold mines will be for gold mines located in Colorado so adding or mapping a DDC number into the metadata record of 622.342209788 may make the Table 2 notation irrelevant. This would not be the case were the database to be expanded to include records from other states or were there to be so many digital images of gold mines in Colorado that a county or local breakdown would be necessary.

On the other hand, the breakdown in DDC Table 2 for Colorado locations may require expansion for this database especially for materials dealing with local history. Classifying materials to the county level in most cases may not be sufficient. Figure 4 from DDC Table 2 illustrates the geographic locations for the Northern counties of the Rocky Mountains of Colorado.

Figure 4

T2--788	Colorado
T2--7886	Northern counties of Rocky Mountains
T2--78861	Clear Creek County
T2--78862	Gilpin County
T2--78863	Boulder County
T2--78865	Grand County
T2--78866	Jackson County
T2--78868	Larimer County
T2--78869	*Rocky Mountain National Park

Table 2 Entries from WebDewey

In Figure 4, none of the counties listed has further geographic, local areas. For example, the Table 2 notation for Boulder County -78863 may not be sufficient when distinctions need to be made (especially for historical documents or photographs) between local cities located within Boulder County, e.g. Boulder, Erie, Superior, Louisville, Longmont, etc. Exactly how this expansion will take place must be determined.

5. Conclusions

The Dewey Decimal Classification seems to offer the most promising method for subject retrieval in a database that has subject vocabulary from multiple thesauri as is evidenced by the research being conducted at OCLC. Further testing is necessary to determine the feasibility of using the above model, and it is hoped that the OCLC SiteSearch software will be enhanced to incorporate use of WebDewey and automatic classification as well as much of the functionality currently available in CORC. DDC numbers will undoubtedly need to undergo human review for quite some time; however, it seems wise to begin incorporating DDC numbers into the CDP database at an early stage. Research will need to be done to determine how the level of specificity of DDC numbers impacts usefulness of retrieval in the CDP union catalogue. Expansion of the Table 2 geographic terms from Colorado must also be investigated. The method and model described in this paper may not be what is chosen by the CDP, but it seems to be a logical place to start in order to achieve consistent subject retrieval for metadata records using multiple subject thesauri.

References

Blackaby, J. R. & Greeno, P. (1988). *The revised nomenclature for museum cataloging: a revised and expanded version of Robert G. Chenall's System for Classifying Man-Made Objects*. Nashville, TN: American Association for State and Local History.

Hickey, T. B. & Vizine-Goetz, D. (1999). The role of classification in CORC, *Annual review of OCLC research*. <http://www.oclc.org/research/publications/arr/1999/hickey/corc.htm>.

Markey, K. (1985). Dewey Decimal Classification Online Project: integration of a library schedule and index into the subject searching capabilities of an online catalogue, *International cataloguing*, 14, 31-34.

The Iter Bibliography: International Standard Subject Access to Medieval and Renaissance Materials (400-1700) (http://iter.utoronto.ca)

Clare Beghtol

Abstract: Iter ("journey" or "path" in Latin) is a non-profit project for providing electronic access to materials pertaining to the Middle Ages and Renaissance (400-1700). Iter's background is described, and its centrepiece, the Iter Bibliography, is explicated. Emphasis is on the subject cataloguing process and on subject access to records for journal articles (using *Library of Congress Subject Headings* and the *Dewey Decimal Classification)*. Basic subject analysis of the materials is provided by graduate students specializing in the Middle Ages and Renaissance periods, and, subsequently, subject access points systems are provided by information professionals. This close cooperation between subject and information experts would not be efficient without electronic capabilities.

1. Iter: Gateway to the Middle Ages and Renaissance

Iter is a non-profit research project dedicated to providing electronic access to all kinds and formats of materials pertaining to the Middle Ages and Renaissance (400-1700). Iter began in 1995 as a joint initiative of the Renaissance Society of America (RSA) in New York City and the Centre for Reformation and Renaissance Studies (CRRS), Univ. of Toronto. By 1997, three more partners had joined: Faculty of Information Studies (FIS), Univ. of Toronto; Arizona Center for Medieval and Renaissance Studies (ACMRS), Arizona State Univ. at Tempe; and John P. Robarts Library, Univ. of Toronto. Iter was funded initially by the five partners and major foundations and, since 1998, has offered low-cost subscriptions to institutions and individuals. When Iter becomes financially self-sufficient, any profits will be used to enhance and expand the project. Iter databases are housed and maintained at the John P. Robarts Library. The interface is a customized version of DRA *WebZ*. A new interface using DRA *Web2* can be searched now and will replace the DRA *WebZ* interface shortly.

Iter was originally conceived as a comprehensive bibliography of secondary materials that would be an alternative to the existing commercial research tools for its period. These were expensive, generally appeared several years late, had limited subject indexing, were inconsistent in coverage, of uneven quality, and often depended on fragile networks of volunteers for identification of materials. The production of a reasonably priced, web-based, timely research tool was Iter's first priority. In addition, the partners wanted to involve graduate students in the project in order to contribute to the scholarly training and financial support of future scholars of the Middle Ages and Renaissance and to utilize as much automation as possible.

As the project matured, Iter supplemented the Bibliography with other kinds of resources. *Baptisteria Sacra: An Iconographical Index of Baptismal Fonts* offers pictures and a detailed descriptions of fonts from the early Christian period to the seventeenth century. Index strings describing font decorations are based on Iconclass, a classification system for the content of art works. *Iter Italicum,* based on Paul Oskar Kristeller's *Iter Italicum: A Finding List of Uncatalogued or Incompletely Catalogued Humanistic Manuscripts of the Renaissance in Italian and Other Libraries*, is a comprehensive listing of manuscripts around the world. Shortly, the *International Directory of Scholars* will be available. This directory provides access to Mediaeval and Renaissance scholars, their affiliations, research interests, and the resources of their institutions. Access to a number of other resources is planned. More detail on the history and plans for Iter appears in Bowen (2000).

2. The Iter Bibliography

The Iter Bibliography is an entirely web-based bibliography of secondary print materials that will be expanded to electronic resources shortly. It contains approximately 230,000 records for articles and reviews from approximately 550 period-specific and general journal titles in many languages. Examples of period-specific titles are: *Ambix: Journal of the Society for the Study of Alchemy and Early Chemistry*; *Milton Quarterly*; *Opportunities for Research in Renaissance Drama*; and *The Sixteenth Century Journal*. Examples of general titles that are culled for appropriate articles are: *Journal of Garden History*; *Physics; Quarterly Journal of Speech Education*; and *Technology and Culture*. Experts in various fields are consulted for lists of appropriate journal titles. New titles are added regularly and a complete list of titles, with coverage dates, appears on the Iter website. The Bibliography is updated daily and about 60,000 new records are added annually. A separate bibliography for books is under construction.

The overall goal of the Bibliography is to provide accessible, authoritative, reliable, and timely information for scholars and students. Three objectives are: 1) to provide comprehensive coverage of print and electronic publications; 2) to involve graduate students in the creation and maintenance of records; and 3) to employ international record format and cataloguing standards. The plan is to include records for all works published from 1700 to the present that concern the period 400-1700. To this end, graduate students at CCRS and ACMRS work on laptops collecting basic data (e.g., author, title, pagination, language) for the entire run of a particular journal. For example, *Quellen und Forschungen aus italienischen Archiven und Biblioteken* has been covered since volume 1, 1898. Data are collected for everything (e.g., articles, catalogues, bibliographies, discographies) in each issue of a period-specific journal. Each issue of a general journal is scanned for relevant materials. Original procedures for data management, some of which have been modified since publication, are discussed in Castell (1997).

2.1 Standard Systems in the Iter Bibliography

In 1996, a pilot project was conducted at FIS to determine what the best standard systems would be for the Bibliography. To address the basic principles of Iter, a number of criteria were considered in the pilot study, e.g., international acceptance and availability of the standard; its regular updating and maintenance; its ability to accommodate the complex data that were expected; its familiarity to potential users of the Bibliography and to graduate students who would be working on it; and the ability of all the standards to work together to create reliable, consistent records. The decision-making process included all the partners of Iter, and the final decision was to use the MARC record format, the *Anglo-American Cataloguing Rules* (AACR2), *Library of Congress Subject Headings* (LCSH), the *Dewey Decimal Classification* (DDC), and Library of Congress authority records. These standards were judged to be the "most stable...and most likely to be employed in other applications with which the current system needs to exchange data" (Borgman, 1997, p. 4). This paper concentrates on the two subject access systems. Further discussion of all the standards appears in Bowen (2000) and Castell (1997).

2.2 Subject Cataloguing Decisions for the Iter Bibliography
Investigation of subject access for the Bibliography uncovered a number of problems. Scholars of the Middle Ages and Renaissance consider this period as their special "subject" of study. For this reason, we initially looked at the possibilities of using an existing thesaurus or constructing our own special thesaurus (cf. *Medici Archive Project*, 2001; *Medieval Feminist Index*, 2001). Research showed, however, that no existing thesaurus could meet the criteria listed above. In addition, creating a new system would mean a considerable delay before any subject access points could be added and also a major commitment to the development and maintenance of the new system itself. It was thus more fruitful to consider the Middle Ages and Renaissance not as a "subject" but simply as a "time period". This point of view acknowledged that any and every kind of thing between the years 400-1700 might become the subject of scholarly research and debate. For example, it would be necessary to specify scientific topics (e.g., medicine, physics, chemistry), technical topics (e.g., bridge-building, agriculture, navigation), social topics (e.g., gender relations, cooking, work practices), and humanities topics (e.g., art, painting, music) for the period. Thus, it become clear that what was needed was a general system for all knowledge.

Both LCSH and DDC are general systems designed to cover the range of human knowledge. They are consistently maintained and updated. They can specify complex subjects, and they can be accommodated in the various MARC formats. Nevertheless, they have some problems in relation to the criteria that had been set out. Both were developed for the subjects of books, which may be less specific than the subjects of journal articles. LCSH is available only in English, and, although it has recently been adopted by the British Library, is primarily a North American system. DDC is the most widely-used classification system in the world and has been translated into numerous languages, but DDC notations as sole subject expressions are not familiar to many. It thus became apparent that the best subject access for international users would be provided by using both systems. The language-independence of DDC notation can offset the English-only LCSH headings. In addition, structured access through an internationally-known classification system using multiple notations would make it unnecessary for users to know an exact LCSH string for searching and would facilitate search narrowing. Thus, the Bibliography would be indexed with both a classified and an alphabetic file and the strengths of the two systems would complement each other. It was decided, also, that the special terminology of journal articles would be best served by adding a field for "uncontrolled keywords" (i.e., non-LCSH terms that appear in an article and are familiar to scholars in the field). The abridged version of DDC was chosen to simplify notational searching and to create broad classes of materials for further search refinement.

2.2.1 Subject Analysis of Materials for the Iter Bibliography
In many bibliographies, subject analysis of the material is done by the same person who provides subject access points. In the Iter Bibliography, however, these two processes are separated. Subject analysis is done by Mediaeval and Renaissance graduate students, called "subject specialists", who work on laptop computers in the library stacks at their own Medieval and Renaissance centre (CRRS and ACMRS). The concentrated examination of articles necessary for subject analysis enhances the students' knowledge of the literature of their chosen field and contributes to the training of these future scholars.

These subject specialists are trained in subject analysis by information professionals on the Iter staff, called "information specialists", who subsequently translate the subject analysis worksheets into LCSH and DDC expressions. Currently, subject specialists are assigned to a run of a particular journal. They input basis bibliographic data for the entire run of the journal on laptops using EndNote software. For articles from 1990 to the present, subject specialists include subject analysis work in the EndNote record. Then, EndNote records are ftp-ed to information specialists in Toronto. The records are mapped to MARC format, and information studies students proofread and format the contents according to AACR2. Subsequently, information specialists in their quarters at the John P. Robarts Library, Univ. of Toronto, produce subject access points for each article. Subject specialists are trained over several days doing exercises with the *Iter Manual for Subject Specialists* (Manual) (2001), which was developed for this purpose. The subject specialists are trained in general principles for subject headings (e.g., full coverage of subject content, specificity, objectivity), and are encouraged to incorporate different approaches scholarly users might take to an article.

Subject analysis for each article has three parts: a descriptive sentence; a time period; and headings. The descriptive sentence is a summary of the whole article and provides a general context on which the information specialists can base subject access points. The following examples are taken from the Manual.

Example 1:

> This article discusses various renditions between the 13th and 15th centuries of the tale of an unfaithful wife surprised by her husband while entertaining lovers; the author offers interpretations from both misogynist and feminist points of view.

Example 2:

> This article discusses the creation of social projects directed at poor relief by Juan Luis Vives, Ignatius Loyola and John Calvin in the context of poor relief in the 16th century; the author suggests that, as a counterpoint to Machiavellian thought, these thinkers promoted a communitarian approach to social problems.

The time period in the article can be a single year or a range of years (e.g., 1621; 1564-1569). When two different time periods occur in a single article, they are combined into one range. For example, if an article covers both the periods 1342-1465 and 1530-1560, the time period of the article is 1342-1560.

Headings provided by subject specialists are highly abbreviated versions of Library of Congress Subject Headings that follow strict guidelines for content and format set out in the Manual. Headings consist of an obligatory main subject and optional geographic area(s) and/or optional subdivision(s). When necessary, subject specialists use square brackets to elucidate specific points for the benefit of information specialists who are unfamiliar with the time period and who do not have access to the article. Contextual information is provided, for example, for various kinds of names (personal, organizational, place), titles of works, events, details of manuscripts, and obscure terminology, e.g.,

Personal name:	Lassus, Orlandus [also known as Orlando di Lasso, Flemish composer, 1532-1594];
Organization:	Franciscan Order [religious order established by St. Francis of Assisi. Italy. Also known as the Grey Friars];
Place:	Parish of Saint-Ouen [in the city of Rouen in France];
Title:	*Kudrun* [anonymous Middle High German epic poem, 13th century, also known as *Gudrun*];
Event:	Peace of Westphalia [1648. France. single treaty that ended the Thirty Years War, 1618-1648];

The Iter bibliography

Manuscript:	Art of shooting in great ordnance [ms. known as MS. Sloane 3651. non-fiction treatise on shooting in England. British Library [London, Eng.]. 1572. English. no facsimile given];
Terminology:	*amor proximi* [love of one's neighbour].

A list of allowable subdivisions and their scope notes is provided in *Subdivision Lists for Iter Subject Analysis* (List) (2001) created for the use of subject specialists, e.g.,

> **Military relations:** for articles discussing the military relations between two places. Make note of the other place involved, e.g., Sicily [Italy]—military relations [Rome, Italy]".

In creating subdivisions, subject specialists are not confined to the subdivisions in the List. If none is appropriate, they add explanatory notes as necessary, e.g.,

> Beheim, Michel [German poet, 1416-1777]—[autobiographical representation in his work]).

Two examples of the kinds of subject analysis provided by subject specialists follow.

Example 1:

Sentence:	An analysis of ritual in 16th century Rouen based on the social aspects of 14th century clothing.
Time period:	1300-1552
Headings:	clothing—France—Rouen—social aspects—1300-1340 rituals—France—Rouen—1503-1552

Example 2:

Sentence:	Article discusses how Vesalius adapted Galen's ideas about the design of human physiology and anatomy, with emphasis on Galen's teleological perspective.
Time period:	1500-1599
Headings:	Galen [classical scholar, 0129-0216]—influence [on Vesalius] Vesalius, Andreas [16th cent. Italian scientist]—criticism and interpretation Vesalius, Andreas—sources teleology human anatomy—Italy human physiology—Italy

2.2.2 Final Subject Access Points in the Iter Bibliography

Information specialists translate the subject specialists' subject analysis work into fully-developed LCSH headings and DDC notations. Throughout this process, the subject specialists and information specialists communicate by e-mail if there are questions about the information given in the subject analysis. The examples below show full subject cataloguing in the Iter Bibliography. (They also incidentally illustrate the inadequacy of title keywords for precise subject searching of journal articles). About 20,000 records currently in the Bibliography have full subject cataloguing. At the moment, the database cannot be searched by DDC notation for technical reasons. The subject headings can be searched through each stage. For example, in "Horse owners—Italy—History—16th century", clicking on "16th century" links to all other records with the entire subdivided heading. Clicking on "History" links to all records with "Horse owners—Italy—History". "Horse owners—Italy" links to records with that heading, and "Horse owners" links to records with the unsubdivided heading only. The following examples have been abridged for this paper.

Example 1:

Title:	Reading through Galileo's telescope: Margaret Cavendish and the experience of reading
Language:	English
Time Period:	1564-1674

Subject Headings:	Galilei, Galileo, 1564-1642. Mensagem das estrêlas. Galilei, Galileo, 1564-1642—Views on books and reading. Galilei, Galileo, 1564-1642—Views on astronomy. Astronomy—Observations. Books and reading—Philosophy. Newcastle, Margaret Cavendish, Duchess of, 1642?-1674. Description of a new blazing world. Newcastle, Margaret Cavendish, Duchess of, 1642?-1674—Views on books and reading. Vision in literature. Experience in literature.
Dewey no.:	028.01 [philosophy and theory of reading] 520.1 [philosophy and theory of astronomy] 808.001 [philosophy and theory of rhetoric] 823 [English fiction]

Example 2:

Title:	Il linguaggio medico e anatomico nelle opere di Dante
Language:	Italian
Time Period:	098-1321
Subject Headings:	Dante Alighieri, 1264-1321. Convivio. Dante Alighieri, 1264-1321. Divina commedia. Dante Alighieri, 1264-1321—Language. Medicine—Terminology. Avicenna, 980-1037. Canon totius medicinae. Avicenna, 980-1037—Influence.
Uncontrolled Keywords:	Medical language; medical terminology; complexio.
Dewey no.:	610.1 [philosophy and theory of medicine] 851 [Italian poetry]

Example 3:

Title:	*Miscellanea curiositae Michelangelae*: a steep tariff, a half dozen horses, and yards of taffeta
Language:	English
Time Period:	1514-1550
Subject Headings:	Michelangelo Buonarroti, 1475-1564—Clothing. Michelangelo Buonarroti, 1475-1564—Friends and associates. Michelangelo Buonarroti, 1475-1564. Risen Christ. Horse owners—Italy—History—16th century. Men's clothing—Italy—History—16th century.
Dewey no.:	391.00945 [costume and personal appearance, Italy] 636.100945 [animal husbandry, Italy] 709.2 [biography of artist]

3. Conclusion

The centrepiece of Iter, the Iter Bibliography, contains unique provisions for subject analysis and access. It uses a combination of multiple LCSH headings and multiple DDC notations for subject specification in order to incorporate the strengths of each system, and it also provides uncontrolled keywords to cater for terms that would be likely to be used by Mediaeval and Renaissance scholars. In addition, subject cataloguing in the Bibliography capitalizes on the strengths of students and graduates in both information studies and Middle Ages and

Renaissance studies by involving them at different stages of the subject cataloguing process. These provisions and the cooperation of the people who put them into practice would not be efficient, and might not have been possible, without the extensive use of technology. The result is a sophisticated resource for international scholars and students of the period from 400-1700 that can be expanded and used as a model for other projects of its kind.

References

Borgman, C. L. (1997). "Multi-media, multi-cultural, and multi-lingual digital libraries: or how do we exchange data in 400 languages?" *D-Lib magazine*, 3 (6) June <httpwww.dlib.org/dlib/june97/>

Bowen, W.R. (2000). "*Iter*: where does the path lead?" *Early modern literary studies,* 5(3). Special Issue 4 (January): 2.1-26. <http://purl.oclc.org/emls/05-3/bowiter.html>

Castell, T. (1997). "Maintaining web-based bibliographies: a case study of Iter, The Bibliography of Renaissance Europe". In *Digital collections: implications for users, funders, developers and maintainers: proceedings of the 60th Annual Meeting of the American Society for Information Science.* Vol. 34. Medford, N.J.: Information Today. Pp. 174-182.

Iter Manual for Subject Specialists: Guidelines and Procedures. (2001) last update. Toronto: Iter .

Medici Archive Project. (2001). <http://www.medici.org> Accessed May 24, 2001.

Medieval Feminist Index. (2001). [2002: name changed *to Feminae: medieval women and gender index*] <http://www.haverford.edu/library/reference/mschaus/mfi/mfi.html>
Accessed 24th May, 2001.

Subdivision Lists for Iter Subject Analysis. (2001) last update. Toronto: Iter.

Session 5

DOMAIN SPECIFIC RETRIEVAL

Subject Access to Web Resources in Education

Michèle Hudon

Abstract: Introduction to various classificatory structures currently used to organize and make collections of Web-based resources in education more accessible to educators, education specialists, and the general public. Presentation of other models which could also be useful.

1. Background

We are currently witnessing a proliferation of attempts at providing thematic access to Web resources to better serve information searchers. A growing number of general and special virtual libraries, defined as *structured collections of active links to preselected electronic resources*, are being set up. Ad hoc thematic organization schemes, often structured around loose categories representing a mix of disciplines, subjects, types of document, and intended audiences, are designed and implemented. These new classification schemes, touted as being more intuitive and user-friendly than those that are applied in traditional libraries, vary considerably from one virtual library to another. A majority of them shares significant weaknesses, such as a lack of concern for conceptual or terminological standardization, and a marked disregard for known theoretical principles of knowledge organization, such as facet analysis, citation order, etc. It should be easier to organize special virtual libraries than general ones, and one would think that more similarities would be observed in the way resources in the same domain are classified. This does not appear to be the case, however, even within domains, Engineering or Law for example, that are rather well structured in the "real world".

In this paper, we present and discuss briefly some observations made in the course of a research project focusing on Web-based resources in the field of education, a most interesting discipline for a study of this nature. Education is a culturally and politically stamped field of knowledge and practice; educational objectives, methods and systems vary from one country to another, and this is certainly an obstacle to efficient information finding and information sharing among educators and education specialists. Yet, the main facets of the field have been identified, defined and used repeatedly to organize and provide access to information found in directories, handbooks, and traditional library collections. As for the terminology that is used to facilitate retrieval and exchange of education-related information, it has been standardized and is made available in specialized dictionaries and reputable thesauri.

On the Web, resources in education may be accessed via general directories (Yahoo!, Excite, Argus Clearinghouse, etc.), as well as in special virtual libraries with systematically organized collections of links to selected pertinent resources.

In virtual as in traditional libraries, organizing and searching for information in education will involve various combinations of two or more of the following essential facets:

Educational level (preschool, primary, secondary, higher, etc.)
Type of education (continuing, remedial, etc.)
Audience (adult, immigrant, etc.)
Agents (teachers, counsellors, etc.)

Subject taught (mathematics, music, etc.)
Geographical location (Québec, France, England, etc.)

2. Education-related information in virtual libraries with general collections
General Web directories act as general virtual libraries. This is where most searchers, novices and specialists alike, will first browse for information. Within the classificatory structures the searcher must go through to access resources, education is not always found in the same or even in comparable locations, and not necessarily where it should logically be. Table 1 shows that education is most often considered important enough to be a first-level entry, but a few directories give it only sub-category status, and position it in such improbable environments as Lifestyles, along with Horoscopes and Recipes, or Reference, with Flags, Museums and Parliamentary practice.

Yahoo! [1]	Home > Education
Excite [2]	Home > Lifestyle > Education
AltaVista [3]	Home > Library and Resources > Education
Google [4]	Home > Reference > Education
Argus ClearingHouse [5]	Home > Education
Librarians' Index to the Internet [6]	Home > Education
La Toile du Québec [7]	Home > Éducation
Yahoo! France [8]	Home > Enseignement et formation

Table 1. Education in general Web directories

Once the education category has been located, a vertical move down the structure reveals a few similarities and important differences in sub-arrangements, both at the conceptual and at the terminological levels. Table 2 presents a sample of second-level headings provided respectively by Yahoo (33 sections), Google (20 sections), and Argus Clearinghouse (6 sections). Three of the essential facets enumerated in the previous section — level, type, and audience — can be identified clearly in the following lists of sub-categories.

An obvious commonality is the use of some or all educational levels as subdividing facet in general organization schemes. Levels are not, however, presented in a consistent manner (e.g. K-12 / K through 12 / Primary and secondary school, or Higher education / Colleges and Universities). Distance education / learning and Instructional technology appear in most structures, but surprisingly enough the facet Subject (i.e. subject taught) does not. Argus seems more focused, with fewer sub-categories to choose from; some of the categories overlap however (Educational institutions and Primary and secondary school), and this generates ambiguity: where then will we find universities and colleges, under Educational institutions or under Higher education?

Yahoo! (excerpts)	Google (excerpts)	Argus
Academic competitions Adult and continuing education Bibliographies Chats and Forums Conferences Distance learning Early childhood education Financial aid Higher education Instructional technology K-12 Policy Theory and methods	Alumni directories Colleges and universities Directories Distance learning Early childhood Educators Home schooling How to study Instructional technology K through 12 Methods and theories Special education Subjects	Adult and special education Educational institutions Higher education Instructional technology and tools Primary and secondary school Teaching and pedagogy

Table 2. Sub-arrangement of education in general Web directories

The classificatory structures of general directories are generally shallow, varying from three levels (a *de facto* standard in most virtual libraries) to a maximum of six levels. Shown below are examples of structural depth offered in selected general virtual libraries.

Yahoo!
Education > Theories and methods > Montessori methods > Teacher education
Google
Reference > Education > Methods and theories > Learning theories> Montessori > Professional development
Yahoo! France
Enseignement et formation > Pédagogie > Problèmes et débats > Échec scolaire > Associations et organismes
Argus
Education > Teaching and pedagogy > Educational standards

The logic of the hierarchies thus created is generally explicit and quite acceptable, with the occasional blurred area (e.g. from Argus: Education > Teaching and pedagogy > Education). Associative relations between sub-categories are few and far between, with Google faring slightly better with useful relationships such as the one established between Reference > Education > Methods and theories > Learning theories and Society > Philosophy > Philosophy of education.

Structural and terminological differences make it more difficult for the educator to find pertinent resources, either through manual browsing or through an automated or semi-automated meta-search. Educators use virtual libraries to browse collections of documents in an area of interest, to keep on top of what is happening in their speciality, and to look for clusters of related resources, but it remains difficult for them to locate quickly a fairly specific subject in the various classification schemes used in general libraries. As a rule, it seems easier to uncover instructional materials and to establish further distinctions using levels or curriculum subjects as specifying criteria than it is to find information about instructional theories and methods; the latter are often found at the lowest level of the hierarchy, where they cannot be linked to a level or a subject.

3. Virtual libraries in education

Virtual libraries in education are established and maintained by governments and other official agencies with an interest and/or responsibilities in education and training, as well as by professional associations of educators and education specialists. There are hundreds of such libraries or portals on the Web, with much duplication in collection contents. Resources may have been selected and organized for the benefit of educators only, for an audience of parents and other taxpayers, for actual and potential students, for mixed audiences of specialists and non specialists. Consequently, conceptual structures and terminology have to be as accessible as those that are used in general directories.

On the whole and as could be expected, organizational schemes in the special libraries are more homogeneous, more focused, and in the top levels of the hierarchies contain only education specific headings. However, significant structural and terminological variations remain.

Education Index [9]	Learning library [10]	AskEric [11]	SOSIG Education [12]
Prenatal and infant	L. theory & research	Counselling	Adult education
Preschool	Measurement & Eval.	Educ. levels	Educ. policy
Primary education	Instructional design	Educ. management	Educ. theory
Middle education	Education admin.	Educ. technology	Elementary educ.
Secondary education	Education topics	ERIC	Further educ.
College education	Technology in educ.	Evaluation	Higher educ.
Distance learning	Counselling & guid.	Family life	Primary educ.
Graduate education	Family resources	General education	Secondary educ.
Continuing education	Special populations	Specific populations	Special educ.
Parenting		Teaching	Teaching methods

Table 3. First level of subdivision in virtual libraries in education

Education Index adopts an interesting Lifestage approach, each stage a close relative of an educational level. Of the four structures shown in Table 3, only the Learning library shies away from using level as a principle of subdivision. Organizing resources by educational level is relatively safe, although not necessarily globally acceptable. Middle or College education, for example, correspond to different realities within various education systems and may not exist at all in some places.

Variations in terminology are numerous, but they rarely reflect variations in concepts. Such variations as Special populations / Specific populations, Educational technology / Technology in education, Educational administration / Educational management, are most unfortunate. They do nothing to add to the clarity of the structure and they complicate needlessly the task of the searcher who must apply his own vocabulary control methods when browsing several collections.

Overall, virtual libraries in education are accessible. As was the case in general Web directories, however, they do not make it easy to separate resources about education from instructional resources. The Education Virtual Library does that well, splitting its virtual collection in two to populate a Curriculum Subject Library and a distinct Learning Library.

4. Library classification schemes and Web-based education resources

Traditional library classification schemes are sometimes selected to organize general virtual library collections set up and maintained by professional librarians. Traditional classification schemes are an interesting option, if only because users are already familiar with the type of hierarchical organization they propose.

In the field of education, traditional schemes such as the Dewey Decimal Classification (DDC), the Universal Decimal Classification (UDC), and the Library of Congress Classification (LCC), have a structural advantage over the general schemes used to organize resources in Yahoo!, Excite, etc. They offer greater internal consistency in the organization of essential facets. Here as in the Web-based schemes, top-level categories are likely to represent educational levels. But the following sub-arrangement, extracted from the much consulted Canadian Information by Subject directory [13], shows that a DDC-based classified guide is not necessarily easy to browse.

3	Social sciences
37	Education
378	Higher education
378.007	Universities and Colleges — Research
378.016	Student exchange programs
378.1	Education higher — Organizations
378.17	College teaching
378.175	Distance education
378.198	College students
378.7	Universities and Colleges
378.711	Universities and Colleges — British Columbia
378.713	Universities and Colleges — Ontario
379.9	Community colleges
379.914	Cegeps

In virtual as in traditional libraries, universal classification schemes are most useful in general collections; they will not be appropriate for use with collections of specialized resources in a single domain of knowledge.

5. Exploring other models

Reference tools commonly used by education specialists appear so far to have been overlooked by the majority of classifiers of virtual resources. As thesaurus developers know, such reference tools do come with scientific warrant, and they contribute significantly to the maintenance of conceptual and terminological consistency in any indexing and retrieval instrument. They include specialized encyclopaedias and thesauri.

Encyclopaedias often provide a systematic structure, and they are a rich source of controlled terminology, part of which, however, may not be the most current. The *Encyclopedia of Education Research* [14] assigns articles to one of sixteen broad categories:

Agencies and institutions related to education
Context of education
Counselling, medical, and psychological services
Curriculum, elementary and secondary
Education of exceptional persons
Education related to identifiable groups

Educational measurement and assessment
Internal operational policies and practices
International differences in education
Levels of education
Methods of inquiry
Occupationally oriented education
Organizational structure and governance
Policymaking arenas
Teachers
Teaching, Instructional systems and strategies.

The *Encyclopedia* offers a three-level deep hierarchical structure which would suit quite well the virtual library in education.

1. Agencies and Institutions
    2. Private companies in education
        3. Textbook publishing companies

1. Organizational structure and governance
    2. Educational administration
        3. Financing schools

All facets of education, with the exception of geographical location, are put to good use in this environment which takes away the emphasis on educational levels characterizing most other organizing schemes in the field.

The thesaurus model should also be examined. Thesauri are normally structured around a loose set of categories and sub-categories, which may or may not be apparent in the display. Some of the categories in the *Thesaurus of ERIC descriptors* [15], for example, are:

Learning and perception
Classroom perspectives
School perspectives
Societal perspectives
Educational levels
Curriculum
Students, teachers, school personnel
Research and theory
Measurement
Test and scales

Because thesaural categories may vary greatly as to their intension and extension, however, and because they are seldom familiar to thesaurus users, they may not be efficient in the provision of access to education-related resources in the virtual library.

On the other hand, hierarchical and associative relationships established between thesaurus terms, can be used to solidify the newly designed classificatory structures. Thesauri should also be used to standardize the terminology within and across Web-based libraries. Finally, major textbooks and handbooks in the field of education can as well suggest a basic organizational structure for specialized concepts and subjects.

6. Conclusion

Classifying Web-based resources in education for maximum retrieval efficiency is obviously no easy task, and there may not be any universally acceptable way of doing so. The difficulties of combining the various facets of the field in a logical, flexible, and intuitive classificatory structure have transferred themselves from the traditional library environment to the virtual one. Old systems and newly created structures have similar strengths and weaknesses, and it is likely equally difficult, but not impossible, for educators and education specialists to locate the most pertinent resources in the virtual library as it is in the traditional one. It could be useful at this point to explore a wider variety of organizing models to try and improve the navigability of existing structures, and to maybe find a way to better differentiate the theoretical from the pragmatic information, resources on education from instructional resources.

Notes:

[1] http://www.yahoo.com

[2] http://magellan.mckinley.com

[3] http://www.altavista.com

[4] http://directory.google.com

[5] http://www.clearinghouse.net

[6] http://lii.org/search/

[7] http://www.toile.qc.ca

[8] http://www.yahoo.fr

[9] http://www.educationindex.com

[10] http://www.byu.edu/ipt/vlibrary/learning/

[11] http://ericir/syr/edu/

[12] http://sosig.esrc/bris/ac.uk/education

[13] http://www.nlc-bnc.ca/caninfo/esub.htm

[14] *Encyclopedia of Education Research.* (1992). Sponsored by the American Educational Research Association. 6th ed. New-York : Macmillan.

[15] *Thesaurus of ERIC descriptors.* (1990). 12th ed. Phoenix, AZ : Oryx Press (for the Educational resources Information Center).

A Multi-Layered, Multi-Dimensional Representation of Digital Educational Resources

Jian Qin and Jiangping Chen

Abstract: Semantic mapping between controlled vocabulary and keywords is the first step towards knowledge-based subject access. This study reports the preliminary result of a semantic mapping experiment for the Gateway to Educational Materials (GEM). A total of 3,555 keywords were mapped with 322 concept names in the GEM controlled vocabulary. The preliminary test to 10,000 metadata records presented widely varied sets of results between the mapped and non-mapped data. The paper discussed linguistic and technical problems encountered in the mapping process and raised issues in the representation technologies and methods, which will lead to future study of knowledge-based access to networked information resources.

1. Introduction

Digital libraries serve diversified user groups—teachers, students, researchers and the general public, to meet their information needs in work and life. To do this job well, digital libraries must have the capabilities to provide intelligent information retrieval. In other words, they should be able to provide a topic-centred access with rich relationships to all associated topics. While this idea is not new, it brings up a fundamental issue of enabling representation architecture and technology that support intelligent navigation and information search.

There are two ways in developing representation architecture and technology: one is the knowledge-based approach that uses controlled vocabularies and classifications, and the other the topic-map (Rath, 2000) approach based on semantics and syntax suitable for database schemas. The boundaries between these two are often less than clear-cut, because their roles in representation are not exclusive to one another, but complementary. In terms of research orientation, the former casts a more theoretical orientation while the latter tends to focus on a more pragmatic naming system that reflects the data content. This paper presents an experiment that combines methods in both knowledge representation and data catalogues to develop a multi-layer, multi-dimensional system for navigational search of information resources in the education domain.

2. Previous Research

2.1 Mapping Knowledge-Oriented Vocabulary Systems

A knowledge-oriented vocabulary system is a classification scheme or thesaurus that organizes knowledge concepts into a hierarchical or an alpha-hierarchical structure. In digital libraries, vocabulary is a central component (Buckland, 1999). Approaches to content representation from the library and information community have been largely focused on creating metadata records in which subject headings and classification numbers are manually assigned. Example projects include the BUBL Subject Tree at Strathclyde University in Glasgow, Scotland (Wood, 1995; BUBL Information Service, 2000), the Scout Report Signpost, and the Engineering Electronic Library, Sweden (EELS). One common characteristic among these Internet-based subject access is the combination of a classification scheme and thesaurus for providing alternative subject-based access, whereby class notations are mapped against the corresponding concepts in a thesaurus or vice versa. For example, the EELS uses the Ei Classification Scheme and Thesaurus, and Scout Report Signpost applies the Library of Congress Classification (LCC) and Library of Congress Subject Headings (LCSH).

This common characteristic resulted from librarians' long time recognition to the limitations of a hierarchical classification's linearity and a thesaurus' non-hierarchical structure of vocabularies. In addition, terminology used in vocabulary systems often differs, even in the same subject domain (Giral & Taylor, 1993; Qin, 2000). Buckland et al. call these "unfamiliar metadata vocabularies" (Buckland & Gey, 1999). He and his colleagues argue that familiarity with the sources being sought is critical for effective, reliable searching. However, as digital resources increase exponentially, effective searching becomes an increasing problem. This is due to the user's unfamiliarity with vocabularies. Librarians started in the 1990s to solve the multi-vocabulary problem in searching online catalogues by painstakingly manually mapping different thesauri (Chaplan, 1995; Olson & Strawn, 1997). As the Web became the standard interface for many information systems, Web-based vocabulary mapping began to draw attention from the research communities. Using what is known as "Entry Vocabulary Modules," Gey et al. created associations between ordinary language and domain-specific technical metadata vocabulary used to describe databases (Gey, et al., 1999). Their project represents a large scale of multi-thesaurus mapping for cross-system resource discovery.

2.2 Topic-Map Style of Representation

In a simple way, the topic map style representation resembles a back-of-book index that has topic names, types of topics, occurrences, and locators. A topic map is an XML document in which different elements are used to represent topics, occurrences of topics, and relationships between topics (Rath, 2001). The application of XML syntax in representing these topic elements makes it convenient to turn the topic map into a database schema. What is more attractive is its capability of separating topic associations from information resources (Pepper, 2001). The separation between the information resources and the topic map makes it possible to create topic maps as portable semantic networks which, in essence, forms a necessary component in knowledge-based information access.

Associations between concepts are crucial for information search and resource discovery because they serve not only as a control mechanism to disambiguate semantic meanings in varying linguistic forms of vocabularies, but also as a linking mechanism to map such varying forms. While each approach has its strengths, a combination of both would add a significant advantage to structured representation in topic maps. In this sense, ontologies fit into the scenario perfectly as they possess a structure appropriate for both knowledge-based and topic-map style representations. In the following sections, we will discuss the kinds of associations which exist among concepts in the case of educational materials and how such associations can be modelled as an ontology and built into the indexing database. The discussion is based on an experiment of mapping controlled vocabulary and keywords in the GEM system.

3. Conceptual Modelling of GEM Controlled Vocabulary

The GEM system is one of the early adopters of the Dublin Core as its metadata format together with expanded local elements. GEM's content representation includes controlled vocabularies including subject categories and a list of keywords. The subject categories describe a resource about what type of material it is, for whom it is intended, for which grade level it is suitable, or what subject the resource is about. Users can browse resources by either keywords or subject categories. The search engine provides simple and advanced (Boolean) search. The challenge here is that, when browsing or searching by using either controlled vocabulary or keywords, associations between subject categories and keywords are covert to users, because such relationships cannot be seen until the user looks at the subject field in these resulting records. There are no cross-references between keywords and subject categories. It is quite possible that, if a user use keywords only, s/he risks missing important relevant information; or if s/he uses subject categories only, then s/he might retrieve a large number of hits with a high rate of irrelevant information. The mapping between the controlled vocabulary and keywords becomes the first step in minimizing the burden of users and maximizing the search effectiveness.

GEM's controlled vocabulary describes a resource from nine dimensions: audience, educational level, format, grade, language, pedagogy, relation, resource type, and subject. Besides the core descriptive elements in Dublin Core (such as author, title, date of creation, and URL), these dimensions represent indicative elements for the content. Figure 1 depicts the dimensions and how they extend to lower levels.

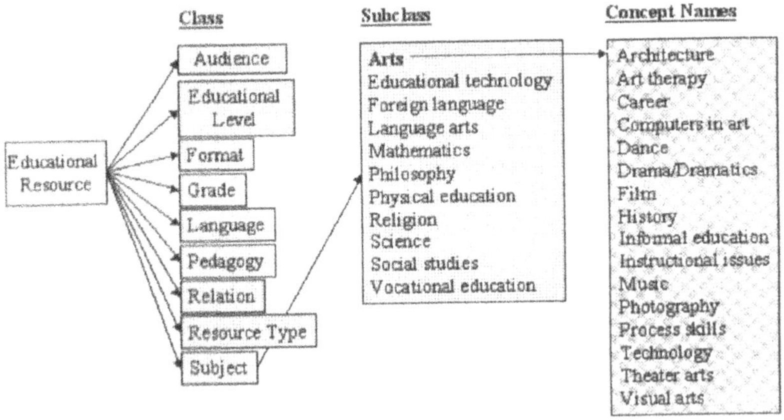

Figure 1. Structure of GEM's controlled vocabulary (source: Qin & Pailing, 2001)

We carefully analyzed the controlled vocabulary and reorganized it into an hierarchical structure of Class (dimension) → Subclass → Concept Name. The nine classes have 106 subclasses and 322 concept names at the time of writing.

GEM contains information about resources. Its metadata records represent nine dimensions for each resource. Choosing resources as the focal concept, we found that each of the remaining dimensions serves a distinctive rôle in characterizing resources. Resource types, for example, are logical subordinate classes for the resource concept, which qualify for a subclass of association with the resource concept (Figure 2). Each resource, no matter what type (resource subclass) it belongs to, has properties such as for whom it is beneficial, in what format it is compiled, what subject it deals with and what pedagogical methods it uses. These properties add discriminating capabilities in metadata which can be a balance force for the mapped (expanded) keywords to control the relevance aspect as well as the volume of information in searching processes. In an ontological view, such properties fit into a "has-a" type of association. In Figure 3, the screenshot image shows the ontology structure for GEM concepts, where each dimension is modeled as a class with corresponding slots (properties). As a result of modelling concepts and relationships into an ontology, we are able to lay the foundation for an association knowledge base for automatic vocabulary mapping in the future.

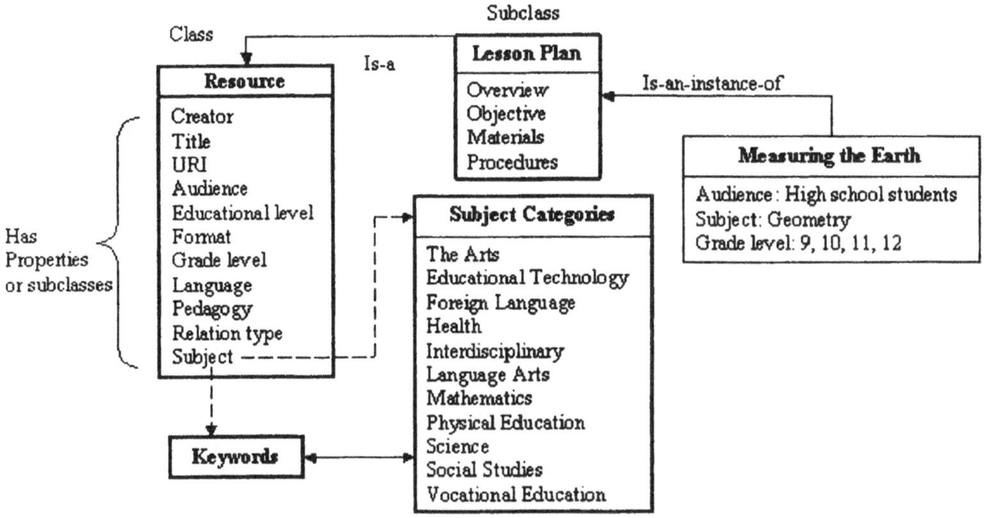

Figure 2. The representation architecture of educational resources

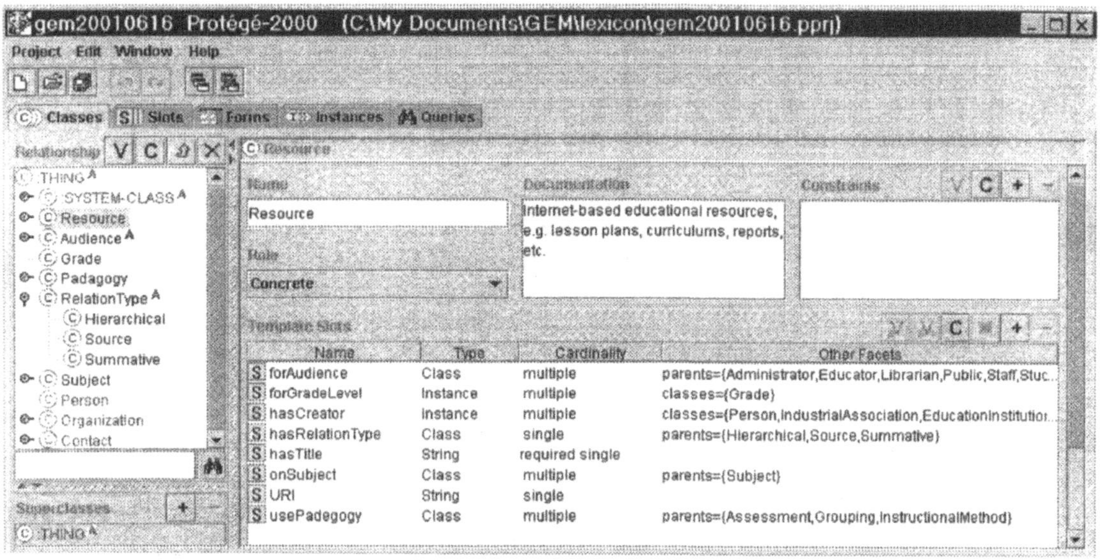

Figure 3. Screen shot of the GEM ontology created by using Protégé, an ontology editor

4. Mapping the Controlled Vocabulary and Keywords

Keywords in GEM include names for persons, organizations, books, animals or things from daily uses, e.g., J.F. Kennedy, American Library Association, Gone with the Wind, tiger, and computers, and terms that are too general to belong to any of the concept names. For example, keywords "absorption" and "acceptance" are so general that they can result in many semantic senses. We decided to exclude personal and organizational names as well as titles of books and movies from mapping due to the time constraint. Animal names were mapped into zoology, since it is the closest concept. Keywords that are very general and broad were set aside and given special codes for future processing. Over 8,500 keywords were suitable for this mapping project and they were examined against concept names only in the pedagogy, resource type and subject classes. For each mappable keyword, we chose the closest concept name(s) and assigned 1-3 concept name ID numbers to that keyword.

The mapping was done manually and we expected to generate a semantic association base that bridges the gap between the two vocabulary pools. We encountered several problems in the manual mapping process:

1) Normalization of keywords: Keywords in GEM's metadata records come with various forms for the same term. The most common is that of singular vs. plural, with a dash vs. without a dash in between two words, and different suffixes for the same word stem (e.g., -ing, -tion, -zation). Our decision was to maintain different forms of these terms but assign the same concept name to the same term with varying forms.
2) New subject categories: A small number of keywords did not fit into any existing categories. These keywords appeared to be general terms in education, information and technology. None of the concept names was suitable for them. Since we did not intend to expand the concept names at this time, these keywords were given special codes rather than concept name IDs for future study.
3) Levels of mapping: Even though the mapping used the lowest level of the concept hierarchy, we found from time to time that the concept names are relatively large-grained classes. The dilemma we had was that, for keywords that are general (e.g., American history, African-American history), the mapping may not add much value but for those that are very specific, the specificity was lost to broad subject categories.
4) Semantic senses of a keyword: Vocabulary mapping is also a process of disambiguating the semantic meaning for words and phrases. The nature of educational materials decides that many keywords are general and can be interpreted in many ways. How to define the disambiguation criteria becomes critical. Although the context was set in the education domain, we still had a hard time to find the most appropriate and accurate concept names for certain keywords.
5) Mode of mapping: At this stage, the semantic mapping is limited to subject categories and text format. While educational materials include a large volume in multimedia format, semantic mapping in the future may go beyond subject categories in the text format.

At the time of writing, we have completed mapping 3,555 keywords with concept names. To test the mapping result, we built a database with 10,000 metadata records and designed a simple search interface that can search the mapped and non-mapped data. We then obtained 50 queries from the GEM search log. Only 17 of them are usable for the test. Table 1 shows that most numbers in the two columns are dramatically different, the ones with mapping far exceeding those without. This informal test did not use any limitations such as grade level, resource type, audience, or access right (free or commercial), nor did it apply any measure for relevance. Nonetheless, these preliminary results reveal at least two deeper issues in subject access to networked resources. The first issue is the mismatch between the representation technology and representation methods. Current knowledge technologies such as ontologies tend to be well structured, i.e. capable of both modelling the knowledge structure and data structure, and work better when the resources bear the same or similar representation structure. However, current practice of indexing and metadata encoding does not generate such a structure, which can be a serious obstacle to applying new representation technologies. Semantic mapping between vocabularies forms only part of the solution; a more fundamental and perpetual solution lies in the construction of a representation architecture that matches between representation technologies and methods.

Table 1. Number of records retrieved from searches with and without mapping

Query ID	Query Sample from GEM's Search Log	Number of Records Retrieved	
		Without Mapping	With Mapping
Q01	Adaptation	21	792
Q02	African American History	123	1114
Q03	Bubbles	1	354
Q04	Design	96	--
Q05	Email and ethics	19	36
Q06	Fractions	39	256
Q07	Gifted	--	--
Q08	Government	13	1470
Q09	Integrated unit plan	27	--
Q10	Introduction to economics	15	261
Q11	Math and United States	101	268
Q12	Math and blueprints	96	1237
Q13	Math travel	115	878
Q14	Renaissance	9	1679
Q15	Snails	3	--
Q16	Technology	96	--
Q17	Who were the immigrants of 1800s and early 1900's and what role did the steamship play in immigrants to the United States	--	--

Another issue is the capability of semantic mapping in dealing with queries such as Q17 in Table 1. Although modern retrieval systems can translate sentence-type queries into an appropriate form, it is still largely a word/phrase matching process. Associations between concepts can be easily misinterpreted or lost in query representation and again in resource representation. Even with the mapping between GEM controlled vocabulary and keywords, we found it difficult properly to dissect Q17 to formulate a word-based query, needless to say, having to undertake another round of matching in the mapped vocabulary pools.

5. Conclusions and Further Study

Subject access to networked information resources relies on a sound representation that includes not only a well-developed vocabulary but also, more importantly, a knowledge representation structure that is in synch with representation technologies. This mapping project built an initial semantic mapping base. This base can serve as a mapping test for bridging different vocabulary pools, as well as a training data set for developing an automatic mapping algorithm in the future. The problems encountered in this project demonstrate a need for semantic mapping to go beyond simply matching words and phrases. The ideal scenario would be to build a knowledge network in which concepts and associations are explicitly specified and modelled in such a way that they can be directly programmed into systems. This knowledge network would be a multi-layered, multi-dimensional representation of resource content. The next phase of semantic mapping will study what knowledge needs to be captured and how the knowledge base works with metadata in enhancing the effectiveness of resource discovery and filtering.

References

Buckland, M. (1999). Vocabulary as a central concept in library and information science. In *Digital Libraries: Interdisciplinary Concepts, Challenges, and Opportunities: Proceedings of the Third International Conference on Conceptions of Library and Information Science (CoLIS3)*, pp. 3-12. <http://www.sims.berkeley.edu/~buckland/colisvoc.htm>. Accessed 20th June 2001.

Buckland, M. & Gey, F. (1999). Mapping entry vocabulary to unfamiliar metadata vocabularies. *D-Lib magazine*, 5(1) January: [http://www.dlib.org/dlib/january99/buckland/01buckland.html]. Accessed 20th June 2001.

BUBL Information Services (2000). *BUBL Link / 5:15*. <http://bubl.ac.uk/link/> Accessed 20th June 2001.

Chaplan, M. A. (1995). Mapping Laborline Thesaurus terms to Library of Congress Subject Headings: implications for vocabulary switching. *Library quarterly*, 65, 39-61.

Gey, F. et al. (1999). Advanced search technologies for unfamiliar metadata. *Proceedings of Meta-Data '99 Third IEEE Meta-Data Conference, 1999.* <http://metaphor.sims.berkeley.edu/papers/gey/advanced-search-ieee.pdf>. Accessed 06/20/01.

Giral, A. & Taylor, A.G. (1993). Indexing overlap and consistency between the *Avery Index to Architectural Periodicals* and the *Architectural Periodicals Index*. *Library resources and technical services*, 37, 19-43.

Olson, T. & Strawn, G. (1997). Mapping the LCSH and MeSH. *Information technology and libraries*, 16, 5-19.

Pepper, Steve. (2001). The TAO of topic maps. [http://www.gca.org/papers/xmleurope2000/papers/s11-01.html]. Accessed 6/20/01.

Qin, Jian. (2000). Semantic similarities in a keyword database and a controlled vocabulary database: an investigation in antibiotic resistance literature. *Journal of the American Society for Information Science*, 51, 166-180.

Qin, Jian & Paling, S. (2001). Converting a controlled vocabulary into an ontology: the case of GEM. *Information research: an international electronic journal*, 6(2) January: [http://InformationR.net/ir/6-2/paper94.html]. Accessed 6/20/01.

Rath, H. H. (2001). Making topic maps more colourful. [http://www.gca.org/papers/xmleurope2000/papers/s29-01.html]. Accessed 6/20/01.

Rath, H. H. (2000). Topic maps: building information and knowledge management. *XML-journal*, 1(6) 8-16.

Wood, Joanne. (1995). Introduction to the BUBL Subject Tree. *Computers in libraries*, 15, 79-80.

General Library Classification in Learning Material Metadata: the Application in IMS/LOM and DCMES Metadata Schemas

Aida Slavic

Abstract: This paper analyses the approach to resource discovery in the educational domain and stresses this community's need for a subject approach to information. The use of both general (Dublin Core) and domain specific (IEEE Learning Object Metadata/IMS Metadata) metadata schemas for learning resource discovery suggests that library classification could be used for subject description. There are several reasons why this indexing language might be suitable for the indexing of education resources. The paper will explain the reasoning behind the application of Universal Decimal Classification in the EASEL (Educator's Access to Services in the Electronic Landscape - http://www.fdgroup.com/easel) project. EASEL deploys two Dublin Core and several different application profiles of LOM i.e. IMS Metadata and this paper will explain how these two types of metadata support the use of classification.

Online education and access to resources

Online education is a large field that envolves many different domains such as academic, publishing, research, government and business. An orientation towards lifelong learning and an interest in distance learning, coupled with the availability of a large amount of digital material facilitated through powerful information and communication technology, leads to a wide range of innovations, products and research in the education arena. A vast number of software tools is available to design and publish learning material and this results in the heterogeneous nature of instructional material that is not easy to discover and reuse. Numerous projects researching these issues have contributed towards the existence of national and international information gateways and services to educational material such as the Education Network of Australia (EdNA - http://www.edna.edu.au/EdNA), European Schoolnet (http://www.en.eun.org/eun.org2/eun/en), The Gateway to Educational Material (GEM - http://www.thegateway.org) and many others. Revolving around general issues of knowledge representation, this domain is very interested in interoperability and information exchange across domains, subject areas, languages and geopolitical boundaries. The educational sector is particularly active in its attempt to harmonize standards and avoid duplication of effort on the level of learning resource management, and metadata in particular. This results in the development of standards for educational metadata that describe resources from the point of view of their role and place in the curriculum and pedagogical context but also from the point of their intellectual content. Some of the fora involved in these issues are European CEN/ISSS Learning Technology Group, Instructional Management Systems (IMS), IEEE Learning Technology Standardization Committee, Education Working Group of the Dublin Core Metadata Initiative (DC Education), Aviation Industry CBT Committee (AICC http://www.aicc.org), Advanced Distributed Learning (ADL http://www.adlnet.org), ARIADNE Foundation (http://www.ariadne-eu.org) etc.(see further in Bacsich et al., 1999). As a consequence of these activities, online education has a strong metadata standard candidate in the IEEE Learning Object Metadata schema (IEEE LOM). The IMS metadata workgroup that contributed to the development of IEEE LOM, has also created an application profile with an XML encoding solution based on the LOM: IMS Meta-data. Amongst the more recent developments that promotes interoperability outside the education sector, is the proposal for the extension of the Dublin Core Metadata Element Set for educational purposes (DCEd).

Information management and resource discovery in the online education
Gateways to online educational material are entirely dependent on metadata based information management and the supporting architecture. This is because of the heterogeneous nature of learning objects and their availability in a variety of forms and formats. Learning material can, for instance, be *passive* (information flow from the resource to the user) or *interactive* (information flow from the user to the learning object). The electronic learning environment can offer material that is adaptive on the basis of different criteria within the user profile (prerequisites, learning preference, learning ability etc.). From the point of view of granularity, learning resources can be anything from the entire material leading to a degree, or a single web page, graph or image. The consequence of this reality is the plethora of metadata schemas and their variants already in use in electronic learning environments worldwide. Typically, metadata implementers would start from simple resource discovery schemas like Dublin Core and then add the elements necessary to describe learning material. This is the situation that prompted the development of the IEEE LOM standard some 6 years ago.

With the objective of providing information access to a specialised profile of users, information services usually choose a "third party view" approach to information management (Vellucci, 1999). This means that information resources are going to be harvested, selected, described and made available by information specialists and the final result will be a repository of standalone metadata records that are used for resource discovery in order to contribute to its effective use. Standalone metadata (metadata repository), or in more traditional terms: *a catalogue of the resources*, becomes the prevalent approach for specialised information services and the educational domain has adopted this model. Information management in online education will thus often be characterised by standalone metadata (usually created by a third-party and not by the author of the resource), XML encoding and an XML metadata repository. As mentioned before, there are numerous schemas in use but those said to be predominant are simply different application profiles of the Dublin Core Metadata Element Set and LOM or IMS (which can be treated as one schema). These two schemas, recommend the use of a bibliographic indexing language, in particular library classification, for subject description. This paper will address some of the practical approaches in the use of library classification in educational metadata using the example of the EASEL project, which is one of many European research projects in this field

Subject description in IEEE LOM /IMS and Dublin Core metadata
The IEEE LOM schema and IMS Metadata profile based upon it have a large number of descriptive elements and attributes organised into 9 descriptive blocks

1 GENERAL (title, language, description, keywords, coverage, catalogue)
2 LIFECYCLE (author, publisher, version....)
3 METAMETADATA (scheme, language, author...)
4 TECHNICAL (format, size, requirements...)
5 EDUCATIONAL (learning time, difficulty level, interactivity level...)
6 RIGHTS (price, copyright)
7 RELATION
8 ANNOTATION
9 EXTERNAL CLASSIFICATION

The standard itself specifies the syntax and semantics of learning object metadata and attributes required to describe a learning object. The elements of this metadata schema are organised into a hierarchical structure. It is also worth mentioning that this schema with XML encoding serves not only as a framework for resource discovery (such as Dublin Core) but is designed both as a metadata schema and format for automated information management. When one examines the area devoted to subject description of a resource, on may find strange that this is divided between *keywords* and *coverage* in block 1 (general) and block 9 - *external classification*. Also, the definition and guideline for *coverage* does not indicate that *coverage* refers to the subject of the document. The names of the elements in this schema are not always self-explanatory and very often the present terminology has an entirely different meaning from the one in bibliographic practice. A good illustration of this is the way the IMS schema uses the terms *classification* or *taxonomy* as explained in the following text by Thomas D. Wason: "...A taxonomy is a controlled vocabulary of terms and phrases... The most typical form of taxonomy is hierarchy.... A taxonomy provides a controlled vocabulary for populating fields or taxonpaths. A taxonomy may be used for two majoru reasons: 1) to limit the choices of field values to a controlled set 2) to use terms that are defined by a known source. The simplest taxonomy is a controlled vocabulary" (Wason, Thomas D., 2000, pp. 1).

It is obvious that "controlled vocabulary" as described here only partly relates to the controlled vocabulary as understood and used in the bibliographic world. The taxonomy Wason describes in his Taxonomy guide could be, for instance, a list of learning resource types such as: exercise, simulation, questionnaire, diagram, figure, graph, index, slide, table, narrative text, exam, experiment, problem statement and self assessment. Or it could be an enumerated list of terms, such as interactivity level: 0 [very low], 1 [low], 2 [medium], 3 [high], or 4 [very high]. At the same time Wason's taxonomy can be *classification* that has *purpose discipline* which is the equivalent to classification in the sense of an indexing language as used in the bibliographic domain. The LOM and IMS schemas (and Wason's explanation), do not make a distinction between vocabulary when used to describe the subject of a resource and vocabulary used to describe its formal characteristics or educational functions. From the point of view of the information model or XML encoding, there is no reason to differentiate the two.

It would be wrong to draw conclusions hastily about the way LOM treats the subject of the resource. This schema gives good provision for subject description. If one ignores the potential terminological dissonance and structural curiosities, it should be noted that the schema offers not only the possibility to describe resources with keywords and coverage but that block *9 external classification* makes good provisions for an indexing language

```
<classification>
     <purpose>discipline</purpose>
     <taxonpath>
          <source>UDC</source>
          <taxon>
               <id>004</id>
               <entry>Computer   science   and   technology.
Computing</entry>
          </taxon>
          <taxon>
               <id>004.7</id>
               <entry>Network</entry>
          </taxon>
          <taxon>
```

```
            </taxon>
            <taxon>
                <id>004.73</id>
                <entry>Network   according   to   the   area
    covered</entry>
            </taxon>
            <taxon>
                <id>004.738</id>
                <entry>Network interconnection</entry>
            </taxon>
            <taxon>
                <id>004.738.5</id>
                <entry>Internet</entry>
            </taxon>
        </taxonpath>
    </classification>
```

This is an example of subject description using UDC classification in IMS metadata in the EASEL project. It is obvious that this schema has a format particularly suitable for machine readability of classification hierarchy and allows an indexing language to be fully exploited. The other schema often used in education, Dublin Core Metadata Set (DCMES), although closer to bibliographic metadata, is actually more rudimentary when it comes to subject description. The reason is the intentional simplicity and interoperability of the format. Nevertheless, Qualified Dublin Core allows keywords and library classification (or some other indexing language to be announced and used in the subject element) and also provides the facilities for element coverage to be used, although again does not explain the close relationship between coverage (temporal and spatial) and subject. In standalone metadata encoded in XML, DCMES would look like the example below:

a) when using *keywords* to describe subject of the resource that speaks about object-oriented databases and object-oriented data model:

```
    <dc>
        <subject>object-oriented data model</subject>
        <subject>object-oriented databases</subject>
        <subject>OODBS</subject>
    </dc>
```

b) when using library classification to describe the subject of the same resource

```
    <dc>
        <subject scheme = "udc">004.652.5</subject>
        <subject scheme = "udc">004.65.045</subject>
    </dc>
```

Educational metadata and classification

Subject access to resources is an important issue for online education. Although this is often stated for the Internet as a whole (Koch, 1997; Kwasnik, 1999; Hodge, 2000), the educational domain is a specific area that might appreciate subject access to resources the most. Education is based on the knowledge framework and scientific consensus that is normally present in accompanying and supporting literature, thus the tools used for information organisation and indexing in libraries can be easily applied to access learning material. It is only logical that library classification has already found its place in learning object metadata as illustrated in the previous section.

There are several reasons why library classification as a knowledge framework has a special place in the representation of learning material. Whenever one needs to index and browse resources that span the whole of knowledge, general library classification is an appropriate aide to this task, whether one uses it as a source of terms or mimic its structure. Gateways to online learning material have to provide very powerful search functionality and enable resource discovery on specific topic levels. Such a gateway should provide the student or educator, for instance in the field of Computer sciences, with the facility to search for specific terms such as e.g. *Bacchus Naur Form* or *BNF* or *normalisation*. It is of equal importance for those involved in education to be able to browse through the subject area and look, for example, at material available in the broader areas of *database management systems*, *database design* or *computer architecture in general*. While classification will not support specific searches and will not provide user friendly terms for the search, it will enable browsing of the subject field . Classification will also help to contextualise search terms to the relevant area. Therefore if the system is designed to support this function a terms such as *architecture* and *design* can be linked using classification structures to either the field of computers or the field of building architecture, and help the user to place his search in to appropriate context.

Often, educational gateways merge material in different languages. Many projects supported by the European Union, for instance, are addressing the issue of international gateways in the area of education. Much learning material on a fine granular level such as images, graphs or sound are not language sensitive, and a large amount of resources used in the field of philology, arts or humanities needs to be in its original language. In these cases, using language independent indexing tools such as classification can help in information exchange and collection merging.

Although the need to deploy library classification might appear obvious, metadata implementers outside the library domain often lack the necessary expertise in deciding which classification, if any, would suit their needs. It is always sensible to suggest to these users, that library classification is a rich vocabulary that can be used as a source of terms and a reference tool for different kinds of taxonomies and relations within a particular subject field. Classification can be used as a control mechanism for the keywords and their distribution in the process of indexing. Once encoded in metadata, classification is a valuable source for a browsing function through fields of knowledge and although hidden from the end user it can always help in subject navigation or mapping to competing indexing languages. Most of these simple tasks can be performed with very little investment in the system.

EASEL: an example of an indexing approach

The EASEL project is one of many European projects concerned with the issues surrounding learning resource discovery. Although EASEL is primarly interested in the reuse of distributed learning material through the function called the *course constructor kit* - the whole concept is based on rich metadata and powerful searching across distant metadata repositories. When looking into subject description, EASEL partners have agreed on the following requirements for indexing tools: a) extensible and flexible alphabetical indexing covering the whole area of knowledge in order to enable user friendly searching, b) a taxonomy to enable hierarchical browsing on the search gateways, c) possible language independent identifiers of the subject for vocabulary control and maintenance.

For the purpose of simplicity it was decided to use natural language terms in the form of keywords that are going to be used alongside Universal Decimal Classification (UDC)[1] in order to enable control and consistency. The reasons UDC was chosen are: size of vocabulary (62000 terms), hierarchical structure, synthetic feature. During the indexing process and metadata population, the UDC schema is used not only for indexing, but also as a source of keyword vocabulary and a reference tool for related subject areas, synonyms or hierarchical relationships. The basic set of keywords is always extracted from the classification schedules and more specific terms are added when appropriate. This is a simple but efficient way of imposing some kind of minimal control during indexing.

With regard to the search gateway, UDC is planned to be used for browsing the taxonomy as well as to contextualise the keywords providing the technology employed will allow the full exploitation of this potential. Learning material available through the EASEL search gateway is described in several metadata schemas and different application profiles of these schemas are encoded in XML. Partners are free to use any metadata providing they submit the XML schema that is used to parse their XML encoding. Some partners have used Dublin Core extended with Dublin Core Education Elements while others are using existing versions of LOM and IMS Metadata. Heterogeneous metadata is the reason for EASEL to explore the Resource Description Framework architecture(RDF) and its potential in the cross metadata and distributed search. The RDF search gateway with a Semantic Registry allows discovery across distributed metadata repositories[2]. An RDF data-model allows expression of properties and relationships for each uniquely identified semantic unit originating from different metadata schemas held in the Semantic Registry. The Semantic Registry could be described as a collection of descriptions of metadata classes, fields and values and the relationships between them. During the search, RDF looks for data elements that describe the content in the remote metadata repository and then looks up their definitions in the Semantic Registry. The RDF schema is extensible and therefore very suitable for the distributed environment and its unpredictable content.

For subject searching, SR could for instance, express the relations of two competing vocabularies through representational facets. In the following graph "hasSubject" is a normal property; "hasUDCRep" and "hasKeywordsRep" are representational facets.

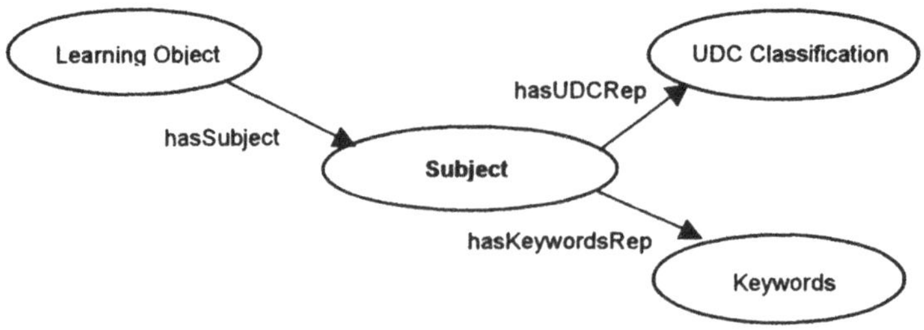

It is the intention of EASEL to explore whether an RDF search gateway based on a similar model can meet expected needs. A Semantic Registry could prove to be a good model of having a classification that helps organisation of information behind the scenes.

It should be noted that metadata is merely a way of structuring and storing data about information resources. How this data is going to be used by the system architecture, and what functions will be based on the available data is not proscribed by the metadata schema or by the information model that is basis of that schema. In the example of the RDF/SR architecture, for instance, it is possible to see technological solutions that may determine the choice of the indexing language or the indexing policy. The evaluation of the EASEL gateway will show whether or not some aspects of classification can be easily implemented and exploited with this technology.

Also when it comes to subject description, metadata schemas do not make any suggestions regarding indexing policy (e.g. exhaustivity, specificity, relations, or the use of compounds or complex terms). The choice or format of indexing terms (keywords or classification numbers) is completely open. Should keywords be in plural or singular should they (e.g. database / databases), should synonyms be listed and acronyms spelled out (e.g. object-oriented databases / OODBS) etc. When it come to classification, the indexing policy is even more important. But even more importantly, the information model that serves as a basis for metadata encoding has to support the decision on how particular elements and terms in classification should be encoded and how to encode hierarchies to make them *machine readable using* XML or *machine understandable* using RDF. These issues would be partly solved if an appropriate standardised format (XML/RDF) for representation of indexing languages would be used to hold classification scheme. Good examples for the better approach in handling vocabularies could be found in the field of lexicography, these are, for instance, OLIF (Open Lexicon Interchange Format) and TMF (Terminological Markup Framework).

Deciding on an indexing policy using traditional and traditionally digitised tools requires expertise in both the indexing language and system architecture. Indexing tools such as classification can be well exploited in many ways in spite of the lack of an appropriate machine readable format. Possible development of new indexing tools requires more expertise, time and money than metadata implementers are prepared to invest and library classification might prove to be good alternative.

Conclusion

The interest in alphabetical indexing languages and classifications stretches beyond the bibliographic/library environment. Communities currently involved in metadata activities, such as education, have already become involved in metadata creation and are interested in deploying existing indexing tools. Metadata standards, such as Dublin Core or IEEE LOM/IMS are making provisions for and are recommending the use of library classification. However, metadata itself only gives the "room" to store classification data while the full exploitation of this data depends on the system.

When classification is chosen, a certain expertise is necessary to recognise whether a particular scheme is suitable for the role and whether the system architecture and metadata encoding can support its full functionality. The EASEL differs from other education projects in that it attempts to make sensible use of library classification. In this project, classification is used as a source of indexing terms and a reference tool to control simple keyword indexing as well as the basis for the subject browsing taxonomy. Full implementation and evaluation of an RDF search gateway with a Semantic Registry capturing classification relationships will show whether or not there is room for improvement in the way classification can be further exploited in resource discovery.

References

Bacsich, P. et al. (1999). The standards fora for online education. *D-Lib magazine*, 5(12) December. <http://www.dlib.org/dlib/december99/12miller.html>.

Dempsey, L. & Heery, R. (1998). Metadata: a current view of practice and issues. *Journal of documentation*, 54, 145-172.

Hodge, G. (2000). *Systems of knowledge organization for digital libraries: beyond traditional authority files*. Washington, DC, Council on Library & Information Resources. <http://www.clir.org/pubs/reports/pub91/contents.html>

IMS Global Learning Consortium (2000). IMS Learning Resource Meta-Data Information Model: version 1.1 – Final specification. http://www.imsproject.org/metadata/mdinfov1p1.html

Institute of Electrical & Electronics Engineers. Learning Technology Standardization Committee. (2000). Draft Standard for Learning Object Metadata: IEEE P1484.12/D4.0 http://ltsc.ieee.org/doc/wg12/LOM_WD4.htm

Koch, T. et al. (1997). The role of classification schemes in Internet resource description and discovery. DESIRE Project deliverable D3.2(3). <http://www.ukoln.ac.uk/metadata/desire/classification/>.

Kwasnik, B. (1999). The role of classification in knowledge representation and discovery, *Library trends*, 48, 22-47.

Sutton, S. (1999). Conceptual design and deployment of a metadata framework for educational resources on the Internet, *Journal of the American Society for Information Science*, 50, 1182-1192.

Vellucci, S. L. (1999). Metadata and authority control, *Library resources & technical services*, 44, 33-43.

Wason, T.D. Dr. Tom's taxonomy guide: description, use and selection. <http://www.imsproject.org/drtomtaxonomiesguide.html>. Accessed 10/10/2000

---

[1] UDC Consortium (http://www.udcc.org) has granted permission for the extraction of the Master Reference File without charge for the research purposes of the project.

[2] EASEL leading partner for RDF Remote Search Gateways / Semantic Registry is the Institute of Learning & Research Technologies (ILRT), Bristol, UK (Jan Grant, jan.grant@bristol.ac.uk)

Session 6

TOOL DEVELOPMENT FOR RETRIEVAL

Personal Construct Theory as a research tool in Library and Information Science. Case Study: Development of a user-driven classification of photographs

Mary A. Burke

Abstract: This paper describes a preliminary research project which applies Personal Construct Theory to individual user perceptions of photographs. The research has both theoretical and practical objectives, namely: to test the validity of Personal Construct Theory (Kelly's theory and corollaries) for subject content analysis of photographs, and to use Personal Construct Theory and repertory grids to enhance retrieval of photographs. The background to Personal Construct Theory and to the use of Repertory Grids is presented and there is an overview of applications of these techniques in library and information science and other disciplines. Research results show a high level of consistency among the personal constructs which participants used to distinguish between photographs. While some problems associated with using Repertory Grids for subject content analysis are identified, the research concludes that they provide a useful method of collecting unbiased data about what users see in visual images and for comparing user perceptions with alternative retrieval vocabularies and methods. Incorporation of a participant's constructs in automatic classification systems for visual images remains a major challenge.

1. Introduction

There is considerable evidence that the description of subject content for visual images is a subjective process in which individual user characteristics play an important role. There are two main categories of solutions to this problem:

- intellectual analysis of content by human indexers with searchers using some combination of free-text, thesaurus terms, or classification codes.
- automatic analysis of content by computer software as exemplified by QBIC (IBM) (2001).

However, neither of these reflects the variety of interpretation of subject content which may occur for a diverse user population, especially in a web-based environment with remote users of digitized collections. Personal Construct Theory, which emphasizes the personal constructs that an individual uses to make sense of his / her world, appears to have tremendous potential to enhance subject based retrieval by identifying the constructs which groups of users consider to be important (Bannister, 1968; Gaines and Shaw, 2000; Kelly, 1955; Kelly, 1970; Shaw, 1980, Shaw, 1981).

This paper describes preliminary research on the application of Personal Construct Theory to the subject content analysis of photographs, using a test collection from the Irish Folklore Archive and participants from the Departments of Irish Folklore and Library and Information Studies in University College Dublin (UCD).

2. Personal Construct Theory and Repertory Grids

Personal Construct Theory was developed by George Kelly in the mid 1950s as a contribution to Psychotherapy. He argued that each person is a scientist who is concerned with prediction and control of his/her environment. He also claimed that each individual develops her own personal repertoire of constructs by means of which s/he structures his/her world and tries to anticipate events. Kelly's fundamental postulate was that 'a person's processes are psychologically channelized by the way in which he anticipates events'. (Kelly, 1955, 46).

Kelly's Postulate and his eleven associated corollaries provide an alternative cognitive model (Bannister, 1968).

There are two main components of Personal Construct Theory: elements and constructs. Elements represent the area to be investigated. They are objects of people's thoughts, e.g., people, books, events, experiences. Constructs are qualities people attribute to those objects, e.g. kindness, level of interest, type of memory or effect on one's mood.

Kelly developed Repertory Grids as a technique for exploring the relationship between constructs and elements in a given context. They present a two-way classification of data and also facilitate the analysis of patterns and the presentation of relationships. They are created from a structured interview situation between the researcher and the participant which normally involves the following steps:

- The participant is shown three elements at random and asked to identify two of these elements which are similar and thereby different from a third.
- The participant then has to say why the two elements are similar and thereby different from the third - this gives the first construct.
- The participant then completes the grid for this construct by rating the remaining elements along a rating scale, between the two poles of the construct.
- The participant then repeats the first three steps to elicit more constructs.

The construct system is then analysed manually and by computer software. There is a wide range of software packages for this purpose, including WebGrid, a web-based version of RepGrid, which allows for multimedia elements and multiple options for data storage and analysis on the Knowledge Science Institute web-site at the University of Calgary (Gaines and Shaw, 2001a; Gaines and Shaw, 2001b).

3. Subject Retrieval of Visual Images

Shatford (1986) develops a broad framework for analyzing the subject of a picture, which expands on earlier work by Markey (1983). She describes the analysis of visual images as being 'of' certain subjects, creatures, places and events, and as being 'about' certain intangibles and then subdivides 'ofness' into 'specific of ' and 'generic of'.

Shatford also takes the tradition of facet analysis as described by Ranganathan (1959) in his work on classification and uses the facets independently for subject analysis of paintings. Facets correspond to different aspects of, or approaches to, a subject, in the same way that the many-sided structure of a gem can reflect different views when examined from different angles. Ranganathan identified five primary facets - Personality, Matter, Energy, Space and Time - which may be applied to subject content analysis of visual images and other media.

Subject analysis is also enriched by the principles of iconography, 'the study of subject matter or meaning in art' (Panofsky, 1962, 3). Panofsky's theory may be applied to all visual images, including photographs, and is not limited to art. This art historian developed a theory which describes three levels of meaning in a visual image, namely:

- primary or natural subject matter,
- secondary or conventional subject matter, and
- intrinsic meaning of content.

A combination of the four approaches to subject content analysis described above, namely 'ofness' and 'aboutness', 'generic' and 'specific', facet analysis, and Panofsky's three levels of meaning, provide a systematic framework for subject content analysis of visual images such as photographs.

4. Research Project on Classification of Photographs

4.1 Research Objectives

The aims of this research were both theoretical and practical. For the former, the researcher wanted to test the applicability of Personal Construct Theory (Kelly's theory and corollaries) for subject content analysis of a collection of photographs. For the latter, the aim was to use Personal Construct Theory and Repertory Grids to enhance retrieval of photographs.

The research intended to answer the following questions:

1. How similar are the constructs of the participants?
2. Is the level of similarity greater within a professional sub-group, e.g. Library and Information Scientists (LIS) and Irish Folklorists (IF)?
3. Will subject experts generate a greater number of constructs and how will these differ from those generated by generalists for the same collection?
4. How similar are the constructs of the participants to those of cataloguers and indexers?
5. Do the constructs reflect Panofsky's primary and secondary levels of meaning, or other theoretical approaches to subject indexing?
6. Does the MPEG-7 Multilevel Indexing Pyramid accommodate these constructs (Jaimes et al., 2000)?
7. What other factors influence the personal constructs, e.g. urban or rural background, nationality, etc.?

4.2 Experimental Methodology

The sample collection consisted of a set of nine digitised photographs from the Irish Folklore Archive at University College Dublin (UCD). The photographs were selected as a stratified sample in order to represent five of the main subject categories in the in-house classification scheme. The photographs were selected randomly within each subject category. The participants came from two subgroups:

- Students on professional post-graduate programme in Library and Information Studies (23 participants);
- Students and staff from the Department of Irish Folklore in UCD (11 participants).

The photographs were classified using the in-house classification scheme of the Folklore Archive and this categorization was used as a baseline for comparison with each participant. Various types of analysis were carried out on the participant's data, including a basic display of the Repertory Grid, a FOCUS cluster analysis, and a PrinCom principal components analysis using software on the WebGrid site (Gaines and Shaw, 2001a).

5. Results

5.1 Summary of Constructs

Overall 264 constructs were identified, with huge diversity in emphasis and structure. These constructs were analyzed for semantic and syntactic similarity and grouped under general headings. Semantic similarity was based on equivalent word meanings at both poles of the construct, e.g. 'people - no people' was deemed equivalent to 'humans - no humans'. Syntactic similarity was based on categorizing the elicited constructs according to Ranganathan's PMEST formula. Constructs were deemed to be equivalent if they had the same semantic and syntactic meaning, this process resulted in 73 unique constructs. It would be possible to reduce this number of unique constructs by applying less rigorous criteria for similarity but this step seemed inappropriate at this stage of the research.

5.2 Consistency of Constructs

The researcher's initial reaction was that there was huge diversity of constructs, with very little overlap among participants. However, on analyzing these constructs more closely, certain patterns emerged. The twelve most frequently used constructs (with eight or more occurrences) account for 156 constructs from a total of 264 (59%), while the 18 most frequent constructs account for 186 individual constructs from a total of 264 (70%).

5.3 Comparison of Constructs for Professional Sub-Groups

There is a slightly greater use of frequent terms by the LIS participants than by the IF participants. Consideration of infrequent terms shows that nine of these terms came from the eleven IF participants (82%), with fourteen from the twenty-three LIS participants (61%). There is a clear pattern of IF participants seeing unique features in photographs, which presumably is due to their more detailed knowledge of the subject area. No difference was observed in the number of constructs generated by members of the IF and LIS sub-groups. All participants were encouraged to generate the same number of constructs, but there was no observable difference between the two sub-groups in terms of their ability or desire to continue generating constructs.

5.4 Comparison with Cataloguers and Indexers

The in-house classification scheme of the Folklore Archive was used to generate a baseline set of constructs for categorisation of the photographs. All but one of the categories used in the in-house classification scheme emerged as constructs in the experiment. However, none of the clusters of photographs which the participants generated was remotely similar to the baseline. Extensive discussion with the curators of the collection indicated that the reason for this lack of similarity was the distinction between the needs of researchers in Irish Folklore and those of generalists looking at photographs. The classification scheme is designed to facilitate research by Folklorists using general subject categories.

Asking people to classify photographs in the context of specific user needs is not the same exercise as asking people to distinguish between them, dissociated from any context. Thus, it is understandable that the classification scheme used in the archive does not correspond to that which users from either participant group see in photographs.

5.5 Comparison of Constructs with Theoretical Approaches to Subject Retrieval

There is complete predominance of Panofsky's first level of analysis, corresponding to identification of primary subject matter which does not require any specialist subject knowledge. There was no identification of specific people or places but the photographs did not lend themselves to this.

When one turns to Shatford's criteria of 'ofness' (generic and specific) and 'aboutness', there is a preponderance of 'specific of' terms (55 from 73, 75%), with 18 'aboutness' examples (25%), and no 'generic of' terms. The 'aboutness' examples reflected the subjective meaning or role of some photographs, including constructs for mood, financial and social conditions, etc. If one takes the frequency of occurrence of each construct into consideration, there was even greater emphasis on the 'generic of' category (242 from 264, 92%).

Ranganathan's PMEST approach to facet analysis provided a sound basis for grouping the constructs, with all five types of facet represented. There was a small number of constructs which corresponded to combinations of terms from two or more facets, e.g. 'young, poor, female - none of these', or 'children playing - no children playing'. These results support the view that facet analysis has much to offer as an aid in classifying and indexing visual images.

5.6 Comparison with MPEG-7 Multilevel Pyramid

Jaimes et al. (2000) outline experiments they have performed for the MPEG-7 standard for describing multimedia objects. They used a ten-level pyramid to classify attributes obtained from images, video and audio. The top four levels of the pyramid deal with the syntax of the object, namely: 1, Type / Technique; 2, Global Distribution; 3, Local Structure; and 4, Global Composition. The bottom six levels of the pyramid deal with semantics, namely: 5, Generic Objects; 6, Specific Objects; 7, Abstract Objects; 8, Generic Scene; 9, Specific Scene; and 10, Abstract Scene. All of the constructs in the Irish Folklore experiment were accommodated by the MPEG-7 multilevel indexing pyramid. Levels 5, 8, and 10 occur most frequently, level 4 is also fairly common and level 7 occurs twice. When frequency of occurrence of each construct was included, Generic Scene (116 from 264, 44%) and Generic Objects (91 from 264, 34%) become even more dominant.

5.7 Other Factors

There was no perceivable connection with personal circumstances but the sample group was fairly homogenous, as all participants were white university students or graduates. Some variations were noted: an overseas student had some difficulty identifying features of the photos which were obvious to Irish students; participants who had experience of photography or analysis of photographs were stronger on compositional and technical elements, etc.

6. Overall Conclusions and Recommendations

This research had both theoretical and practical objectives. It showed that Personal Construct Theory and Repertory Grids are applicable to research on what participants see in visual images. The nature of the difference between asking people to classify objects in the context of specific user needs and merely asking people to distinguish between objects out of context merits further research. Considerable analysis has yet to be done on the data collected in this experiment. Analysis so far has focused on the constructs; the next stage will do cross comparisons of the 34 subjects by comparing the clustering of photographs using shared constructs.

A new phase of the research would generate a core set of constructs from this experiment and use these as the basis for a new experiment with a different set of photographs and a different group of participants. This would enable testing of the independence of the constructs of a group of users and of a set of photographs and also provide a better basis for comparison of clustering by participants. The researcher already has a parallel collection of nine photographs with same distribution across subject categories.

Alternatively, one could also allow complete freedom of constructs; it is even possible for a participant to avoid naming a construct at all and to rank photographs based on his/her unarticulated understanding of it. This facility proved useful already when one participant had difficulty articulating a construct, which was recorded as 'value 1 - value 5' on the grid.

A longitudinal study would be needed to determine how the constructs used by an individual change as s/he develops expertise in his/her subject. It would be interesting to execute a similar experiment for a different collection, e.g. a general photographic collection without the Irish Folklore specialization. There is tremendous potential for cross-cultural comparison, e.g. with ethnic minorities in Ireland or with international partners and for demographic and social studies. An upgraded version of WebGrid III which enables the image of each photograph to be shown on screen during the ranking will be used in subsequent research (Gaines & Shaw, 2001b).

It is difficult to assess the possible effects of the results of the research for operational visual image databases and search engines. This would require a user interface which would enable users to filter large image collections by selecting a construct value from a range of options. The range of options would be created from personal construct experiments with previous users of the collection. These would be likely to include generic and specific people, animals and objects, activities and events, and time and place.

As part of this link with operational systems an important next part of the research will be to test the correspondence between the WebGrid categorization and that of an automatic indexing system, e.g. QBIC (IBM) (2001). Query by information content (QBIC), an IBM search and access development, allows users to search a collection's media objects by colour, texture, shape and size. A query may be expressed graphically, for example, by specifying colours from a colour wheel or selecting textures from a list of sample images. Once a user finds one fairly useful item, he or she can then request other 'similar' items. The constructs could be included as a basis for similarity.

Personal Construct Theory and Repertory Grids have potential for enhancement of retrieval for other media, e.g. video and film material, leisure books, Web resources, etc.; indeed for any materials which lend themselves to subjective interpretation. They have much to offer other areas of Library / Information Science, e.g. user studies, human resources management, etc. Many surveys of user needs and of library / information service performance would be enriched by using Repertory Grids to identify constructs which are important to users and to measure users' rankings of relevant elements for these constructs. McKnight's research on personal construction of information space is an encouraging move in this direction (McKnight, 2000).

Personal Construct Theory provides a neutral framework for comparison of subject vocabularies and for many areas of study of human behaviour in an information society. It is encouraging that many diverse strands of research subject retrieval are converging on new applications of traditional tools to a multimedia web-based environment. The real challenge, however, will be to implement user interfaces which exploit this greater awareness of how users perceive photographs and other visual images.

Acknowledgements
The author would like to express her gratitude to all participants in the experimental part of this study and to colleagues in the Departments of Irish Folklore, Library and Information Studies, and Psychology in UCD who facilitated the research in many ways. Particular recognition and thanks go to Professor Brian Gaines and his colleagues at the Knowledge Science Institute, University of Calgary, for providing WebGrid software on the Web and for their gracious technical support and advice. Any errors or weaknesses in the paper are the author's sole responsibility.

References

Bannister, D. (1968). Personal construct theory: a summary and experimental paradigm. *Acta psychologica,* 20, 104-120.

Gaines, B.R. & Shaw, M.L.G. (2000). *Personal construct psychology.* <http://repgrid.com/pcp>. Accessed 27.06.2001

Gaines, B.R. & Shaw, M.L.G. (2001a). *WebGrid II.* <http://repgrid.com/>. Accessed 27.06.2001

Gaines, B.R. & Shaw, M.L.G. (2001b). *WebGrid III.* <http://gigi.cpsc.ucalgary.ca/>. Accessed 05.11.2001.

Jaimes, A. et al. (2000). Experiments in indexing multimedia data at multiple levels. In *Classification for User Support and Learning. Proceedings of the 11th ASIS&T SIG/CR Classification Research Workshop,* held at the 62nd ASIS&T Annual Meeting, Chicago, IL, Nov. 12, 2000. Silver Spring, MD: American Society for Information Science and Technology. Pp. 163-168.

Kelly, G. A. (1955). *The psychology of personal constructs.* New York: Norton. 2 vols. (2nd printing, London: Routledge, 1991).

Kelly, G. A. (1970). A brief introduction to personal construct theory. In *Perspectives in Personal Construct Theory,* ed. D. Bannister. London: Academic Press. Pp. 1-29.

McKnight, C. (2000). The personal construction of information space, *Journal of the American Society for Information Science,* 51, 730-733.

Markey, K. (1983). Computer-assisted construction of a thematic catalog of primary and secondary subject matter, *Visual resources,* 3, 16-49.

Panofsky, E. (1962). *Studies in iconology: humanistic themes in the art of the Renaissance.* New York: Harper and Row.

QBIC (IBM) (2001). <http://wwwqbic.almaden.ibm.com/>. Accessed 27.06.2001

Ranganathan, S. R. (1959). *Elements of library classification.* 2nd ed. London: Association of Assistant Librarians.

Shatford, S. (1986). Analyzing the subject of a picture: a theoretical approach, *Cataloguing and classification quarterly,* 6(3) 39-62.

Shaw, M. L. G. (1980). *On becoming a personal scientist: interactive computer elicitation of personal models of the world.* London: Academic Press.

Shaw, M. L. G. (Ed.) (1981). *Recent advances in personal construct technology.* London: Academic Press.

Improving Subject Retrieval with Frame Representations

Carol A. Bean and Rebecca Green

Abstract: Frames are integrated structures that address equivalence, hierarchical, and associative relationships. The richness of their internal organization and external relationality provide power and flexibility in meeting user needs for both high recall and high precision, as required.

1. Introduction

The use of synonyms, quasi-synonyms, lexical variants, etc., contributes to a many-to-many relationship between words and meaning. Equivalence relationships are commonly established in thesauri so the nonfunctional relationship between words and meaning will not interfere with retrieval by concept (that is, by meaning) when we use words as our intermediaries in the retrieval process (Aitchison et al., 1997, 47-52). If retrieval performance is improved by controlling equivalence relationships between word-level units, it stands to reason that performance could also be improved by controlling equivalence relationships between higher-level units (e.g., clauses, propositions). Indeed, the degree to which these higher-level meanings can be paraphrased in natural language is potentially greater than the base occurrence of word-level synonymy, since ideas can often be conveyed in ways that differ by more than just the substitution of equivalent terms. For example, *Mary returned home from New York by way of Philadelphia* and *Mary traveled from New York to her home, making a stop in Philadelphia en route* convey roughly the same information, as do *Peter sold his bike to Marcia for $200* and *Marcia paid Peter $200 for his bike.*

TRAVEL	COMMERCIAL TRANSACTION
Traveler [Mary]	Buyer [Marcia]
Originating location [New York]	Seller [Peter]
Destination location [Mary's home]	Merchandise [Peter's bike]
Intermediate location [Philadelphia]	Price [$200]

Figure 1. Frame representations common to various paraphrases

The control of equivalence relationships between such higher-level units can be achieved through the use of frame representations—integrated structures used here to convey relational configurations of various types of events or situations.[1] Such frames standardize syntagmatic relationship types on the conceptual level. Frames can be defined for general states, activities, and processes and then instantiated to represent specific occurrences of such predicates. For example, each of the pairs of sentences cited above could be represented (simplistically) by a single frame representation without significant loss of propositional information, as in Figure 1. The primary purpose for controlling equivalence relationships is to increase retrieval recall. In a networked environment, the potentially overwhelming size of retrieval sets often prompts reactions that increased recall is the last thing we need! Accepting low recall result sets is, however, not the appropriate response to the retrieval conundrum. Coupled with high recall searches, we need high precision searches, and we need appropriately ranked results. The good news is that frame representations can be used not only to increase recall, but also to increase precision and to rank retrieval sets in an intelligent manner.

COMPARISON
Entity A [ ]
Entity B [ ]
Comparative evaluation, B to A [<, >, ≤, ≥, =, ≠, like, unlike]

LOCATION
Entity A; patient [ ]
Entity B; landmark [ ]
Direction [ ]
Distance [:*number*]

Figure 2. Examples of vocabulary control over frame slot values

STATE-a
Patient [Tom]
Attribute type [Height]
Attribute value [5'8"]

STATE-b
Patient [Chris]
Attribute type [Height]
Attribute value [5'10"]

COMPARISON
Entity A [STATE-a:Attribute value]
Entity B [STATE-b:Attribute value]
Comparative evaluation, B to A [>]

Figure 3. Examples of frame slot values as pointers to other frames/slots

In proposing the application of a frame-based system for subject retrieval, two primary issues need attending: Representations of items and queries on the one hand, and on the other the closely related issue of identifying, characterizing, and capturing potential relationships of relevance between them. This paper will focus on the organizational and structural elements of frames that support the objectives of subject retrieval and briefly address the representation in frame structures of items and queries and the relationships that link them.

2. Organizational Structure of Frame Representations

Internally, frames consist of some number of "slots" (e.g., Traveler, Originating location, Buyer, and Merchandise from the examples above), which can be characterized alternatively as semantic argument types for the conceptual predicate represented by the frame or more directly as participant types in the state, activity, or process type represented by the frame. Frames are instantiated by assigning values to these slots. In addition to being assigned specific values (e.g., the name of a person, a type of object), slots may also be given generic values (e.g., value not applicable, value unknown). An instantiated frame reveals syntagmatic relationships between the fillers of its various slots.

Vocabulary control should be exercised over the values assigned to slots. In some cases this may involve identifying a specific set of permissible values or at least the semantic type of permissible values; see Figure 2. In other cases the set of permissible values is more open-ended, in which case values could be drawn from an extant thesaurus of the more traditional sort. Since complex events may incorporate one or more events in their representation, in yet other cases slot values may be pointers to other frames (or to specific slots within them); see Figure 3.

We assume a situation in which vocabulary control is imposed not only over the values used to fill slots, but also over frame configurations, so that relationships between frames are evident in part in the sets of slots they incorporate. For instance, a TRAVEL frame includes slots for Originating location and Destination location. In the parlance of thematic roles, these are specifications of Source and Goal, respectively. Other frames may also include some notion of Source and Goal, with 'travel' between them often being metaphorical. For example, a GIFT frame would include a Giver, who is a Source, and a Recipient, who is a Goal; the Gift is the'Traveler' who journeys between Source and Goal. Thus, when frame slots are identified, they may carry both a frame-specific characterization, such as Originating location, and, whenever appropriate, a generic characterization, such as Source.

Given the internal structure of frames, the relational structure among frames is potentially quite rich. First, frames can be organized hierarchically, based on such factors as (a) the presence of a slot in one frame that is absent from another, (b) the greater specificity of some slot in one frame vis-à-vis another frame, or (c) the greater specificity of the value of a slot filler in one instantiation of a frame vis-à-vis another instantiation of the same frame. Figure 4 illustrates these situations.

Another way that frames may be specified to a greater degree is by setting constraints on the permissible number for a slot's values. For example, a PATH frame with one Origin and two Destinations may be used to represent a SPLIT or FORK; likewise, a PATH with two Origins and one Destination describes a MERGE or UNION conceptual structure.

Additionally, when generic slot types recur in combination with each other, as Source and Goal do in TRAVEL, GIFT, COMMUNICATION, TEACHING, and (Number) RANGE, among others, another type of relational structure emerges. Such common elements linking disparate frames together create extended structural "families" supporting the transfer of underlying gestalts, such as with metaphors.

	(a) Slot presence	(b) Slot specificity	(c) Slot filler specificity
General	ACTION-PROCESS Action [ ] Process [ ]	EXPERIENCE Experiencer [ ] Experience [ ]	ACTION Agent [Pitcher] Activity [Throw]
Specific	PRODUCTION Action [ ] Process [ ] Material [ ]	COGNITION Knower [ ] Known [ ]	ACTION Agent [Mike Mussina] Activity [Throw]

Figure 4. Hierarchical relationships between frames

Finally, multiple distinct individual frames may be joined on the basis of common elements to form a third independent conceptual structure. The resulting composite frame is both more specific and more complex in its representation than would be permitted by a simple binary association of the component frame structures: The whole is greater than the sum of its parts.

For example, a CONDUIT frame may be seen as the compositional joining of the more primitive CONTAINER and PATH frames; the conceptual structure for the PATH frame itself incorporates elements of a LOCATION frame joined with a LINK frame, as shown in Figure 5.

LOCATION	+	LINK	→	PATH
Entity A; patient [ ]		Entity A [ ]		Source [ ]
Entity B; landmark [ ]		Entity B [ ]		Destination [ ]
-----		Link [ ]		Path [ ]
Direction [ ]		-----		Direction [ ]
Distance [ ]		-----		Distance [ ]

Figure 5. PATH as a composite of LOCATION and LINK

3. Indexing

To use frame representations to full advantage, we assume a policy of indexing as specifically as user needs warrant. A given concept may be represented at the level of frame, slot, or value depending on the body of knowledge within the domain and the needs of the users of the knowledge base. Representing concepts at higher orders of specificity provides increasing contextual detail: A slot bears additional meaning in the context of a frame, and the meaning of a value is dependent on specific context of a slot in the specific context of a frame, supporting relevance to a third degree of specificity. Specific indexing can thwart high recall searches at the same time that it promotes higher precision. In order to support higher retrieval recall when such is called for, we also assume automatic upward posting of specific slot values to slot values at the basic level, where such can be identified.

We further assume a subject indexing policy of high importance exhaustivity, to which the use of weights is added. High viewpoint exhaustivity is promoted in turn by the internal structure of frames, which remind the indexer of subject aspects that might otherwise be overlooked, a pattern seen in the use of MedIndEx (Humphrey, 1994, 166).

With these policies in place, a frame-based indexing scenario would essentially fulfill all the desiderata set out in (Soergel, 1994, 598) for retrieval systems sufficiently flexible to meet the requirements of a broad array of searches: high viewpoint exhaustivity, high importance exhaustivity, weights, specific indexing, inclusive searching, a well-structured hierarchy, and the ability to express syntagmatic relationships.

A potential disadvantage of frame-based indexing is the additional effort required of an indexer to use such a highly structured tool. This raises the question to what extent frame-based indexing, more specifically, the selection of appropriate frames and frame values, could be supported automatically.[2] While we have as yet no definitive answer to this question, there is significant relevant ongoing research in both the linguistics and computational linguistics communities. Computer-aided frame-based indexing is a more likely prospect than completely automatic selection of frames and assignment of frame slot values.

As just noted, the problem involves two distinct parts, one, the selection of appropriate frames, and the other, the selection of appropriate values to fill slots within the frames. On some level, the first problem is perhaps the more difficult, if only because it has received less attention. Any approach to frame selection will build on the evoking of frames by lexical items. Thus, if a lexical item in a specific sense evokes a specific frame, frame selection must incorporate word sense disambiguation. For example, frame selection could be addressed through the intersection of frames potentially evoked by the lexical items of a sentence (or a set of nearby sentences).

More progress has been made with respect to the automatic selection of values to fill frame slots. The FrameNet project (Baker et al., 1998; http://www.icsi.berkeley.edu/~framenet) has annotated selected portions of the British National Corpus to show how slot fillers correspond to lexical units in sentences, providing significant data on how frames could be instantiated from natural language text. The FrameNet data could also be used in an analysis of correlations between lexical items and frames, thus addressing the prior frame selection task. Research in information extraction (for example, Riloff & Lorenzen, 1999) is also relevant to the task of identifying slot filler values, in this case, from domain-specific texts; given the domain specificity, information extraction would not be expected to shed light on the frame selection problem.

4. Searching

Subject retrieval depends crucially on accurate and appropriate representation, both of the items as described above and of the user needs. Not surprisingly, many issues of indexing with frame-based systems are mirrored on the searching side of the track. As with traditional descriptor-based indexing and searching, a frame-based retrieval system relies upon the specific relationships linking user needs with items potentially relevant to those needs. However, a frame-based system would differ from the descriptor-based system in at least two crucial ways: The relationships could be explicit rather than necessarily implicit, and it permits far more, and more complex, concepts to be captured on both sides of the process.

Searching would take the form of instantiating some number of frames to represent the user need for comparison against a database of index frames. The rich hierarchical structure of frames noted above, along with knowledge of presuppositional and logical relationships between frame structures, will enable the search system to identify index frames related to the search frames in numerous ways. Expert searchers might need to limit which (kinds of) extensions from search frames to index frames are allowed. For example, a searcher might supply values for all slot values in a frame but one, only wishing to see index frames that match (more or less) the slot values supplied and that also supply a value for the unfilled slot.

The overarching objective of retrieval is to provide some avenue for meaningful access (intellectual or physical; actual or pointer) to items relevant to user needs. Although it has been well-established that such user relevance goes far beyond topicality, the issue of subject retrieval centers operationally on topical relevance. Other, non-topical perspectives on user relevance may also be addressed profitably using a frame-based system, but such a discussion by definition falls outside the scope of subject retrieval, per se.

Topical relevance extends beyond topic matching, or content similarity between a user's need and an item that satisfies that need. We have argued in other venues the importance of taking a relational perspective on topical relevance. Our 1995 study (Green & Bean, 1995) of the topical relationships that obtained between user needs and texts judged a priori to be relevant identified three main clusters of semantic relationship types. In addition to the conventional topic matching relationships of equivalence presumed by extant systems, we also identified hierarchical relationships (both taxonomic and meronymic), and what we termed 'structural relationships,' to describe the syntagmatic relationships in complex conceptual gestalts (structures) and their components, as well as metaphorical devices. Frame structures can be employed at all levels (frame, slot, value) for each type of relevance relationship to improve the representation of concept linkings by relationships of equivalence, as well as permit the capture and expression of hierarchical and associative conceptual relationships.

Thus in addition to questioning-answering searches that seek to fill blank slots in a query frame, a frame-based system is also responsive to more generalized user needs that seek information relevant to a particular topic in a variety of ways. Such a system can specify or generalize at the slot level either sequentially or simultaneously through the invocation of other concepts or frames related hierarchically or associatively in a structured knowledge base. As a simplistic example, consider the user who wants information on drug withdrawal. This query has two essential subject components: Drugs of addiction and Withdrawal symptoms. A potentially relevant item on morphine tolerance would be missed by a conventional Boolean search ANDing these as index terms, a natural language search seeking to match either the entire string and/or its components in some proximity, and even one that incorporates synonymous term mapping. In contrast, the frame-based system would be able to link these concepts in a query frame to those in an indexing frame via hierarchical and associative relationships manifest in the knowledge base. Using hierarchical linkages, morphine is found to be a member of the class of opioid compounds, which in turn belong to the class comprising common drugs of abuse. In a similar manner, associative relationships between query and indexing frames may be revealed: Drug tolerance is a precursive component of drug withdrawal symptomology, and both together contribute to the defining characteristics of drug addiction.

CONTAINER
Interior [ ]
Boundary [ ]
Exterior [ ]

LOCATION
Entity A; patient [CONTAINER.Interior]
Entity B; landmark [CONTAINER.Boundary]
Direction [within]
Distance [ ]

FORCE-a
ACTION; force [ ]
PATH [PATH-a]
PROCESS; effect [ ]
Impediment [CONTAINER.Boundary]

FORCE-b
ACTION; force [ ]
PATH [PATH-b]
PROCESS; effect [ ]
Impediment [CONTAINER.Boundary]

PATH-a
Source [CONTAINER.Interior]
Destination [CONTAINER.Exterior]
Path [ ]

PATH-b
Source [CONTAINER.Exterior]
Destination [CONTAINER.Interior]
Path [ ]

Figure 6. Inferences for CONTAINER

Ranking of results would take into account any weights supplied in the index and search frames, the nature of the relationships between search and index frames and their slot filler values, and user preferences.

Families of conceptual structures linked by common elements are capable of supporting the retrieval of texts that are analogically relevant to a user's request rather than topically relevant. This might apply, for instance, to the retrieval of such didactic texts as parables and fables, whose configurational structure might match a user's request only on a generic thematic role level. The retrieval of non-didactic texts on this same basis of shared generic relational configuration might also be effective in cases where the user is trying to solve a problem and could be creatively inspired by a text outlining a parallel situation in another domain.

Because of the propositional nature of frames, various presuppositional and logical relationships can be established between them, which can also be manipulated in the search process. Figure 6 illustrates frame relationships that can be inferred from the CONTAINER frame: The Interior of a Container is within its Boundary, while its Boundary is an impediment blocking movement between its Interior and its Exterior, in both directions. These inferences are stated in one LOCATION frame, two FORCE frames, and two PATH frames.

5. Conclusion

The representational power of frames presents significant improvements for the control of equivalence relationships at the propositional level, which is required for high recall searches. Frames also promote high recall through a rich hierarchical structure at frame, slot, and slot value levels, as well as giving access to relevant literature via non-matching relationships and analogy.

In a context where text is increasingly available electronically, this power to locate a high proportion of relevant documents must be balanced by precision-enhancing mechanisms. This frames have in being structured with slots, which provide a natural expression of syntagmatic relationships.

Notes

1. In artificial intelligence applications, frames are often used to represent physical objects (for example, their parts, their properties, relationships they enter into). Our concern here is primarily with their use to represent the participant structure of semantic predicates.
2. The question assumes that we have first identified a viable set of frames and corresponding slots, a task that is itself under investigation (Green, 2000).

References

Aitchison, J. et al. (1997). *Thesaurus construction and use: a practical manual.* 3rd ed. London: Aslib.

Baker, C.F. et al. (1998). The Berkeley FrameNet Project. In *COLING-ACL '98: 36th Annual Meeting of the Association for Computational Linguistics and 17th International Conference on Computational Linguistics.* Pp.86-90.

Green, R. (2000). Automated identification of frame semantic relational structures. In *Dynamism and Stability in Knowledge Organization: Proceedings of the Sixth International ISKO Conference, 10-13 July 2000, Toronto, Canada*, ed. C. Beghtol et al. Würzburg: Ergon Verlag. Pp.193-199.

Green, R. & Bean, C.A. (1995). Topical relevance relationships. II. An exploratory study and preliminary typology, *Journal of the American Society for Information Science*, 46, 654-662.

Humphrey, S.M. (1994). Knowledge-based systems for indexing. In *Challenges in indexing electronic text and images*, ed. R. Fidel et al. Medford, N.J.: Learned Information. Pp.161-175

Riloff, E. & Lorenzen, J. (1999). Extraction-based text categorization: generating domain-specific role relationships automatically. In *Natural language information retrieval*, ed. T. Strzalkowski. Dordrecht: Kluwer. Pp.167-196.

Soergel, D. (1994). Indexing and retrieval performance: the logical evidence, *Journal of the American Society for Information Science*, 45, 589-599.

Features of an Integrated Thesaurus Management and Search System for the Networked Environment

Marcia Lei Zeng & Yu Chen

Abstract: Reports an integrated system that employs an open structure for managing the distributed resources (thesauri and databases) and integrates a thesaurus management system with a cross-thesaurus search system. Describes the functions of the system that highlight the unique design for the networked environment.

1. Introduction

This paper reports an integrated thesaurus management and cross-thesaurus search system designed for an international collaborative project *CAMed*, a comprehensive resource for complementary and alternative medicine (CAM). The ultimate goal of developing such a system is to provide a gateway to facilitate the search across distributed CAM bibliographic databases and other resources.

In the design process, we have considered functions of this system beyond what a full-text search system usually could achieve. The ideal functions of the system would benefit both end-users and database managers. These include:

a) For the end-users, knowledge of various controlled vocabularies used by the databases is not a prerequisite. This would require that the system have capabilities including (1) searching terms across-thesaurus, (2) online-displaying the overall structure of a main component of a thesaurus as well as the details of each thesaurus term entry, (3) dynamically presenting thesaurus contents as they are updated, and (4) enabling direct searching of document records using the selected terms.
b) For the database managers, the processes of editing and updating their thesauri would be done online through a web interface, no matter where they are and when they want to do it.
c) For the thesaurus developers, managers and editors, the system also provides a full online thesaurus editing program so that various additional thesaurus components (different displays) can be automatically generated based on either a hierarchical list or an alphabetical list after it is imported into the database.

A review of the available literature and products reveals that these functions do exist, but mostly they are not integrated. In summary, the major limits of the existing products are:

- the tools used for thesaurus constructing and database searching are usually separated;
- most thesaurus construction systems do not have an open structure which would allow 24x7 time and worldwide access;
- the methods of online database searching using online thesauri either do not provide the cross-thesaurus searching function (like DIALOG's EXPEND command used in single database searching) or cannot keep dynamic updating between the vocabulary and the data indexed by the vocabulary (like the former BRS's file of multiple thesauri);
- most search systems are designed for searching one type of resource, i.e., for searching databases, searching Webpages, or searching the internal Website. They

would seldom allow searching all of these resources after a user selected a term from a thesaurus.

The reason of the existence of these limitations can be traced back to the environment in which thesaurus tools and search tools were invented and gradually developed: stand-alone computers and software, non-graphical user interfaces, dedicated telecommunication lines for accessing the online databases and centralized resources (databases or thesaurus). At that time there was no networked environment. It is our intent to overcome these limits and to build an integrated thesaurus management and search system for the networked environment.

2. Structure and Functions

The overall structure and functions of this integrated system can be illustrated by the following figure:

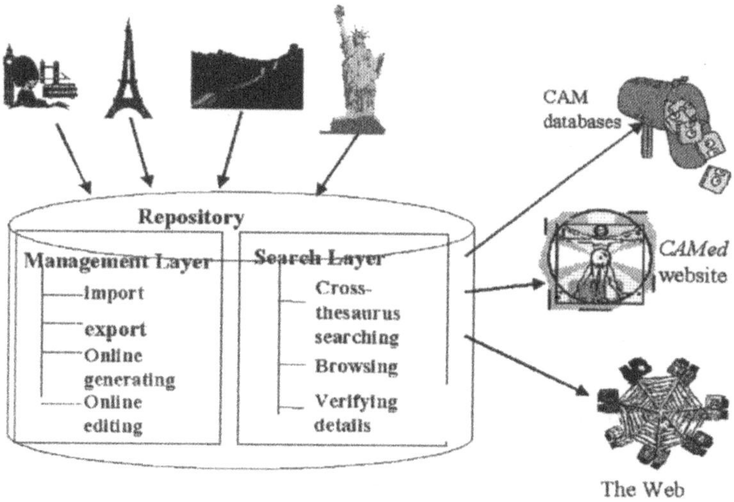

Figure 1. Structure of the system

As illustrated in the above figure, there are two layers in the system. End-users will be given the options at the *search layer*. Database managers and thesaurus developers/editors will be given the options at the *management layer*, in addition to those in the search layer. We have designed a Web interface that brings all available functions to the user. The following sections introduce the functions of the system:

2.1 Browsing various thesaurus components

The system provides various online display options such as hierarchical, alphabetical and rotated displays, which are the standard thesaurus display formats specified by the ISO 2788 standard. (See Figure 2). Users can either browse various components of a thesaurus or print a hard copy from here. The difference in our thesaurus displays from other printed or online displays is that these displays are dynamic. The software generates any of the displays when a request is sent through a mouse-click.

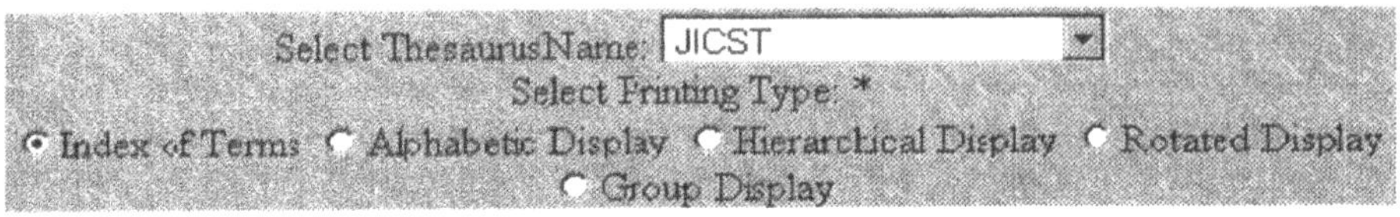

Figure 2. Browsing and printing options

2.2 Cross-thesaurus searching

More importantly, the system enables users to conduct cross-thesaurus searching and to examine the details of the matching terms used in each thesaurus. In the following example, the word "acupuncture" is typed into the search box (Figure 3):

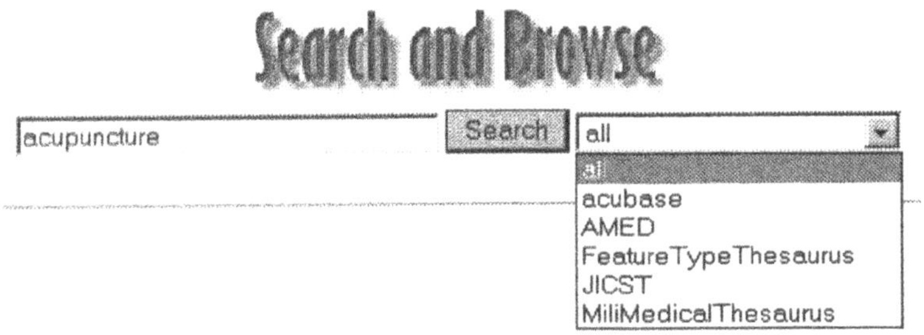

Figure 3. Searching thesaurus terms in selected thesauri.

The system matches the query against the thesauri and gives back all fully- or partially-matched thesaurus terms. In this example, because it is an "all" thesauri search, the result shows the exact match and partial match of the word 'acupuncture' in each of the thesauri hosted at the repository, as shown in Figure 4:

Exact Term: *acupuncture*

Term	Thesauri
acupuncture	JICST
ACUPUNCTURE	AMED

Other Related Term for *acupuncture*

Term	Thesauri
acupuncture therapy	MiliMedicalThesaurus
ACUPUNCTURE THERAPY	AMED
CLASSICAL TEXT ON ACUPUNCTURE AND MOXIBUSTION	acubase
COMPENDIUM OF ACUPUNCTURE AND MOXIBUSTION	acubase
EAR ACUPUNCTURE	AMED
ELECTROACUPUNCTURE	AMED
ELECTROACUPUNCTURE	acubase
new acupuncture therapy	MiliMedicalThesaurus
PARANEURAL ACUPUNCTURE	acubase
SCALP ACUPUNCTURE	AMED
scalp acupuncture therapy	MiliMedicalThesaurus
SOMATIC ACUPUNCTURE	acubase
therapy of acupuncture and moxibustion	MiliMedicalThesaurus
therapy of acupuncture point	MiliMedicalThesaurus

Figure 4. Cross-thesaurus search results

2.3 From selected terms to the searches of the databases, *CAMed* website, and the Web
The search results can lead to the direct database search, as illustrated in Figure 5.

First of all, when a term is selected from the search results (from Figure 4), a user can see the details of a thesaurus term entry and continue selecting among the terms displayed. For example, the user may choose "acupoints" to see the entry under that term. (See Figure 5).

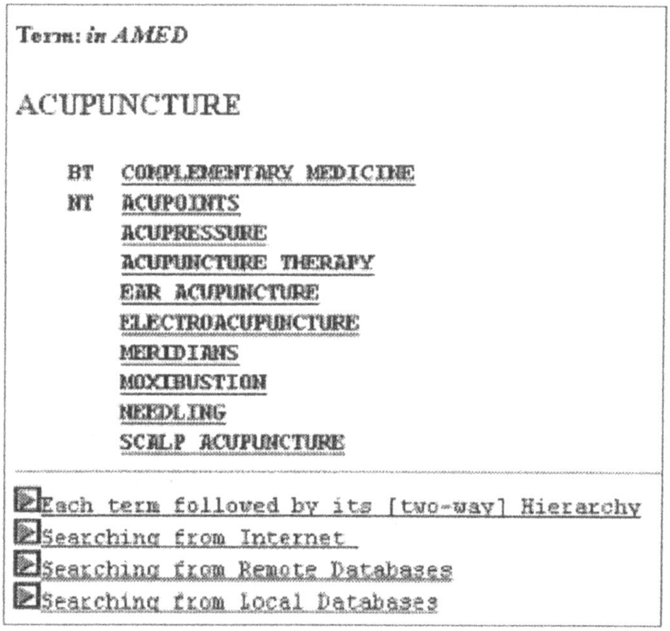

Figure 5. Detailed display of thesaurus terms and the extended search options.

Secondly, the term(s) selected can be used directly in extended searches:

a) The option for *Searching from Remote Databases* enables the search of the thesaurus term (through the web server at SLIS of KSU) to a search of four bibliographical databases (samples, hosted at Columbia University Health Science Library) that we have successfully integrated in our *CAMed* prototype. The search results are bibliographic records that meet the search criteria.

b) The option for *Searching from Local Databases* extends the thesaurus term search to the full-text search of all resources in *CAMed*, a web-based comprehensive resource for CAM. Webpages which have "acupuncture" in a <title> ... </title> tag are considered as exact match. URLs of these pages are provided to the searcher at the first section of the search result screen. Webpages that contain the word "acupuncture" in the main text body are considered as partial matches and their URLs are displayed in the second section of the search result screen.

c) The option of *Searching from Internet* links a searcher to the common Internet search engines. Once this option is selected, the selected thesaurus term can be automatically "filled" in to a selected search engine's search box, hence a search on the Web is conducted.

2.4 Online generating other components of a thesaurus

For the thesaurus developers, this system is also a thesaurus construction software. A developer is given the access to define a new thesaurus first. After a form that describes types of relationships to be included in the thesauri is filled out and submitted, a database table will immediately be created by the system. The database name will be added to the list of hosted thesauri and provided with three options for *more details* (view facts and statistics about a particular thesaurus), *delete it* (delete the whole database, including the thesaurus registration information (title, author, types of relationships, etc.), and *clear it* (only clear the thesaurus terms stored in a database, so that the user can upload a new version of his thesaurus to the server).

Pre-prepared text files of a thesaurus can be directly imported into the repository through the web interface. A thesaurus developer or manager will select the thesaurus name from the list of the hosted thesauri, select the types of files he is going to import (structured or unstructured), and click the *Select Thesaurus* button. This will lead to a screen navigating his local desktop drives and directories, thus the pre-prepared file can be uploaded easily.

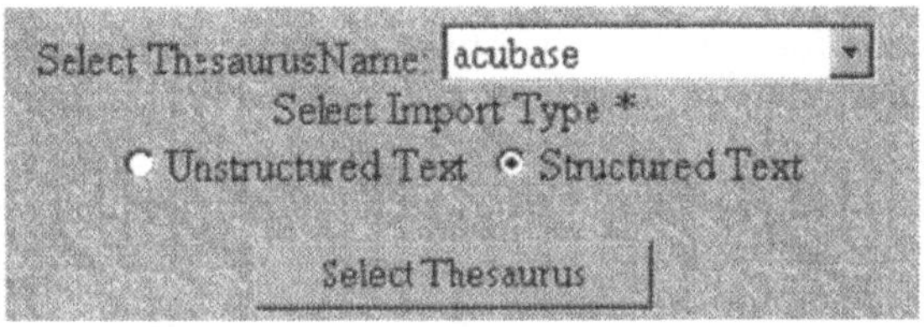

Figure 7. Options of import thesaurus

In the uploading process, the *Unstructured Text* refers to a term list that does not contain any cross-references, hierarchies, etc. In this situation, text will be imported into a source file for further editing. Usually a prepared thesaurus alphabetical display or hierarchical display is considered as *Structured Text*. Text will be imported into a database for automatically generating other components of a thesaurus. For example, if a hierarchically-structured thesaurus component is imported into the database, the alphabetical display and the rotated display of the same thesaurus are generated automatically by the system and can be browsed, exported, or printed at anytime.

2.5 Online editing

The system presents two online editing templates to the thesaurus editors. The first template is to be used to **define** terms and term relationships. With all imported terms available in a pull-down list, one can easily add related information to a thesaurus term entry, including facet/category, second language term, scope note, and relationships such as USE, UF, BT, NT, RT, TT, and CC. In the whole process, one can either select a term from the pull-down list or just enter a term.

The second template deals with **changes** to be made for a particular entry. This includes deleting a term from a current thesaurus or source table, modifying term relationships, replacing a term while keep all old relationships and changing USE-UF relationships. Again, one can select the terms from a pull-down list.

All editing results are updated in the database simultaneously; therefore, any new display or search will be based on the newly updated information. Because of the use of an online table through the pull-down lists, consistency and error-free quality are ensured in the editing process.

3. Conclusion

The system's open structure for distributed resources (thesauri and databases) and the integration of a thesaurus management system with a cross-thesaurus search system highlight the unique design for the networked environment. At the beginning of the paper, we listed the limits of current available systems. In responding to these limits, our system is successful in breaking through them, because:

- the tools used for thesaurus constructing and database searching ARE NOT separated;
- the thesaurus construction system HAS an open structure which would allow 24x7 time and worldwide access;
- the method of database searching using online thesaurus DOES provide cross-thesaurus searching and CAN keep dynamic updating between the vocabulary and the data indexed by the vocabulary;
- the search system IS NOT just designed for searching one type of resource, i.e., for searching the databases, searching the Web, or searching the internal website; it allows to search all of them after a user selected a term from a thesaurus.

We would like to share the experiences gained from the design and testing of this system. To see the system running in *CAMed*, please go to: http://circe.slis.kent.edu/mzeng/macmed/tmshome.html. To use the system to create your thesaurus, please go to http://circe.slis.kent.edu/mzeng/macmed/thesaurishome.html. Two instructional documents are available at these websites. We would also appreciate your comments and suggestions.

Session 7

TRANSFORMATION OF TRADITIONAL TOOLS FOR THE WEB ENVIRONMENT (1)

From Library Authority Control to Network Authoritative Metadata Sources

Maria Inês Cordeiro

Abstract: *Authority control* is a quite recent term in the long history of cataloguing, although the underlying principle is among the very early principles of bibliographic control. Bibliographic control is a field in transformation by the rapid expansion of the WWW, which has brought new problems to information discovery and retrieval, creating new challenges and requirements in information management. In a comprehensive approach, authority control is presented as one of the most promising library activities in this respect. The evolution of work methods and standards for the sharing of authority files is reviewed, showing the imbalance in developments and practical achievements between name and subject authority, in an international perspective. The need to improve the network availability and usability of authority information assets in more effective and holistic ways is underlined; and a new philosophy and scope is proposed for library authority work, based on the primacy of the *linking function* of authority data, and by expanding the *finding, relating* and *informing* functions of authority records. Some of these aspects are being addressed in several projects dealing with knowledge organization systems, notably to cope with multilingual needs and to enable semantic interoperability among different systems. Library practice itself should evolve in the same direction, thereby providing practical experience to inform new or improved principles and standards for authority work, while contributing to enhance local information services and to promote their involvement in the WWW environment.

1. Information retrieval, the WWW and subject access

Existing library frameworks and services do not cope easily with the diversity and scale of changes introduced by the Internet in the information landscape. Yet they remain valid and necessary and are beginning to be extended to selected networked resources by incorporating them into library catalogues. This incremental change grows slowly from within libraries to the external environment, towards the so-called "hybrid" model, while the development of digital libraries (DL) – as purposeful collections of selected and entirely digital materials – ends by finding organization models and information retrieval (IR) tools that do not differ so much in concept from those underlying the traditional library. Although DL may have to face additional IR issues if they are to render non-traditional services, e.g,. full text searches, differences are principally at the level of technological services for resource usage, archiving and management. Both traditional or hybrid and digital libraries have to cope with knowledge organization (KO) problems, and these require intellectual assets for information management that are independent of technology, although they may be facilitated by technological tools. Because DL first developed within the computer scientists' community, we have been witnessing a growth in interest in all sorts of KO tools outside the traditional library field. Despite much of this interest being focused on subject retrieval, namely classifications and controlled vocabularies, the problems of controlling names of individual entities of any kind are not less important.

Along with the DL developments, solutions for interoperability also expanded, in order to provide for simultaneous and seamless access to disparate networked systems. Such solutions rely on automated mediation services – broker or gateway solutions – that realize primarily (or at the very least) a level of integration that is structural and functional, without necessarily attaining complete semantic interoperability, *e.g.* by overcoming inconsistency in access points among the different data sources. Constraints at this level are not new in the bibliographic environment, as the experience with Z39.50 demonstrates: the less successful aspects reveal mostly difficulties and problems that are not of a technological nature and go beyond data structures. These are problems at the level of data content, since different representations of the same information object or entity are not unusual (Moen, 2000) and especially affect assigned access points among which subject access points are the most vulnerable to differences and the less predictable. Furthermore, differences in language particularly restrict the usability of subject access especially when a coded classification scheme is not used. All these are usual problems to cope with in IR integration services of either traditional, hybrid or digital libraries, especially if integration is hoped for already existing systems. For all of them, the shareability of information that controls access points is vital.

But the current scene of IR problems is far more complex because of the wide (and wild) publishing environment of the WWW. Its diversity, dispersal and dynamic nature have been adding new concepts and new types of solutions: it is the realm of *information discovery* (Proper & Bruza, 1999) and of search engines. The capabilities of Web search engines have been continuously improved, with different methodologies and devices, aiming at reducing the randomness of discovery, and the lack of sources for consistent identification and description of resources (Kobayashi & Takeda, 2000). However, all of them still face severe limitations that cannot be overcome by technology alone, if the resources themselves do not provide better conditions for more sophisticated automated processing, namely in terms of machine understandable logical structure and semantic value. In this context the need appeared for enhancing Web publishing with open standards capable of improving Web architecture (Lee, 1999), by common representation languages and data content organization of and about individual information objects. Specifications such as XML (Extensible Markup Language), RDF (Resource Description Framework) and metadata schemes address these needs, paving the way for structural regularities that will be foundational to the so called "semantic Web" (W3 Consortium, 2001). Semantic interoperability in a wider environment is, therefore, the main reason for the new metadata initiatives (Dovey, 2000). New descriptive metadata schemes such as Dublin Core, offer data structures for interoperability that are a promise for bibliographic control and access issues. But the overall success of such data structures being applied by a wide variety of metadata producers - with an equally wide variety of motivations, concerns and skills - will depend on the quality of the metadata content they provide (Vellucci, 1999). And the problems to face in the WWW environment are not less difficult than those already described about semantic interoperability among different structured systems (databases); on the contrary, IR problems are scaled up to unknown dimensions, more diverse and complex, because they are not confined to well-known technical and organizational frameworks. So far, most attention in metadata initiatives has been focused on information models and data structures, old and new, on establishing *crosswalks* among them, and on providing authoritative sources for their use and maintenance, through *registries*. Although more difficult, the level of *data content* should follow the same path: conceptual models more transversal, means to use different systems' representations interchangeably and from trusted and maintained sources.

This is the field of library authority files in general and of all other kinds of tools aiming at intellectually unified and organized representations of the real world entities, concrete and abstract, like ontologies, taxonomies, nomenclatures, etc. The field embraces several areas of academic and professional activity beyond information management, such as logic, computation, cognitive sciences and linguistics, all of them contributing to illuminate or solve particular aspects of IR problems, but not making them less elusive and difficult. This underlines the pragmatic value of existing intellectual assets for information management practice, such as authority files, which can be exploited and evolve to the benefit of an environment wider than that of its origins. Despite all criticisms that can be made of them, they are unique as they have long been built upon accumulated knowledge about the real world of information; the information world is not changed from day to night with the appearance of the WWW, rather it still encompasses the kind of concepts and entities already existing in the offline world, which has not been without evolution down the years.

My approach to library authority work and authority files is essentially a comprehensive one although this conference is devoted specifically to *subject access*. Two main reasons justify such an approach: first, the distinction among different types of authority files (notably names *versus* subjects) has created separate traditions, workflows and conditions of availability of KO resources and this has not contributed to enhance the *linking function* of authority work as a multifaceted function for the catalogue as a whole; on the contrary, it has contributed to the concentration of concerns and objectives of such work in the choice and validation of *headings* by type, which is a limited vision; the second reason, anchored in the first but not less important, is that subject access is not exempt from the problems of naming individual entities and subject search strategies do not exclude them; this was demonstrated by studies on online searching behaviour, in the late 80s, as J. Younger reminds us, stressing the importance of names as *handles* to information (Younger, 1994,135-136). If this is true with online catalogues, we have no reason to suppose that the WWW will create different behaviours, when (and while) most of web search tools rely on random full text indexing and have no means of offering alternative types of search approach.

2. Authority work and authority information: a long way to internationalisation

This is not the place to elaborate on the history of bibliographic control, or even of authority control, as such. They have long been discussed in the professional literature. Nevertheless, it is useful to review some general aspects that can illuminate the shortcomings of contexts and of theories and practices followed so far. In the history of bibliographic control the theoretical and normative basis did not develop in the same way regarding the two main perspectives of a library catalogue: on the one hand, its function as a tool for describing individual information objects and discriminating among them; on the other hand, its function of clustering information objects with one or several information characteristics in common. The first view, *i.e.* the creation of distinctive surrogates, has been the predominant one, as the theory behind cataloguing remain mostly document centred; in this respect, international standardization has attained the levels needed to render quite easy and successful the sharing of bibliographic data. The second view concerns the syndetic structure of the catalogue and relates directly to standards for the building and maintenance of tools supporting such a structure, based on authority data; these only began to appear in the 80s, in the form of guidelines for data model and formats for record creation and transmission[1]. The practice of authority work as we know it is quite recent and developed with library automation, at a time where the capabilities of online catalogues – namely keyword searching – shook the belief about the need for the costly authority procedures and the library budget constraints had arrived to stay (Younger, 1994); besides, bibliographic distribution services already provided records with authority-controlled headings. Besides the lack of a wide and well-established culture of authority work, the achievements in consensual practices and cooperation have been virtually restricted to the field of *name authority*, closer to cataloguing; this has received much more attention than subject authority from bodies concerned with policies of bibliographic control, like IFLA and national bibliographic agencies. Name authority has been the focus of several international studies, recommendations (Willer, 1996; IFLA Working Group on MLAR and the ISADN, 1998) and feasibility projects, such as AUTHOR (Zillhard & Bourdon, 1998), as well as international cooperative services, as NACO and AAAF (Dansky, 1998). Ongoing developments born from this movement on name authority files include the current activities of the IFLA Working Group on Functional Requirements and Numbering of Authority Records (FRANAR) [1] which may come to offer a more structural and comprehensive approach.

With respect to the *subject field* – controlled vocabularies, subject headings and classifications – new specific standard developments arrived almost ten years later and have been of little practical effect: *GSARE - Guidelines for Subject Authority and Reference Entries*, issued by IFLA in 1993; *USMARC Format for Classification Data*, by the Library of Congress in 1990, and a draft for a *UNIMARC Classification Format* is still open to discussion, under the auspices of the IFLA UBCIM [2]. But overall, at the level of international standards, the field still lives by guidelines that deal with partial aspects only and that have long been considered insufficient or in need of revision (Williamson, 1996:168, 2000:272-273); this is the case with the ISO standards 5963 (1985), 2788 (1986) and 5964 (1985), respectively regarding methods for analyzing work contents and selecting subject indexing terms and for the construction of monolingual and multilingual thesauri. [3]. The need for criteria and methods for automated thesaurus development and management, including standard support for interoperability protocols, structures and/or semantics applicable to thesauri is currently being addressed (NISO & ASI & ALCTS, 1999; Taylor, *et al.*, 1999). The lack of wide conceptual and practical standards has been alleviated by some KO tools being used as *de facto* standards (Williamson, 1996), notably classification schemes that are universal in scope, like UDC and Dewey; and also, to a certain extent, by alphabetical subject systems used by large groups of bibliographic agencies pertaining to the same linguistic group, as it happens with LCSH, or dealing with the same subject area, *e.g.* AAT (*Art and Architecture Thesaurus*) or MeSH (*Medical Subject Headings*). Most of these widely-used systems are utilized without structured electronic sources, *i.e.* in the form of authority files with a common source; exceptions, however, already provide some experience about not only sharing data but also on collaborative development and maintenance, like SACO and RAMEAU [4]. Apart from centrally managed systems of this kind, there is still a general lack in structures and services for online subject authority data sharing. But the global network environment has also magnified other aspects that affect the reach of alphabetical subject systems, particularly multilingual needs. In this area one cooperative project in place is MACS [5], providing several national catalogues with multilingual subject access by enhancing this feature in their respective authority files. Again, this is an exception, not a standard practice for which a different philosophy on authority data and more than usual resources would be required. The same may be said of mapping across different subject indexing languages, another strategy being envisaged in specialized fields, of which one of the best examples is UMLS [6]. The current general situation is still that of linguistic boundaries and local practices from database to database, with multiple cultural factors affecting concepts/terminological choices and evolutions within each language, as well as a proliferation of overlapping indexing languages for different purposes and communities, making it complex to cope with predictability and transferability across systems (Maniez, 1997). To sum up, although the usefulness and power of structured alphabetical languages within the network environment is widely recognized (*e.g.* Batty, 1998; Milstead, 1998; Chan, 2000; Studwell, 2000), solutions for dealing with linguistic barriers and terminological differences are costly and are difficult to prove in the short term without enormous investment. This is why the potential of classifications has been especially highlighted for the organization of resources in the network environment (Vizine-Goetz, 1996, 1998; Koch *et al.*, 1997; Kwasnnik, 1999; Wheatley, 2000; Broughton & Lane, 2000). A comprehensive bibliography on this trend is provided by Candy Schwartz (Schwartz, 2000). Although the most used classifications systems originate in the library field, library authority work does not have a long tradition in relation to classifications, because they have been mostly used as externally produced and maintained tools. This, in turn, may explain why classification systems have been so under-exploited in library OPACs.

3. A new philosophy and scope for authority resources

From the overview provided above it is evident that considerable changes are ongoing but it is also clear that the field is still markedly biased by the centrality of document cataloguing and the prominence of the goal of heading consistency, at the local level. Therefore, the philosophy and extent of authority files have been principally those of tools and practices internal and subsidiary to the major objectives of catalogues. Although there is progress in the availability of KO tools in electronic form, either offline and online, for reuse in libraries, both in name and subject authority, such availability is still irregular; besides, it has been mostly motivated by the need to optimise resources, avoid redundancy of work and therefore provide for self-sustainability of local libraries, rather than to expand and integrate their function into a wider space. It is also clear that in order to enhance the shareability of authority files, the standards level has to be reinforced and deepened, both in conceptual and technical aspects, and this is taking place in several frameworks. But while this happens, changes in practice may develop that can raise experience and inform a new vision for authority work, which can in turn contribute to new or improved standards: it is a vision that promotes the *linking function* of authority files, within a catalogue, among the library community of catalogues and within the wider network space of resources.

The *linking function* is, therefore, one of the aspects that I want to underline with a comprehensive view of library authority work. In such a view, *linking* is much more than linking authority and bibliographic records for the sake of data consistency. It is much more than catalogue headings and cross references. In a way this relates closely to the *access control* view which has been defended for several years (*e.g.*, Barnhard, 1996; Tillett, 1988, 2000); in this view, the major point is to provide for more flexibility in the user (professional or end-user) choices of heading use and display, thereby liberating the concept of an "authorized" and "unique" that cannot be adequate for all situations. Promoting the linking function goes beyond the "selection" issue, as it is about aggregating useful information and different sources in order to expand the *finding, relating* and *informing* functions of authority records, which can be much more dynamic than the essentially static bibliographic surrogates. In this sense, a new dimension can be built for authority files, that exceeds the traditional function as an internal and almost exclusively library professional mechanism (Hodge, 2000; Tillett 2000); such dimension can be realized by enriching records with more than the sources and information strictly needed to justify headings' choice, to provide for natural language synonymy control or to interlink among system's contained headings. Beyond these features – which have been managed under a strong economy of input – authority files deserve a new strategy and investment (human, technical and financial) in order to embrace orientations to cope with multilingual and multi-systems goals, with information needs from a variety of user types, as well as with relationships to works held in sources external to the local system, namely in the WWW. Such an evolution is possible if authority control is considered far more than a sub-activity of bibliographic processing, therefore not depending so much on the future of cataloguing, at least in all aspects that do not deal with bibliographic (work) relationships. This new dimension would require consistent, relevant and sustainable policies in order to be workable and focused. In practical terms, it would contribute to the effacing of the somewhat artificial partition between names and subjects (this should be enabled by the search option or view selection); assist in enhancing essential information about the recorded entities; help to overcome language constraints and to enable alternate forms of controlled representations, adding modes of understanding by different communities (Buckland, 1999); *e.g.*, by linking to scientific taxonomic sources, currently the focus of international efforts of utmost importance and mutual benefits (Calhoun, 1998). As public information, these enriched records should be provided as an information product of their own (why not a public display of authority records, even as they currently are?) and not only as scattered references and notes, added to the entries of bibliographic catalogue indexes. The reference information provided by libraries would be enhanced in a lively way, and this would be relevant for many more of libraries' activities other than cataloguing or local catalogue searches. Network technology has the potential to facilitate this, namely by active links, and the library automated systems we have nowadays need no big improvements to enable them to accept these changes or to make the most of more diverse information to expand searches within a catalogue and to the network environment.

For purposes other than library services, both internal and for end-users, there is also the need to provide quality metadata content for network information providers. Also at this level, which is a function of major authority files and of bodies in charge of managing important KO systems, most of the enhancements suggested above are relevant, especially the linking function, regarding alternative systems and languages. Furthermore, they should be particularly concerned with improving awareness and trust, by means of KO tools registries[7], as well as with means of availability not restricted to professional uses. This is a point where KO systems should change, especially those managed outside library systems, whose tradition has been to provide unique views; this has not facilitated wide awareness and usability, and it is not any more justified in the automated environment. The change is meant for a final product designed to serve professional and non-professional usages simultaneously. On the other hand, qualitative changes in the availability of KO systems should comprise data portability among different systems, support for optimised linking and searching, *e.g.* by developing unique identifiers, beyond a choice of online different displays and functionalities for the range of purposes needed. How this can be achieved in practice, namely in terms of models of services, centralized or distributed, who are the stakeholders involved, and how it will fit in and evolve with the bibliographic control framework, is something difficult to foresee (Lynch, 2000). Yet it is a matter that needs to be addressed, as it seems unlikely that the future of bibliographic control will be achieved by simply scaling up the current cooperative models (Calhoun, 1998).

Whatever the solutions, the major underlying change is mostly strategic: it relies on concepts, policies, methods and on allocation of resources and responsibilities, rather than on specific technological innovations only. I believe this is the understanding behind several action lines being raised in different fronts of the large information management community, such as IFLA, CLIR, NKOS, Getty Vocabulary Programme, OCLC and the Library of Congress. The recently issued Library of Congress Action Plan (Library of Congress, 2001) is especially noteworthy because of its comprehensiveness and wide range of collaborators. While standard and strategic developments evolve towards a less transitional state of affairs, a great deal can be done to improve and expand the actual role of existing authority files and similar tools, capitalizing on information and functionality that can always be reframed later on. In this sense, and despite all the difficulties that have delayed the internationalisation of authority data, even within the library community alone, the field of authority work appears as one of immediate feasibility and effect by which libraries can gain ground in the Internet environment. It does not represent investments from scratch, it carries an added value that is almost a library exclusive and it has a strong learning and linking potential for the integration of traditional library activities in the interactive network reality. It is like finding a market niche for owned and under-exploited values, with the advantage of contributing to help libraries' penetration in the WWW environment, while maintaining their traditional role of bibliographic control, extending it to the Web resources, at their own pace. It is, in a way, calling for the urgency of ensuring a qualitative role, so very important as libraries cannot yet ensure the means to cope with quantitative aspects, *i.e.*, the scale of the WWW. And this is precisely the dimension I tried to stress for the offering of library authority files to the wider Internet metadata community: as intellectual assets for information management that are *authoritative* in the sense of being well informed and trustworthy, because they are built on the needs of the real information world, and reliable, because they are dynamically and permanently maintained.

---

[1] *GARE – Guidelines for Authority and Reference Entries*, first issued in 1984, by the IFLA International Programme for UBC; *USMARC format for authority data* appeared first in 1981 and the corresponding international format – *UNIMARC/Authorities* was first made available provisionally in 1989 and published officially in 1991.

[1] FRANAR was established in 1999 to address pending aspects of international standardization on authority data, namely the feasibility of the long postponed ISADN, and to define functional requirements of authority records, following the same line as *Functional requirements of bibliographic records* (FRBR), issued in 1998.

[2] This format may have future structural impact on the use of classification schedules as authority data within bibliographic systems, if used by classification publishers to transfer classification files to professional users. Besides, if used by different classification systems, it may facilitate the interlinking of mapping values among them. The draft format is available at http://www.ifla.org/VI/3/p1996-1/concise.htm.

[3] An IFLA working group was established in 2000 to draft new guidelines for multilingual thesauri (Riesthuis, 2000).

[4] Managed respectively by the Library of Congress (http://lcweb.loc.gov/catdir/pcc/saco.html) and the Bibliothèque nationale de France (http://www.bnf.fr/web-bnf/infopro/rameau/).

[5] Multilingual Access to Subjects (http://infolab.kub.nl/prj/macs/).

[6] Unified Medical Language System (UMLS) is a metathesaurus developed by the National Library of Medicine, linking more than 40 different systems for various medical specialties, from a wide range of organizations not limited to the library field (http://www.nlm.nih.gov/research/umls/).

[7] *E.g.*, the NKOS proposal for a Thesaurus Registry (http://nkos.slis.kent.edu/Thesaurus_Registry.html).

References *(all URLs accessed 2001.07.29)*

Barnhart, L. (1996). Access control records: prospects and challenges. In *Authority control in the 21st Century: an invitational conference, OCLC* <http://www.oclc.org/oclc/man/authconf/barnhart.htm >

Batty, D. (1998). WWW - wealth, weariness or waste: controlled vocabulary and thesauri in support of online information access. *D-Lib Magazine*, Nov. 1998. <http://www.dlib.org/dlib/november98/11batty.html >

Broughton, V. & Lane, H. (2000). Classification schemes revisited: applications to Web indexing and searching In *Internet searching and indexing*. New York: The Haworth Press. Pp.143-155.

Buckland, M. et al. (1999). Mapping entry vocabulary to unfamiliar metadata vocabularies. *D-Lib Magazine*, 5 (1) < http://www.dlib.org/dlib/january99/buckland/01buckland.html >

Calhoun, K. (1998). A bird's eye view of authority control in cataloging. In *Proceedings of the Taxonomic Authority Files Workshop, Washington DC.* < http://research.calacademy.org/taf/proceedings/Calhoun.html>

Chan, L. M. (2000). Exploiting LCSH, LCC and DDC to retrieve networked resources. In *Bicentennial Conference on Bibliographic Control for the New Millenium, Library of Congress, 2000.* <http://lcweb.loc.gov/catdir/bibcontrol/chan_paper.html>

Danskin, A. (1998). International activities in authority, *Library Review*, 47, 1998, 200-205.

Dovey, M. J. (2000). "Stuff" about "Stuff": the different meanings of metadata, *VINE*, 116, 6-13.

Hodge, G. (2000). *Systems of knowledge organization for digital libraries: beyond traditional authority files*. Washington, DC, Council on Library & Information Resources. <http://www.lcweb.loc.gov/catdir/bibcontrol/lynch.html>

Maniez, J. (1997). Database merging and compatibility of indexing languages, *Knowledge organization*, 24, 213-224.

Milstead, J. L. (1998). Thesauri in a full-text world. In *Visualizing subject access for the 21st century information resources. Proeeeding of the Clinic on Library Applications of Data Processing, 1997.* Champaign, IL: University of Illinois at Champaign-Urbana, School of Library and Information Science. Pp.29-38.

Moen, W. (2000). Resource discovery using Z39.50: promise and reality. In *Bicentennial Conference of Bibliographic Control for the New Millenium, Library of Congress, 2000.* <http://lcweb.loc.gov/catdir/bibcontrol/moen.html >

NISO & ASI & ALCTS. (1999). *Workshop on electronic thesauri: planning for a standard.* < http://www.niso.org/thesau99.htm >

Proper, H.A. & Bruza, P.D. (1999). What is information discovery about? *Journal of the American Institute of Information Science*, 50, 737-750.

Riesthuis, G. J. A. (2000) Multilingual subject access and the guidelines for the establishment and development of multilingual thesauri. In *Dynamism and stability in knowledge organization: Proceedings of the Sixth International ISKO Conference, 10-13 July 2000, Toronto, Canada*, ed. C. Beghtol et al. Wurzburg: ERGON Verlag, 2000. Pp.131-135.

Schwartz, C. (2000). *Classification on the net.*

<http://artemis.simmons.edu/~schwartz/myclass.html>

Studwell, W. (2000). USE, the Universal Subject Environment: a new subject access approach in the time of the Internet. In *Internet Searching and Indexing*. New York: The Haworth Press, 2000:197-209.

Taylor, M. et al. (1999) *Zthes: a Z39.50 profile for thesaurus navigation.* < http://lcweb.loc.gov/z3950/agency/profiles/zthes-03.html >

Tillett, B. B. (1988). International shared resource records for controlled access. *ALCTS Newsletter Online*, 10 (1) 1988. < http://www.ala.org/alcts/alcts_news/v10n1/gateway.html >

Tillett, B. B. (2000). Authority control on the Web. In *Bicentennial Conference on Bibliographic Control for the New Millenium, Library of Congress, 2000.* < http://lcweb.loc.gov/catdir/bibcontrol/tillet.html >

Vellucci, S. (1999). Metadata and authority control, *Library resources & technical services,* 44, 33-43.

Vizine-Goetz, D. (1998). OCLC investigates using classification tools to organize Internet data. In *Visualizing subject access for the 21st century information resources. Proceedings of the Clinic on Library Applications of Data Processing, 1997*. Champaign, IL.: University of Illinois at Champaign-Urbana, School of Library and Information Science. Pp.93-105.

W3 Consortium (2001). Semantic Web activity statement. < http://www.w3.org/2001/sw/Activity >

Whetley, A. (2000). Subject trees on the Internet: a new role for bibliographic classification? In *Internetsearching and indexing*. New York: The Haworth Press. Pp.115-141.

Willer, M. (1996). Authority control and international standard data numbers: need for international cooperation. Paper presented to *Authority Control in the 21st Century: an Invitational Conference, OCLC.* <http://oclc.org/oclc/man/authconf/willer.htm>

Williamson, N. J. (1996). Standards and rules for subject access, *Cataloging and classification quarterly*, 21, 155-176.

Williamson, N. J. (2000). Thesauri in the digital age: stability and dynamism in their development and use. In *Dynamism and stability in knowledge organization. Proceeding. of the Sixth International ISKO Conference, 10-13 July 2000, Toronto, Canada*, ed. C. Beghtol et al Wurzburg: ERGON Verlag. Pp.268-274.

Zillhard, S. & Bourdon, F. (1998). *Project Author: final report*. [Available from the authors].

FAST: Faceted Application of Subject Terminology

Edward T. O'Neill, Eric Childress, Rebecca Dean, Kerre Kammerer, Diane Vizine-Goetz,
Lois Mai Chan, Lynn El-Hoshy

Abstract. The Library of Congress Subject Headings schema (LCSH) is by far the most commonly used and widely accepted subject vocabulary for general application. It is the de facto universal controlled vocabulary and has been a model for developing subject heading systems by many countries. However, LCSH's complex syntax and rules for constructing headings restrict its application by requiring highly skilled personnel and limit the effectiveness of automated authority control. Recent trends, driven to a large extent by the rapid growth of the Web, are forcing changes in bibliographic control systems to make them easier to use, understand, and apply, and subject headings are no exception. The purpose of adapting the LCSH with a simplified syntax to create FAST is to retain the very rich vocabulary of LCSH while making the schema easier to understand, control, apply, and use. The schema maintains upward compatibility with LCSH, and any valid set of LC subject headings can be converted to FAST headings.

1. Introduction

The enormous volume and rapid growth of resources available on the World Wide Web as well as the emergence of numerous metadata schemas have spurred a re-examination of the way subject data are provided for Web resources. There is broad agreement that a subject schema for metadata must exhibit both simplicity and interoperability. Simplicity refers to the usability by non-cataloguers. Interoperability enables users to search across both discipline boundaries and across information retrieval and storage systems. Additional requirements identified by ALCTS/SAC/Subcommittee (1999) specify that the schema should:

- Be simple and easy to apply and to comprehend,
- Be intuitive so that sophisticated training in subject indexing and classification, while highly desirable, is not required in order to implement,
- Be logical so that it requires the least effort to understand and implement,
- Be scalable for implementation from the simplest to the most sophisticated.

Another central issue involving the syntax revolves around the choice of pre-coordination or post-coordination. Both have precedence in cataloguing and indexing practices. Subject vocabularies used in traditional cataloguing typically consist of pre-coordinated subject heading strings, while controlled vocabularies used in online databases are mostly single-concept descriptors, relying on post-coordination for complex subjects. For the sake of simplicity and semantic interoperability, the post-coordinate approach is more in line with the basic premises and characteristics of the online environment. Chan et al. (2001) provides additional background on the metadata requirements particularly as they relate to Dublin Core applications.

The ALCTS/SAC/Subcommittee recommended that metadata for subject analysis of Web resources include a mixture of keywords and controlled vocabulary. The potential sources of controlled vocabulary the Subcommittee identified included:

- Using an existing schema(s),
- Adapting or modifying existing schema(s),

- Developing new schema(s).

Each of these options offers clear advantages. The use of an existing schema is certainly the simplest approach if a suitable one can be found. Of the existing schemas, LCSH is the most obvious choice, but its complexity greatly limits its use by nonprofessionals. There are many excellent subject specific schemas available but, since the Web is so interdisciplinary, combining diverse schemas is likely to create significant interoperability problems. Obtaining rights to the required schemas could also pose a serious problem.

At first glance, developing an entirely new schema appears to be very attractive. However, the effort required to develop a new subject indexing system appears considerably less attractive upon further examination. The cost would be very high without any guarantee the new schema would necessarily be superior to one of the existing schema. It is quite possible that a new system could trade a set of known problems with its own set of unknown problems. It became quickly clear that attempting to develop a system as comprehensive as LCSH would be very challenging. As was concluded by the ALCTS/SAC/Subcommittee, the options of modifying an existing schema appeared more attractive. As a result, the FAST project team concluded that the most viable option for a general-purpose metadata subject schema was to adapt LCSH.

This new schema, known as FAST (Faceted Application of Subject Terminology), is derived from LCSH but will be applied with a simpler syntax. The objective of the FAST project is to develop a subject heading schema based on LCSH suitable for metadata that is easy-to-use, understand, and maintain. To achieve this objective, this new schema is being designed to minimize the need to construct new headings and to simplify the syntax while retaining the richness of the LCSH vocabulary.

2. Library of Congress Subject Headings

LCSH is the most widely-used indexing vocabulary and offers many significant advantages:

- Its rich vocabulary covers all subject areas,
- It has the strong institutional support of the Library of Congress,
- It imposes synonym and homograph control,
- It has been extensively used by libraries,
- It is contained in millions of bibliographic records, and
- It has a long and well-documented history.

While LCSH have served libraries and their patrons well for over a century, its complexity greatly restricts its use beyond the traditional cataloguing environment. It was designed for card catalogues and excelled in that environment. However, because real estate on a 3x5 card is limited and each printed subject heading requires a new card, the number of headings per item that can be assigned was severely restricted. Since the card catalogue is incompatible with post-coordination, the pre-coordinated headings were the only option available.

LCSH is not a true thesaurus in the sense that it is not a comprehensive list of all valid subject headings. Rather LCSH combines authorities, now five volumes in their printed form, with a four volume manual of rules detailing the requirements for creating headings that are not established in the authority file and for the further subdivision of the established headings. Only about 3 percent of all the topical and geographic headings in OCLC's WorldCat are fully established. The remaining 97 percent of the headings are created, correctly or incorrectly, based on these rules.

The rules for using free-floating subdivisions controlled by pattern headings illustrate this complexity. Under specified conditions, these free-floating subdivisions can be added to established headings. The scope of patterns is limited to particular types (patterns) of headings. For example, **Burns and scalds—Patients—Family relationships** is a valid heading formed by adding two pattern subdivisions to the established heading **Burns and scalds. Patients** is one of several hundred subdivisions that can be used with headings for diseases and other medical conditions. Therefore it can be used to subdivide **Burns and scalds.** However, the addition of **Patients** changes the meaning of the heading from a medical condition to a class of persons. Now, since **Family relationships** is authorized under the pattern for classes of persons, it can also be added to complete the heading.

While the rich vocabulary and semantic relationships in LCSH provide subject access far beyond the capabilities of keywords, its complex syntax presents a stumbling block that limits its application beyond the traditional cataloguing environment. Not only are the rules for pattern headings complex, their application requires extensive domain knowledge since there is no explicit coding that identifies which pattern subdivisions are appropriate for particular headings. Although FAST will retain headings authorized under these rules, they will be established in the authority file, effectively hiding the complexity of rules under which they were created.

The LCSH environment has resulted in a complex system requiring skilled professionals for its successful application and has prompted several simplification attempts. Among these, the Subject Subdivisions Conference (The Future of Subdivisions, 1992) attempted to simplify the application of LCSH subdivisions. Recently, the ALCTS/SAC/Subcommittee on Metadata and Subject Analysis (Subject Data in the Metadata Record..., 1999) recommended that LCSH strings be broken up [faceted] into topic, place, period, language, etc., particularly in situations where non-cataloguers are assigning the headings. The Library of Congress has also embarked on a series of efforts to simplify LCSH.

3. The FAST Schema

After reviewing the previous attempts to update LCSH or to provide other subject schema, OCLC decided to develop the FAST schema. While FAST is derived from LCSH, it has been redesigned as a post-coordinated faceted vocabulary for an online environment. Specifically it is designed to:

- Be usable by people with minimal training and experience,
- Enable a broad range of users to assign subject terminology to Web resources,
- Be amenable to automated authority control,
- Be compatible with use as embedded metadata,
- Focus on making use of LCSH as a post-coordinate system in an online environment.

The first phase of the FAST development includes the development of facets based on the vocabulary found in LCSH topical and geographic headings and is limited to four facets: topical, geographic, form, and period. In later phases, it is anticipated that additional facets will be added for personal names, corporate names, conference/meetings, uniform titles and name-title entries. With the exception of the period facet, all FAST headings will be fully established in a FAST authority file.

4. Topical Facet

The topical facet consists of topical main headings and their corresponding general subdivisions. FAST topical headings look very similar to the established form of LCSH topical headings with the exception that established headings will include all commonly used (i.e., free-floating) topical subdivisions and each of the common multiple headings will be individually established. FAST topical headings will be created from:

- LCSH main headings from topical headings (650) assigned to MARC records,
- All associated general ($x) subdivisions from any type of LCSH heading,
- Period subdivisions containing topical aspects from any type of LCSH heading,

All topical headings strings will be established in an authority file. Examples of typical FAST topical headings are shown below:

Industrial project management—Data processing
Colombian poetry
Blacksmithing—History
Epic literature—History and criticism
Pets and travel
Quartets (Pianos (2), percussion)
Natural gas pipelines—Economic aspects
School psychologists
Blood banks
Loudspeakers—Design and construction
Burns and scalds—Patients—Family relationships

FAST headings retain the hierarchical structure of LCSH, but only topical subdivisions can be combined with topical headings.

5. Geographic Facet

The geographic facet includes all geographic names. In FAST, these place names will be established and used in indirect order. For example, **Ohio—Columbus** is the established form in FAST rather than the direct order form, **Columbus (Ohio)**. In LCSH, place names used as main headings are entered in direct order, but when they are used as subdivisions, those representing localities appear in indirect order. First level geographic names in FAST will be far more limited than in LCSH. They will be restricted to names from the *Geographic Area Codes* table. Other names will be entered as subdivisions under the name of the smallest first level geographic area in which it is fully contained. For example, the Maya forest, which spans Belize, Guatemala, and Mexico, would be established as **North America—Maya Forest** instead of simply as Maya Forest. Qualifiers will only be used to identify the type of geographic name (Kingdom, Satellite, Duchy, Princely State, etc.). As with topical headings, all geographic headings will be established in an authority file. Some examples of FAST geographic headings and their corresponding Geographic Area Codes are:

Bolivia—Cochabamba (Dept.) [s-bo]
England—Coventry [e-uk-en]
Great Lakes [nl]
Great Lakes—Lake Erie [nl]
Italy [e-it]
Maryland—Worcester County [n-us-md]
Ohio—Columbus [n-us-oh]

Ohio—Columbus—Clintonville [n-us-oh]

The same geographic names may appear significantly different in their direct and indirect forms. In LCSH, North Carolina as a first level entry or as a subdivision, is spelled out but, as a qualifier, it is abbreviated as N.C. (e.g., Chapel Hill (N.C.)) To ensure a comprehensive search, users frequently must search for multiple forms of the same name. Unless sophisticated post-processing is performed, identical names of local places located in different areas will be displayed together. For example, a search of WorldCat for the city of *Charlevoix [Michigan]* results in 51 unique names, 29 entries from Michigan and 22 from Québec. An alphabetical display of the names intermixes the entries for Charlevoix, Michigan with those in Québec. The display also includes multiple entries for the same entry resulting from the direct and indirect forms of the name. When all of the names are in the indirect form as used in FAST, the 29 Michigan entries are reduced to the 12 entries shown below:

Michigan—Charlevoix
Michigan—Charlevoix County
Michigan—Charlevoix County—Deer Creek Watershed
Michigan—Charlevoix County—Holy Island
Michigan—Charlevoix County—Horton Creek
Michigan—Charlevoix County—Beaver Island
Michigan—Charlevoix County—Marion
Michigan—Charlevoix County—O'Neill Site
Michigan—Charlevoix County—Peaine Township
Michigan—Charlevoix Harbor
Michigan—Charlevoix, Lake
Michigan—Charlevoix Region

In this case, the entries for Michigan and Québec are clearly grouped in the display of the indirect names. The hierarchical structure could also be used to further reduce the size of the display to five entries by initially displaying only first and second level entries.

Linking the first level entries with the Geographic Area Codes provides additional specificity and hierarchical structure to the headings. In this way, the Geographic Area Codes can be used to limit a search. Searching for *Charlevoix* with the Geographic Area Code *n-us* would improve precision by limiting the above search to the United States.

6. Form Facet

The form facet includes all form subdivisions. The form headings were established by extracting all form subdivisions from LCSH topical and geographic headings. Since many form subdivisions are currently still coded as **x** instead of subfield ***v*** in LCSH headings, they were algorithmically identified and re-coded as *v* prior to their extraction. O'Neill et al. (Forthcoming) provides the details of the algorithm used to identify the form subdivisions for re-coding. Some examples of FAST form subdivisions are:

Translations into French
Rules
Dictionaries—Swedish
Controversial literature—Early works to 1800
Translations into Russian
Statistics—Databases

Textbooks for foreign speakers—English—Juvenile literature
Slides
Directories
Correspondence—Juvenile literature
Records

As with the topical and geographic facets, all form headings will be established in the authority file.

7. Period Facet

The period facet follows the practice recommended at the Airlie Conference: Chronological headings will reflect the actual time period of coverage for the resource. All period headings will be expressed as either a single numeric date or as a date range. Since the only general restriction on periods is that when a date range is used, the second date must be greater than the first, there is no need to routinely create authority records for period headings.

The *MARC 21 Format for Bibliographic Data* does not currently provide for separate identification of periods as main headings and the format will require the approval of a new field for period subjects if that facet is to be treated similarly to the other facets. Chronological subdivisions are established in the *MARC 21 Format for Authority Data* as X82 fields. If the same relationship between main headings and their corresponding subdivisions is used for periods, the X52 fields would be the logical tagging pattern for periods. Therefore a proposal to MARBI is being drafted, requesting that the 652 tag be authorized in bibliographic records. The X52 tag group is currently being used in the development of FAST authority files but will be revised, as necessary, after being reviewed by MARBI.

Period subdivisions in LCSH frequently contain valuable information beyond the chronological information. For example, if the subdivision **Song dynasty, 960-1279,** was replaced by simply 960-1279, useful information would be lost. In cases where the period heading contains information that cannot be captured in a numeric date range, the subdivision will also be retained as part of the topical heading.

8. Creation of the FAST headings

FAST headings are being derived from headings enumerated in LCSH and from the set of LCSH headings assigned to the records in WorldCat by faceting them into the four facets. There are approximately eight million unique topical and geographic headings in WorldCat. Each of these headings has been extracted and parsed into the appropriate facet. For example, the topical heading **Slavery $z United States $v Fiction** would be faceted into the following three FAST headings:

Slavery (Topical)
United States (Geographic)
Fiction (Form)

The geographic heading **France $x History $y Wars of the Huguenots, 1562-1598 $v Sources** would be faceted into:

History—Wars of the Huguenots, 1562-1598 (Topical)
France (Geographic)
1562-1598 (Period)
Sources (Form)

FAST

The faceting process has been completed and we are now in the process of validating the headings and creating the authority records. Not surprisingly, these initial files of faceted headings contain a large number of incorrect or other variant headings. Some of these errors are minor, such as variations in capitalization or spacing, but some are more significant such as incorrect spellings, invalid constructions, or the use of obsolete headings. The details of the validation process are beyond the scope of this paper but it is expected that when the validation process is complete, the error rate in the FAST files will be very low.

Once the FAST headings are validated, authority records will be created for each valid heading. It is expected that the *MARC 21 Format for Authority Data* with some modifications will be used for the FAST authority records. Links from the FAST authority records back to their corresponding LCSH records will be maintained whenever possible using the 7XX fields. When appropriate, the cross-references from the LCSH authority records will also be included in the FAST authorities.

Conclusions

Although much work remains before the FAST authorities files are complete and ready for use, the project has demonstrated that it is viable to derive a new subject schema based on the terminology of the Library of Congress Subject Headings but with a simpler syntax and application rules. Upon completion, the FAST authority records will be extensively tested and evaluated. After the evaluation, we will know if we have achieved our goal of creating a new subject schema for metadata that retains the rich vocabulary of LCSH while being easy to maintain, apply, and use.

References

Chan, L. M. Et al. (2001). A faceted approach to subject data in the Dublin Core metadata record. *Journal of Internet Cataloging,* 4, 35-47.

The future of subdivisions in the Library of Congress Subject Headings System: report from the Subject Subdivisions Conference May 9-12, 1991, ed. M. Hara. (1992). Washington, D.C.: Library of Congress, Cataloging Distribution Service.

O'Neill, E. T. et al. [Forthcoming] Form subdivisions: their identification and use in LCSH.*Library Resources & Technical Services.*

Subject data in the mtadata rcord recommendations and rationale: a report from the ALCTS/SAC/Subcommittee on Metadata and Subject Analysis. (1999). http://www.govst.edu/users/gddcasey/sac/MetadataReport.html

Faceted Indexing Application for Organizing and Accessing Internet Resources

Francis J. Devadason

Abstract: Organizing and providing access to the resources on the Internet has been a problem area in spite of the availability of sophisticated search engines and other software tools. There have been several attempts to organize the resources on the WWW. Some of them have tried to use traditional library classification schemes such as the Library of Congress Classification, the Dewey Decimal Classification and others. However there is a need to assign proper subject headings to them and present them in a logical or hierarchical sequence to cater to the need for browsing. This paper attempts to describe an experimental system designed to organize and provide access to web documents using a faceted pre-coordinate indexing system based on the Deep Structure Indexing System (DSIS) derived from POPSI (Postulate based Permuted Subject Indexing) of Bhattacharyya, and the facet analysis and chain indexing system of Ranganathan. A prototype software system has been designed to create a database of records specifying Web documents according to the Dublin Core and input a faceted subject heading according to DSIS. Synonymous terms are added to the standard terms in the heading using appropriate symbols. Once the data are entered along with a description and URL of the Web document, the record is stored in the system. More than one faceted subject heading can be assigned to a record depending on the content of the original document. The system stores the surrogates and keeps the faceted subject headings separately after establishing a link. Search is carried out on index entries derived from the faceted subject heading using chain indexing technique. If a single term is input, the system searches for its presence in the faceted subject headings and displays the subject headings in a sorted sequence reflecting an organizing sequence. If the number of retrieved headings is too large (running into more than a page) then the user has the option of entering another search term to be searched in combination. The system searches subject headings already retrieved and look for those containing the second term. The retrieved faceted subject headings can be displayed and browsed. When the relevant subject heading is selected the system displays the records with their URLs. Using the URL the original document on the web can be accessed. The prototype system developed under Windows NT environment using ASP and web server is under rigorous testing. The database and indexes management routines need further development.

1. Introduction

Some of the recent findings about the Internet are that (a) it is huge (it has exploded to more than 800 million Web pages), (b) it is growing very fast, (c) search engines cover only a small fraction of the web, (d) even the combined indexes of the major search engines cover only a small fraction of the Web and (e) even the most dedicated surfer using the best search system would be able to find barely one-third of the pages (Dahn, 2000). There is no simple way to index and organize the resources on the Internet. Several search engines using different methods of indexing the resources are being used and their number is steadily growing. Meta-search facilities that offer several engines to be used in parallel to search for information are available. However, "the goal of information systems is to create order in a collection of documents so that an information searcher need not scan the entire collection in an attempt to find information of interest" (Fugmann, 1999). There have been several attempts to organize electronic resources including the use of traditional Library Classification Schemes such as, Dewey Decimal Classification, (Mundie) Library of Congress Classification, Universal Decimal Classification as well as special subject classification schemes for Medicine, Computing etc (McKiernan, 1997). Moreover several subject-based information gateway projects have been on-going (Kerr & MacLeod, 1998), (Mitchel & Mooney, 1996) to provide organized access to electronic resources. Use of classification schemes, although it though helps in organizing electronic documents broadly and help browsing, cannot be used to organize the resources precisely and function as an effective retrieval tool. Analysis of some of the websites using standard classification schemes for organizing the resources (Williamson, 1997) (McIlwaine & Williamson, 1999) identified the fact that the application of classification at the sites was often superficial and poorly executed. This becomes an acute problem as the electronic documents are mostly on recent, developing and yet to be developed subject fields and facets. Relying on such classification schemes may not fully serve the purpose as e-documents get updated fast and may change their subject with each modification and updating. Moreover, assignment of class numbers is needed for documents in a library as it is necessary to restore documents to the shelves in the classified sequence once they are borrowed and returned or their arrangement disturbed otherwise. In other words class numbers are used to mechanize the arrangement of documents on the shelves. In the case of documents on the web, it is only their surrogates that are organized and the sequence of these surrogates is not disturbed by the users. In fact there is no need for the assignment of class numbers to restore their sequence in a mechanical way. What is needed is a tool that provides a standard frame-work/ formula for the e-document developers to fill-in as a subject heading which will have the capacity to produce an organizing sequence when sorted using the assigned subject heading as key as well as provide the necessary index terms or keywords or search terms to provide access. Such a heading can be incorporated as a Meta tag in the resources and used for both organizing and indexing the resources. This paper describes a prototype of such a system that can provide organized access to networked resources.

2.Deep Structure Indexing System (DSIS)

2.1 Categories of DSIS

Kaiser's "Systematic indexing" (Kaiser, 1911) was perhaps the first category based subject indexing system. The Deep Structure Indexing System (Devadason, 1986) is based on the Postulate-based permuted Subject Indexing (POPSI) (Bhattacharyya, 1979) derived from the Chain Indexing system of Ranganathan especially his concept of facet analysis as applied to subject headings (Ranganathan, 1964). The component ideas in a subject heading can be deemed to fall into any one of the Elementary Categories or Facets : Discipline (Base), Entity (Core), Property and Action. Each of these may admit of sub-divisions: species/type, and part. The Entity may have constituents too. In the case of `bamboo'; `arundinarisae', `bambusa lineata', `Brazilian bamboo' are species/types; `bud' `flower', `leaf', `rhizome', `culm', `root' are parts; `ash', `lignin', `peptin', `cellulose' etc., are constituents. Apart from the elementary categories, a special component called Modifier is recognized. For example: "red" in 'red rose', "concrete" in 'concrete bridge'. A modifier generally creates a species/type of the concept modified. Modifiers can be Common Modifiers like Form, Time, Place and Environment and Special Modifiers, which can be based on any of the elementary categories. Generally common modifiers can modify a combination of two or more category occurrences in a subject heading. There are also two other kinds of special modifiers. Independent modifiers can modify the focus independently without depending on any other modifier. Dependent modifiers cannot modify the focus directly but can modify only another modifier of the focus; for example: Temperature, High temperature, Very high temperature. When concepts are represented by terms there may be cases wherein a term (composite term) may have to be broken down (factored) into two or more constituent terms and each one of them identified as belonging to one or the other of the elementary categories. In Kaiser's systematic indexing system agriculture is represented as a combination of land + cultivation corresponding to his categories concrete and process. A composite term is considered as a synonymous term to the combination of the factored constituent terms.

2.2 Syntax of the Subject Headings

The basic rule of syntax for formulating subject headings is DISCIPLINE (BASE) followed by ENTITY (CORE) which is followed by PROPERTY and/or ACTION. PROPERTY and/or ACTION may be further followed by PROPERTY and/or ACTION as the case may be, followed by COMMON MODIFIERS. The SPECIES/TYPES and/or MODIFIERS and/or PARTS and/or CONSTITUENTS for each of the Elementary Categories follow immediately the manifestation to which they are respectively SPECIES/TYPES or MODIFIERS or PARTS or CONSTITUENTS without the manifestation of any other Elementary Category intervening. The rules of syntax give rise to a context-dependent sequence of the components in the subject heading.

2.3 Indicators of the Structure

Certain numeric codes have been prescribed to indicate the categories and their subdivisions to which individual concepts belong. One set of these codes is shown below:

0 Form Modifier	9 Discipline
2 Time Modifier	8 Entity
3 Environment Modifier	.2 Property
4 Place Modifier	.1 Action

SUBDIVISIONS
.3 Constituent
.4 Part
.5 Modifier of Kind 1 including Phase Relation Modifier
.6 Species/Type, including those created by Modifiers of Kind 2

In the subject headings the indicators precede the components to which they are indicators. The indicators for property and action as well as the sub-divisions (species, part etc.) are attached to the indicators for the elementary categories to which they are respectively property or action or sub-divisions.

3. Formulation of Subject Headings

Taking the title of the resource as the starting point each of the specific subjects dealt with in the resource are expressed in natural language. Each of the specific subjects (topics) may warrant a separate subject heading. Each of the component ideas corresponding to each of the elementary categories that are implied is explicitly stated to form expressive titles. Let one of the expressive titles be "In Leather technology, dry salt curing of pig skin in Thailand". This is then analyzed to identify the elementary categories and their sub-divisions to which each of the components in the expressive title belong. All composite terms are factored into their constituent terms and identified as belonging to one of the elementary categories. The component terms are written down as a formalized expression following the rules of syntax, as given below:

(Discipline/Base) Leather Technology (Entity/Core) Pig skin (Action) Dry salt curing (Place Modifier) Thailand.

Each of the component terms in the subject heading is then analyzed to find out its super-ordinate terms. This is done by finding out "of which the concerned component is a species/ type, or part or constituent" in the context of the subject as a whole. This process is continued with each of such super-ordinates recognized in the process till it ends up with the concept of the elementary category. For this purpose terminological sources such as thesauri, glossaries, dictionaries etc., are to be used. Each of the super-ordinates thus recognized is fixed prior to the concerned term successively giving rise to a 'modulated' subject heading as follows:

(D/B) Leather technology (E/C) Hide and skin (Part of E) Skin (Type of E) Pig skin (A) Beam-house operation (Sub-action) Curing (Type of A) Salt curing (Type of A) Dry salt curing (Common modifier) Thailand.

NOTE: The reason for making each of the super-ordinates precede the respective component terms is to endow the subject headings with the capacity to produce an organizing sequence effect resembling the sequence of class numbers when sorted alphabetically along with similarly formulated other subject headings. Moreover, this will facilitate search using any of the super-ordinate terms also.

Each of the component terms in the subject heading is replaced with standard terms and the synonyms are attached to the standard terms with an appropriate symbol such as an equals sign (=). For this purpose vocabulary control tools such as thesauri, classauri (Bhattacharyya,1982) (Devadason & Ramanujam, 1982) (Devadason, 1985) are used. Appropriate indicators for the elementary categories, their sub-divisions, and common modifiers of different kinds are inserted in the appropriate places. The resulting subject heading is as follows:

Leather technology 8 Hide and skin 8.4 Skin 8.6 Pig skin 8.1 Beam-house operation 8.1.4 Curing 8.1.6 Salt curing 8.1.6 Dry salt curing 4 Thailand

4. Organizing Sequence in Alphabetical Arrangement
A set of subject headings formulated according to this system when sorted alphabetically resembles an organizing (classified) sequence as illustrated below:

Subjects according to Colon Class numbers:

L"aN5	= Medicine, Bibliography, 1950s
L"k1, N3	= Medicine, Dictionary.
L"v1'N	= Medicine, History, 19th century
L"44'N	= Medicine, History, India, 19th century
L	= Medicine
L, 0;2	= Medicine, Anatomy
L,0;3	= Medicine, Physiology
L,0;4	= Medicine, Disease
L,0;4:3	= Medicine, Disease, Diagnosis
L,0;4:6	= Medicine, Disease, Treatment
L,9C	= Medicine, Child
L,9C;4	= Medicine, Child, Disease
L,9C;42	= Medicine, Child, Disease, Infectious disease
L,9C;42:6	= Medicine, Child, Disease, Infectious disease, Treatment

L,9C,4;4 = Medicine, Child, Respiratory system, Disease
L,9C,45;4 = Medicine, Child, Respiratory system, Lung, Disease

The same subjects with headings formulated according to the indexing system and sorted alphabetically:

Medicine 0 Bibliography 2 Nineteen fifties
Medicine 0 Dictionary
Medicine 0 History 2 Nineteenth century
Medicine 0 History 4 India 2 Nineteenth century
Medicine 1
Medicine 8.1 Physiology
Medicine 8.2 Anatomy
Medicine 8.2 Disease
Medicine 8.2 Disease 8.2.1 Diagnosis
Medicine 8.2 Disease 8.2.1 Treatment
Medicine 8 Child
Medicine 8 Child 8.2 Disease
Medicine 8 Child 8.2 Disease 8.2.6 Infectious disease
Medicine 8 Child 8.2 Disease 8.2.6 Infectious disease 8.2.1 Treatment
Medicine 8 Child 8.4 Respiratory system 8.2 Disease 8.2.6 Infectious disease 8.2.1 Treatment
Medicine 8 Child 8.4 Respiratory system 8.4 Lung 8.2 Disease 8.2.6 Infectious disease 8.2.1 Treatment

It may be seen that the two sequences are almost similar. In other words it is possible to bring an organizing sequence effect in the alphabetic arrangement of subject headings. Once the sequence is obtained, the indicators may be suppressed in the display or changed to suitable punctuation marks.

5. Prototype System for Web Resources

A prototype system has been built which has three main parts:
1) *input site -Using Dublin Core elements* for data entry.
2) *Maintain database* - Browse the records to update or delete.
3) *Search* - Search records for the web documents.

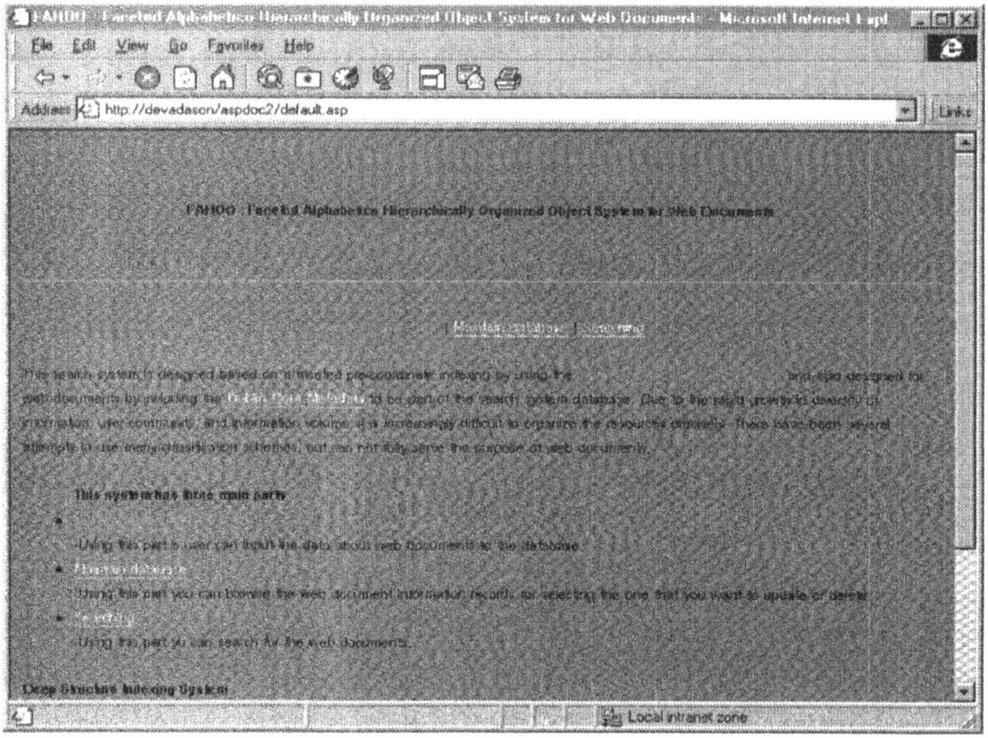

Figure 1. First screen of the prototype
Figures 2-4. (below) Input template

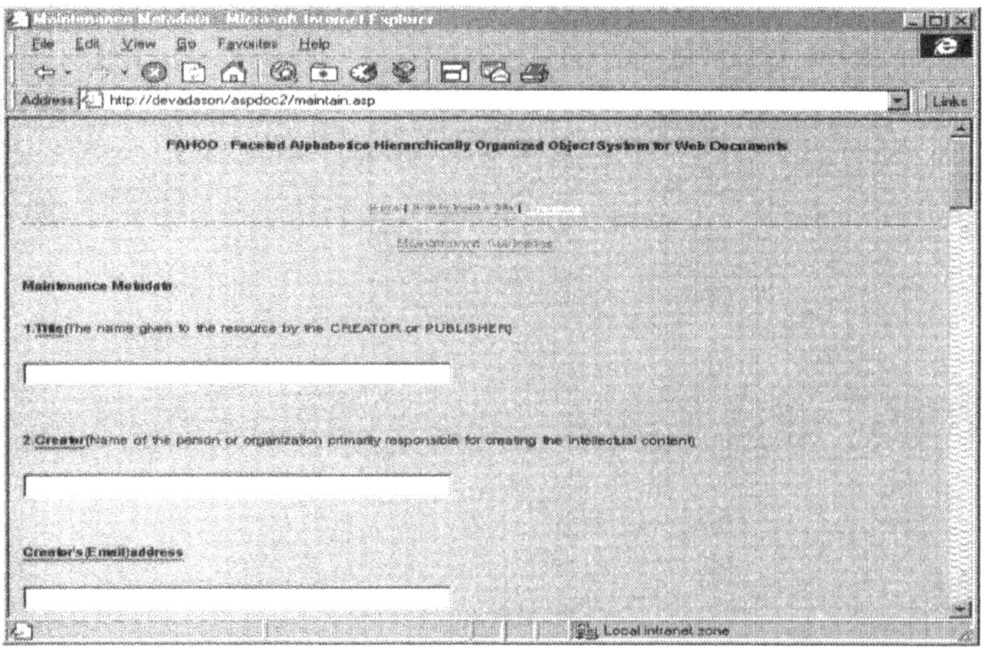

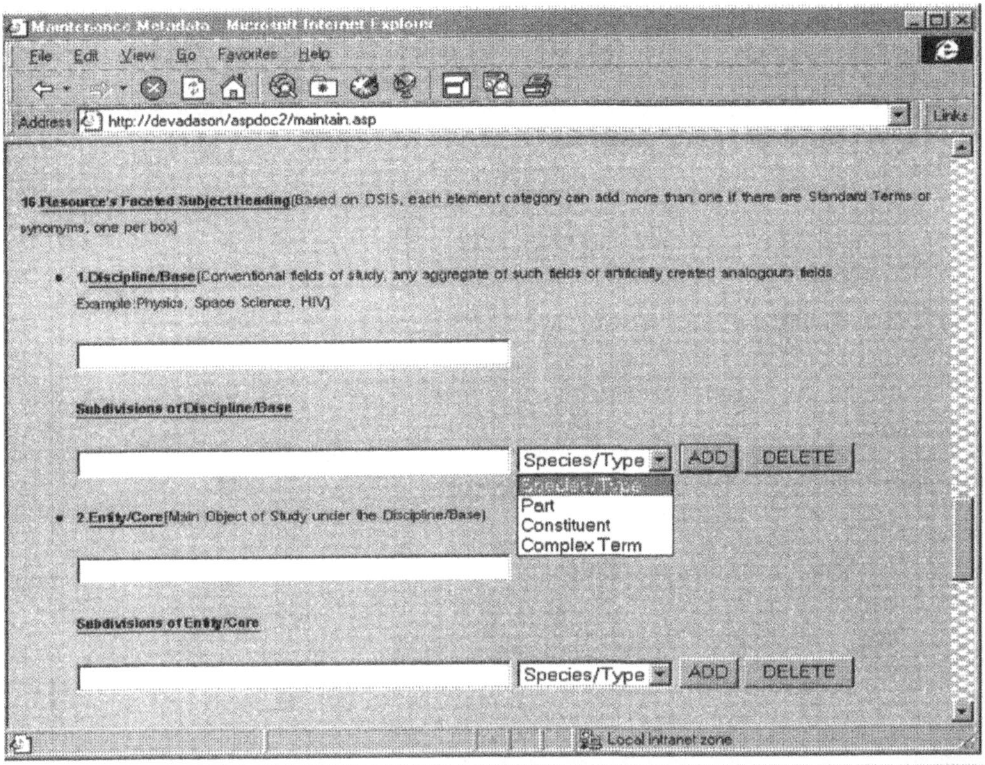
File Edit View Go Favorites Help
Address http://devadason/aspdoc2/maintain.asp
Links
16.Resource's Faceted SubjectHeading(Based on DSIS, each element category can add more than one if there are Standard Terms or synonyms, one per box)
1.Discipline/Base(Conventional fields of study, any aggregate of such fields or artificially created analogous fields
Example:Physics, Space Science, HIV)
Subdivisions of Discipline/Base
Species/Type
ADD
DELETE
Part
Constituent
Complex Term
2.Entity/Core(Main Object of Study under the Discipline/Base)
Subdivisions of Entity/Core
Species/Type
ADD
DELETE
Local intranet zone

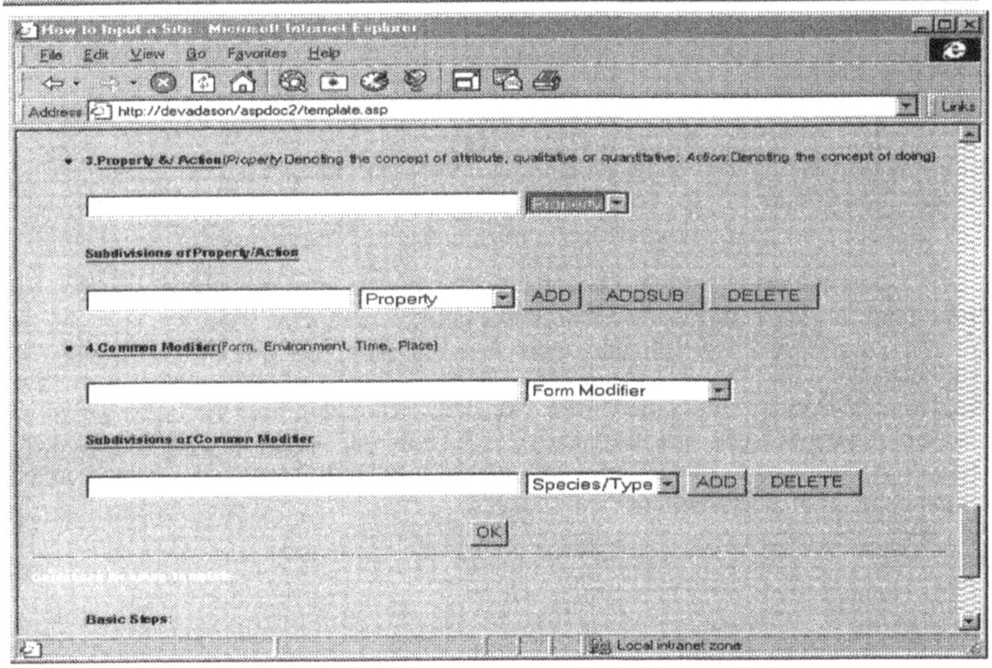
File Edit View Go Favorites Help
Address http://devadason/aspdoc2/template.asp
Links
3.Property &/ Action(Property:Denoting the concept of attribute, qualitative or quantitative; Action:Denoting the concept of doing)
Subdivisions of Property/Action
Property
ADD
ADDSUB
DELETE
4.Common Modifier(Form, Environment, Time, Place)
Form Modifier
Subdivisions of Common Modifier
Species/Type
ADD
DELETE
OK
Basic Steps:
Local intranet zone

Figure 3 and 4 show the portion of the input template that allows the faceted subject heading to be input. The Categories Property and Action are repeatable so also the addition of species and parts. Once the data are entered the record can be browsed and edited and corrected. The desired record can be retrieved by entering some of the input data, edited and modified. Figure - 5 shows the record while browsing.

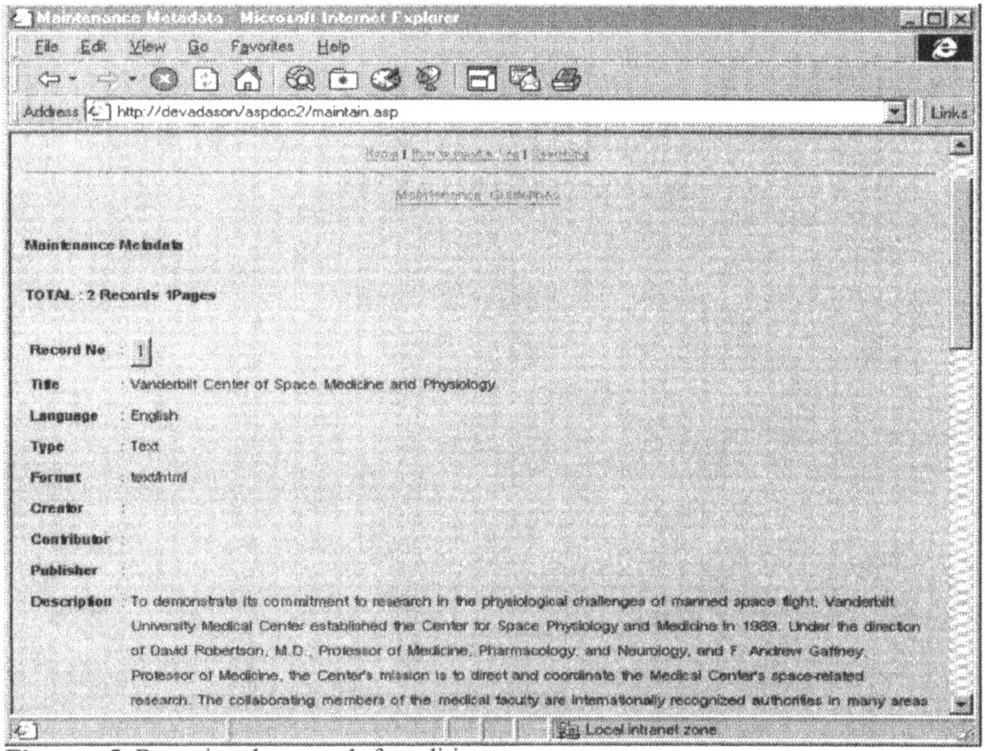

Figure – 5. Browsing the records for editing.

Figure - 6 shows the search screen. Once a search term(s) is input the system searches for faceted subject headings having the term(s) and displays in sorted sequence as shown in Figure - 7. If the subject headings span more than one page, you can browse through the pages to select the subject heading that best describes your query or input another term to be searched in combination. The faceted subject headings containing both the terms would be selected and displayed along with the number of records that would be retrieved for each. The records can be displayed by clicking this number at the right hand side. Clicking on the URL can access the original resource.

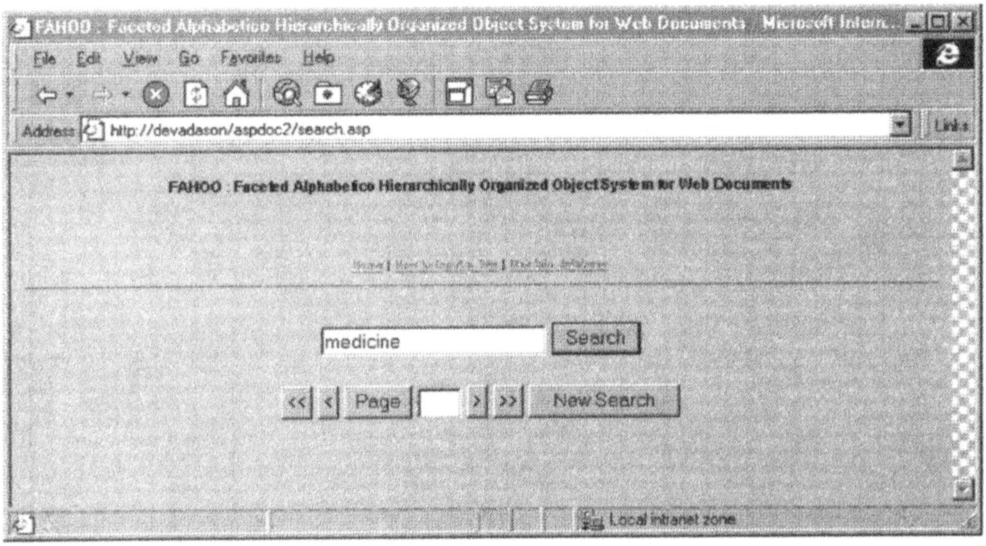

Figure 6. Search screen.

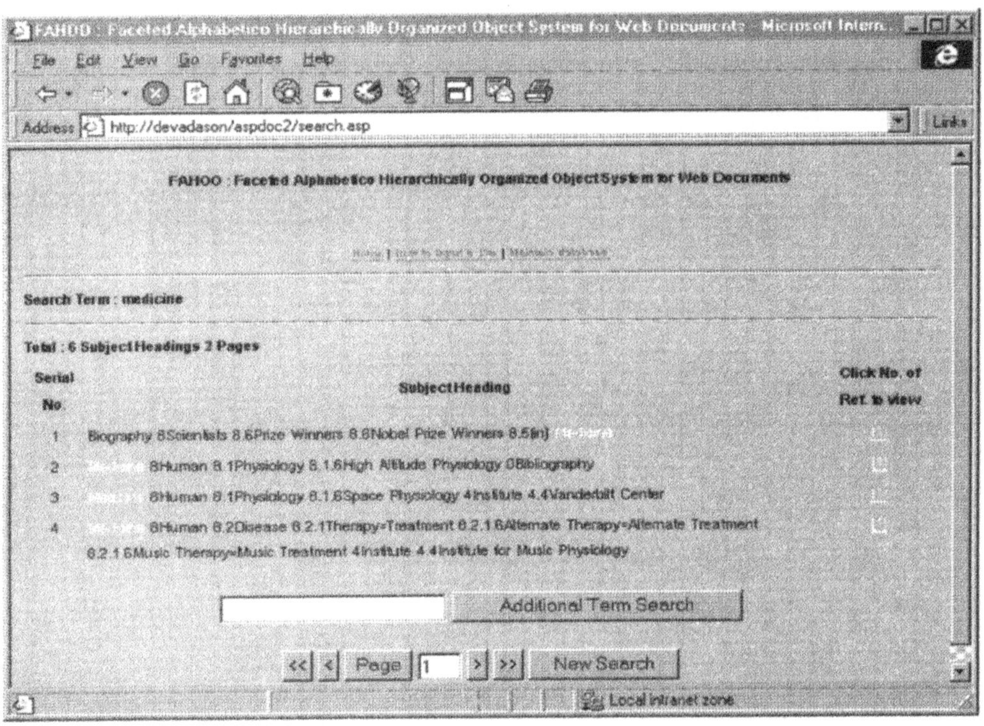

Figure 7. Selected faceted subject headings

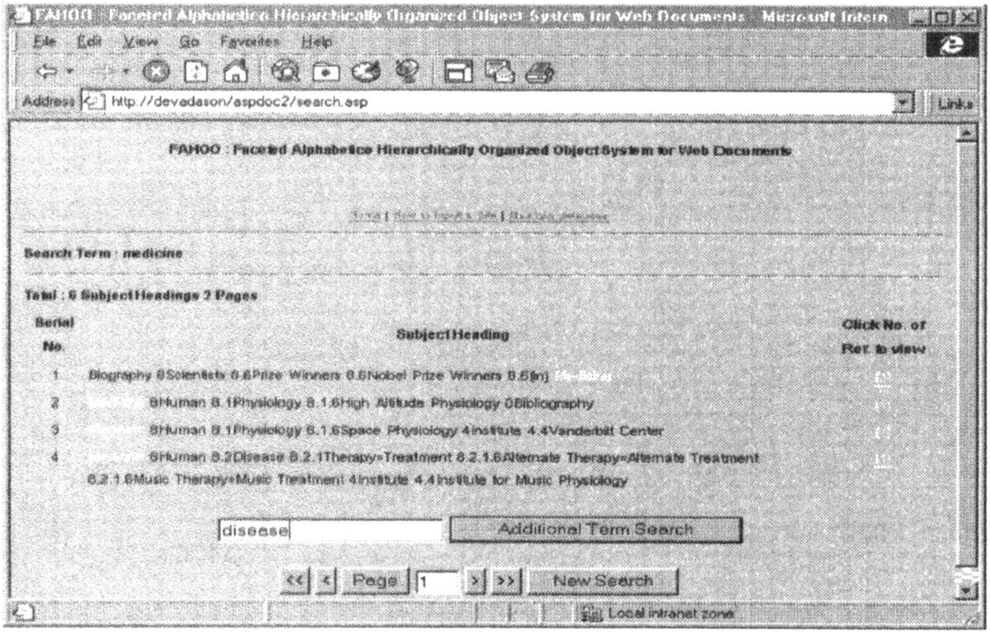

Figure 8. Searching for another term in combination on the retrieved subject headings

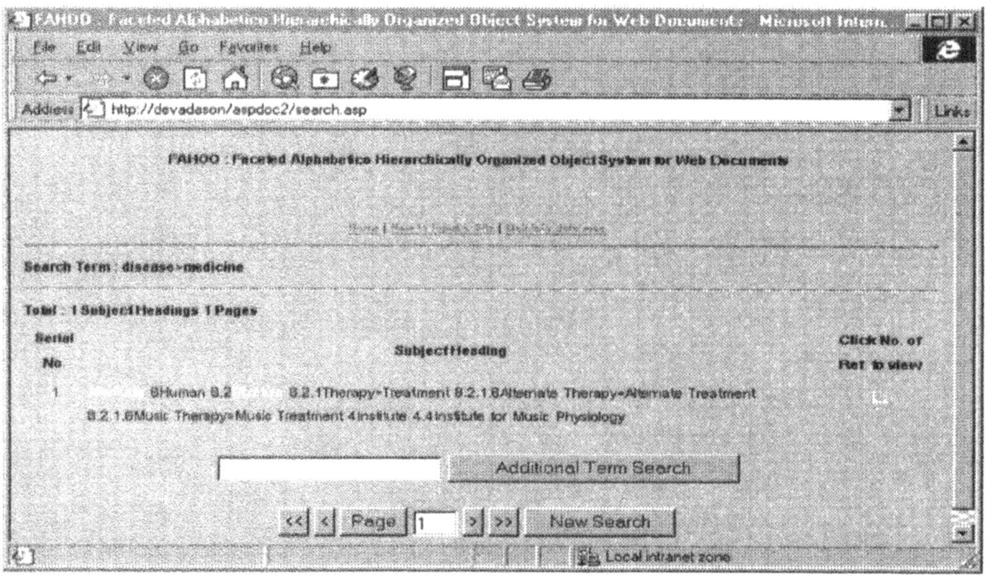

Figure 9. Retrieved subject heading

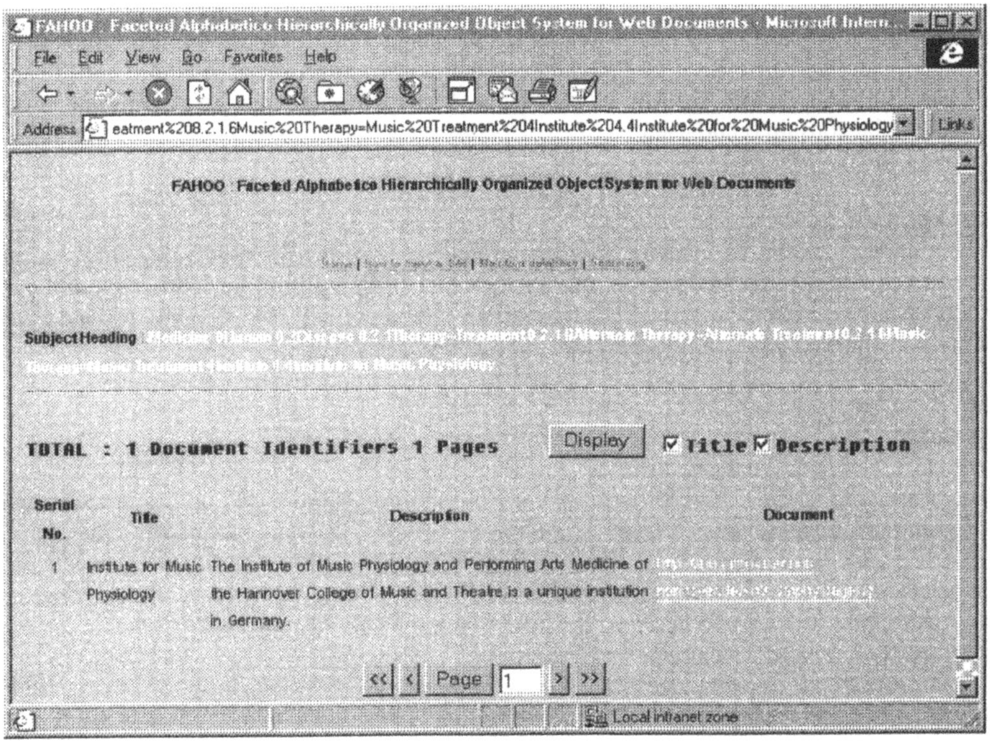

Figure 10. Display of retrieved record

It is possible to change the display to produce an organized index of different levels to make browsing easy. By bringing the required category (along with its subdivisions) to the beginning of the subject chain, the organizing effect can be changed. The sequence can be varied according to the user. It can be presented as discipline-based if the user of the system is an academic. It can be changed to entity (object) based or action (process) based. When resources are collected for indexing and to build search files, it may be possible to exercise control over synonyms and standardize the terms used. It may also be possible to switch from non-standard terms used by the searcher to the standard ones. When any term used by the searcher is poly-hierarchic, then the subject chains in which the term occurs (only the super-ordinates in the category to which the term belongs) can be displayed, perhaps along with the term denoting the discipline or base in reverse order and the user can be asked to select the appropriate chain representing his/her query. It is possible to incorporate synonyms due to semantic factoring so that the system searches for the combination of factored terms to be present in faceted subject headings. It is possible to sort the headings and present higher level indexes for easy browsing. It is also possible to resolve the meaning of homonyms by displaying the full faceted subject headings having the term and asking the user to select the subject heading that represents the intended meaning of the searcher.

6. Limitations

An indexing approach of this analytical type using facet analysis perhaps is best suited for scholarly academic resources having educational and research value. Moreover there may be cases wherein it would be difficult to recognize the categories in certain subjects in spite of illustrative examples. Provision of such subject chains for a resource as a whole and for the significant sub-units would be time consuming as terminological sources of different types may have to be consulted and used.

7. Conclusion

As mentioned by Weinberg (1996) "it is hoped that the systems for organizing information developed earlier will not be ignored, that their design flaws will not be replicated, and that our increasing knowledge of human factors will be incorporated into systems for indexing the Internet". Further work in this direction is on going in our school.

References

Bhattacharyya, G. (1979). POPSI: its fundamentals and procedure based on a general theory of subject indexing languages, *Library science with a slant to documentation* 16, 1-34.

Bhattacharyya, G. (1982). Classaurus : its fundamentals, design and use. In *Proceedings of the 4th International Study Conference on Classification Research, Augsburg, June 28-July 2,* 1982. Frankfurt: Indeks Verlag. Pp. 139-148.

Dahn, M. (2000) Counting angels on a pinhead: critically interpreting web size estimates, *Online* 24 , 35-36, 38- 40.

Devadason, F.J. and Kothanda Ramanujam, M. (1982). Computer aided construction of 'alphabetic' classaurus. In *Proceedings of the 4th International Study Conference on Classification Research, Augsbur, June 28-July 2, 1982.* Frankfurt: Indeks Verlag. Pp. 173-182.

Devadason, F.J.(1985). Online construction of alphabetic classaurus: a vocabulary control and indexing tool, *Information processing and management,* 21, 11-26.

Devadason, F.J. (1986). *Computerized Deep Structure Indexing System.* FID/CR Report. Frankfurt: Indeks Verlag, 1986.

Fugmann, R. (1999). The empirical approach in the evaluation of information systems, *Knowledge organization,* 26, 3-9.

Kaiser, J. (1911). *Systematic indexing: the card system series,* Vol. 2. London: Pitman.

Kerr, L. & MacLeod, R. (1998). Subject-based information gateways, *Ariadne.* <http://www.ariadne.ac.uk/issue18/subject-gateways/>

McIlwaine, I.C. & Williamson, N.J. (1999). International trends in subject analysis research, *Knowledge organization,* 26, 23-29.

McKiernan, G. (1997). Hand-made in Iowa: organizing the web along the Lincoln highway, *D-Lib magazine*, 3 (2) February. http://www.dlib.org/dlib/february97/02mckiernan.html>

Mitchel, S. & Mooney, M. (1996). INFOMINE: a model web-based academic virtual library, *Information technology and libraries,* 15 (1). <http://lib-www.ucr.edu/pubs/italmine.html>

Mundie, D. A. Organizing computer resources; or, how I learned to stop worrying and love the DDC. http://ivory.lm.com/~mundie/CyberDewey/organizing_computers.html [Link not functioning 2002]

Ranganathan, S.R. (1964). Subject heading and facet analysis, *Journal of documentation,* 20, 109-119.

Tinker, A.J. et al. (1999). The Dewey Decimal Classification and the transition from physical to electronic knowledge organization, *Knowledge organization* 26, 80-96.

Weinberg, B. H.(1996). Complexity in indexing systems - abandonment and failure - implications for organizing the Internet. *ASIS 1996 Annual Conference, 19-24 Oct,* 1996. < http://www.asis.org/annual-96/ElectronicProceedings/weinberg.html>

Williamson, N.J. (1997). Knowledge structures and the Internet. In *Knowledge Organization for Information Retrieval: proceedings of the 6th International Study Conference on Classification Research, University College London, 16-18 June 1997.* The Hague, International Federation for Information and Documentation. Pp. 23- 27.

Session 8

TRANSFORMATION OF TRADITIONAL TOOLS FOR THE WEB ENVIRONMENT (2)

The Library of Congress Classification as a Knowledge Base for Automatic Subject Categorization

Carol Jean Godby and Jay Stuler

Abstract. This paper describes a set of experiments in adapting a subset of the Library of Congress Classification for use as a database for automatic classification. A high degree of concept integrity was obtained when subject headings were mapped from OCLC's WorldCat database and filtered using the log-likelihood statistic.

1. Introduction

We are interested in using the Library of Congress Classification (LCC) to classify Web resources and other full-text documents. Our research project has three goals:

- To adapt the LCC for use as a knowledge base for automatically classifying full text.
- To exploit the LCC's structure for online subject-oriented browsing.
- To make the results of our work freely available to the library community.

Our interest is consistent with OCLC's six-month-old Global Product Strategy, whose cornerstone is a proposal to make OCLC's WorldCat database the database of choice for Web users wishing to access the high-quality resources that are held in or described by the world's libraries. We agree with Chan (2000) that the adaptation of library classification schemes for Internet resources would permit semantic interoperabilty between the large store of MARC records and the new resources and would obviate the need to re-invent or re-discover the principles of classification.

However, the LCC presents some well-known obstacles for projects like ours. The complete set of LCC schedules has nearly a quarter of a million sparse class definitions, whose literary warrant is derived primarily from books published in the United States. Moreover, the class notation favours hospitality over economy or consistency and the schedules are not designed for automatic processing.

Nevertheless, many researchers believe that these obstacles can be overcome. The landmark study of Larson (1992) evaluated the suitability of the LCC as a knowledge base for the automatic classification of bibliographic records. Working with Schedule Z, *Bibliography and Library Science*, he concluded that, once the schedule was simplified and additional subject headings were imported, the resulting knowledge base could be used to cluster bibliographic records by subject, a possible first step in the creation of a fully classified record. More recently, several digital library projects that recognize the utility of the LCC as a classification scheme for Internet resources are exploring ways to adapt the LCC for this new application. For example, The Columbia University Digital Libraries Project[1] created browsable hierarchical displays of the LCC, enhanced the subject terminology in consultation with the LCC editors, and linked some of their Web resources to it. CyberStacks[2] and The WWW Virtual Library[3] show the results of similar efforts, though their collections of resources are more narrowly focused by subject.

Our work shares the high-level goals of these projects. The visible result is a demonstration using a fragment of the LCC to organize and access Internet and other full-text resources.

2. Adapting the LCC schedules for automatic classification

Because our project requires that documents be classified automatically, we build on Larson's research and extend its applicability to full-text documents. We selected Schedules Q, *Science*; R, *Medicine*; S, *Agriculture* and T, *Technology* for a pilot study that would shed light on how the LCC should be adapted to accomplish this goal. The topics represented in these schedules provide reasonably broad coverage for a prototype system but present a good test of the system's ability to discriminate among similar subjects.

Previous research in document categorization suggests that a large number of sparsely populated classes present too many spurious targets for an automatic classifier. Accordingly, about 85% of the classes in Schedules Q, R, S and T were deleted using simple heuristics. All classes whose hierarchy contains cross-references to other LCC schedules or that mention geographic names and names of genres were eliminated. The effect of these reductions is shown in the fragment from Schedule S in Figure 1. Only the class shown in italics, *SD426-SD428.22*, is retained. The result is that the essential topic is identified but often at the cost of a flattened LCC hierarchy and a class definition represented as a range of LCC numbers. We made these simplifications for several reasons. First, we believe that topical assignment is the most pressing need for an automatic classifier designed for large collections of Web documents whose subject matter is unknown. Second, many of the genre names that result in a proliferation of LCC class definitions may be irrelevant to descriptions of Web resources that do not fit very well into taxonomies of traditionally published material. Finally, in applications where the information omitted from our system is important, we believe it can be added—algorithmically, in some cases, or with human intervention in a computer-aided classification system.

SD426 – SD428.22 *Forestry. Conservation and protection. Forest reserves.*
- **SD426.A1-SD426.Z** Forestry. Conservation and protection. Forest reserves. United States. General.
  - **SD426.A1-SD426.A5** Forestry. Conservation and protection. Forest reserves. United States. General. Documents.
    - **SD426.A5** Forestry. Conservation and protection. Forest reserves. United States. General. Documents. By date
  - **SD426.A6-SD426.Z** Forestry. Conservation and protection. Forest reserves. United States. General. General works.

Figure 1. A fragment from Schedule S showing an enumeration of genres.

The definitions of the remaining classes were enhanced using two sources of terminology, the Library of Congress Subject Authority (LCSA) File and OCLC's WorldCat database of bibliographic records. Both sources of terminology have class assignments that are more specific than the modified schedules. An algorithm that correctly assigns the terminology must identify the LCC class with the most specific range that contains the LCC number listed in the source record, which requires numeric as well as alphabetic comparisons. For example, the LCSA record that assigns the headings *iron ores* and *manganese ores* to QE390.2.I76 is mapped to **QE390.Q.2.A-QE390.2.Z** Geology. Mineralogy. Special groups of minerals. Ore minerals. Special ore minerals A-Z, to which *platinum ores*, *nickel ores*, *rare earths*, and *antimony ores* have also been applied using our processes. The algorithm rejects an assignment to the more generic class **QE389-QE390.5** Geology. Minerology. Special groups of minerals, which contains mapped terms such as *ores*, *geochemistry* and *hydrothermal alternation*.

This procedure is sufficient for mapping terminology from LCSA records but the subject headings obtained from WorldCat must undergo an additional processing step. While the class assignments in the LCSA file were created for the purpose of improving the LCC as a classification scheme, the WorldCat headings are only indirectly relevant to this goal, since their presence in a bibliographic record serves primarily to enhance subject access to the item being described. To simulate the editorial task of defining an LCC class by assigning a subject heading to it, we need to identify the most stable headings—the headings that most commonly appear with a given range of LCC numbers and do not appear elsewhere in the WorldCat sample.

Figure 2 illustrates one result. It shows an LCC class from Schedule R that has been enhanced with data from the LCSA file and from bibliographic records in a 140,000-record sample of WorldCat that contain class assignments from Schedule R paired with Library of Congress subject headings. The class defines a timely and popular subject, with the result that approximately 4000 subject headings from the WorldCat sample can be mapped to the LC class numbers in the range *RJ370-RJ520*. Since 4000 headings are unwieldy and possibly misleading, the subject-heading/class-number pairs are filtered using the log-likelihood statistic (Dunning 1993), which measures the strength of pairwise associations and is commonly used in information retrieval and computational linguistics research. The highly associated terms, such as *attention-deficit hyperactivity disorder* and *autism in children*, are highly relevant to the definition of the class and are only rarely paired with other LCC class numbers. Conversely, headings such as *adjustment (psychology)* and *first aid* are given low association scores by the log-likelihood measure. Though they may legitimately refer to a facet of a given work about diseases of children, they are only tangentially related to the meaning of the class in Figure 2 because they are paired with a large number of other LCC class assignments in the WorldCat database.

Class number:
RJ370-RJ520

Hierarchy:
Pediatrics.
Diseases of children.

High associations:
Chronically ill children, mentally ill children, epilepsy in children, speech therapy for children, attention-deficit hyperactivity disorder, autism in children, pediatric neurology, rheumatoid arthritis in children, chronic diseases in children

Low associations:
Medical emergencies, child health services, stress (psychology), resuscitation, telephone, children, adjustment (psychology), first aid, disabled, family therapy, diseases, risk, physical fitness, child nutrition, infants (newborn), youth, cerebral palsy, nervous system

LCSA headings:
Adolescent psychopathology scale, aps (adolescent psychiatry), psychiatric rating scales, electroconvulsive therapy for children, electroconvulsive therapy for teenagers, violence in children, child psychopathology, children and violence, violence in adolescence, adolescent psychopathology, fragile x syndrome, syndromes, x-linked mental retardation

Figure 2. An enhanced LCC record from Schedule R *Medicine*.

3. An evaluation

The major outcome of this project is a database design that can be used for the automatic classification of full-text documents. Each record is an LCC class that has been enhanced with subject headings from OCLC's WorldCat database and the Library of Congress Subject Authority File.

The database was constructed from three sources: machine-readable files of the LCC Schedules Q, R, S and T obtained from the Library of Congress; a machine-readable version of the Library of Congress Subject Authority File; and a subset from WorldCat, extracted in April 2000, which contains every bibliographic record that has a Dewey Decimal Classification (DDC) as well an LCC assignment. Though the DDC assignment is irrelevant to the present study, this criterion produces a large but manageable sample of records with a broad distribution of subjects. Most of the records are also indexed with Library of Congress subject headings. The pairing of these headings with LCC numbers constitute the raw data for this study. Table 1 shows their distribution for Schedules Q, R, S and T. From the WorldCat sample, 865,881 pairs of class numbers and subject headings were generated. By contrast, Larson (1992), who reported guarded conclusions about the utility of the LCC as an automatic classifier, conducted his tests with only 30,000 pairs.

LCC Schedule	WorldCat records	LCC class/ subject heading pairs
Q *Science*	326,391	637,470
R *Medicine*	139,280	374,465
S *Agriculture*	83,818	154,400
T *Technology*	314,357	269,546
Total	863,846	865,881

Table 1. Subject heading assignments in a WorldCat sample.

Using the heuristics for simplifying the LCC schedules described in the previous section, we eliminated 91% of the classes, with the result that 6314 potential concept definitions have been extracted from the four schedules. Table 2 shows the distribution of the two classes of subject headings after they have been mapped to the simplified LCC schedules.

The raw data generates two hypotheses that motivate the present study. First, the editorial mappings from the LCSA file, though highly trustworthy, are inadequate for creating the class definitions required for an automatic classifier because they populate only 9% of the classes in the simplified schedules, compared to 86% for headings obtained from WorldCat. Second, the extremely large standard deviations in the distributions of the mappings from WorldCat records present problems for an automatic classifier and suggest that these data must be further processed. The second half of Table 2 shows the results when the terminology obtained from WorldCat is trimmed to the mean, the 120 most highly associated pairs of subject headings and LCC class assignments as measured by the log-likelihood statistic. Logically, this change has the effect of consolidating the locations of the mapped terms in the LCC class structure and reducing the mean, standard deviation and maximum to values close to those found when the Dewey Decimal Classification is converted to a database for automatic classification (Thompson, et al 1997).

LCC Schedule:	Source of Headings: WorldCat	LCSA
Q,R,S and T		
Total	5460/6313 (86%)	618/6313 (9%)
Mean	120	13
Standard deviation	477	18
Largest number of headings in a single record	12,320	1036
Q,R,S and T (filtered)		
Total	5460/6313	Same
Mean	36	
Standard deviation	45	
Largest number of headings in a single record	120	

Table 2. Mappings of two sources of subject headings to the LCC.

The database design was evaluated with the so-called self-match test that was used by Thompson, et al. (1997) to test the suitability of the Dewey Decimal Classification as a knowledge base for automatic classification. Databases were created using OCLC's Scorpion[4] software and indexed with the subject headings found in the LCC hierarchy for each record, as well as those applied from the LCSA file and the WorldCat sample. The baseline database contained terms only from the first two sources, while two additional test databases included Library of Congress subject headings: one that had every heading found in the WorldCat sample, and one that contained only the most highly associated terms for each class, as summarized in Table 2. All three databases contained 6314 records corresponding to the classes in the set of truncated LCC schedules. To test the databases, a set of queries were generated that consisted of the same 6314 records. These were run individually against each database to generate result sets of twenty items that could be interpreted as ranked lists of LCC class assignments.

A self-match occurs if the query retrieves itself as the highest ranked result, a test which measures the concept integrity of the database and hence the classification scheme from which it is derived. Accordingly, if the subject headings that define the LCC classes are randomly scattered throughout the database, the query would fail to retrieve itself as the top-ranked record because many other records would be highly similar. But if the terminology is distributed to form meaningful, distinct concepts, the number of self-matches should be high. Figure 3 has a fragment of a sample run, showing a successful self-match for the LCC class illustrated in Figure 1.

Query: RJ370-RJ520 Pediatrics. Diseases of children.
Ranked results:

1. RJ370-RJ520 Pediatrics. Diseases of children.
2. RJ499-RJ507 Pediatrics. Child psychiatry. Diseases of children. Mental disorders of children and adolescents. Child psychiatry. Child mental health services.
3. RJ506.A-RJ506.Z Pediatrics. Diseases of children. Mental disorders of children and adolescents. Child psychiatry. Child mental health services. Specific disorders A-Z.
4. RJ503.7.A-RJ503.7.Z Pediatrics. Diseases of children. Mental disorders of children and adolescents. Child psychiatry. Child mental health services. Examination. Assessment. Diagnosis.
5. RJ496-A-RJ496.Z Pediatrics. Diseases of children. Diseases of the nervous system. By disease, A-Z.

Figure 3. A sample result from a self-match experiment.

Table 3 is a summary of the results from the self-match test on all three databases. The difference in first-ranked self-matches between the baseline and the database with filtered WorldCat terms is over 22%. This difference suggests that subject headings from an external source can be used to define distinct concepts, and are, perhaps, necessary for converting the LCC into a knowledge base for a useful automatic classification system. However, the results from the database with the unfiltered WorldCat headings suggest that the headings must be properly processed because they can also introduce noise that severely degrades performance.

	Database:	Baseline	with WorldCat headings	with Filtered WorldCat headings
Rank:	1	4325 (68.5%)	1725 (27.3%)	5755 (91.1%)
	2	910 (14.4%)	1659 (26.3%)	161 (2.50%)
	3	246 (3.89%)	1243 (19.7%)	24 (0.38%)
	4	137 (2.17%)	817 (12.9%)	19 (0.30%)
	5	71 (1.12%)	277 (4.38%)	12 (0.19%)

Table 3. The top five results for the self-match test on three databases.

4. Future work

The system we have described uses a library classification scheme, the Library of Congress Classification, to classify full-text documents automatically. Our experiments to date have focused on adaptations and enhancements that are possible with a set of subject headings and class assignments produced by cataloguers who create bibliographic records, but the same model is extensible, in principle, to terminology that has been automatically extracted from documents that have been automatically classified. Depending on the application, resources that are successfully mapped to a record such as the one shown in Figure 1 may or may not be considered fully classified. If the goal is a collection of high-quality bibliographic records, an automatic classification that results in an assignment to a range of LCC class numbers would probably have to be made more specific with a human-mediated process. But if the goal is subject access to a collection of resources where none existed before, the links to well-established subject hierarchies and subject headings made possible by an automatic classifier based on the LCC may be valuable raw material for a resource that facilitates searching and browsing by subject.

Our project Web page[5] can be monitored for further progress reports and demonstrations.

References

Chan, L. M. (2000). Exploiting LCSH, LCC and DDC to retrieve networked resources: issues and challenges. In *Bicentennial Conference on Bibliographic Control in the New Millenium, Library of Congress, November 2000.*
http://lcweb.loc.gov/catdir/bibcontrol/chan_paper.html

Dunning, T.(1993). Accurate methods for the statistics of surprise and coincidence, *Computational linguistics*, 19, 61-74.

Larson, R. (1992). Experiments in automatic Library of Congress Classification. *Journal of the American Society for Information Science*, 43, 130-148.

Thompson, R. et al.(1997). Evaluating Dewey concepts as a knowledge base for automatic subject assignment. In *First ACM Digital Libraries Workshop, January 1997.* http://orc.rsch.oclc.org:6109/eval_dc.html

Notes

[1] Accessible at: <http://www.columbia.edu/cu/libraries/digital/>

[2]Accessible at: http://www.public.iastate.edu/~CYBERSTACKS/

[3] Accessible at: http://vlib.org/

[4] Accessible at: <http://orc.rsch.oclc.org:6109/>

[5] Accessible at http://staff.oclc.org/~godby/auto_class/auto.html

The UDC and the World Wide Web

I.C. McIlwaine

Abstract: The paper examines the potentiality of the Universal Decimal Classification as a means for retrieving subjects from the World Wide Web. The analytico-synthetic basis of the scheme provides the facility to link concepts at the input or search stage and to isolate concepts via the notation so as to retrieve the separate parts of a compound subject individually if required. Its notation permits hierarchical searching and overrides the shortcomings of natural language. Recent revisions have been constructed with this purpose in mind, the most recent being for Management. The use of the classification embedded in metadata, as in the GERHARD system or as a basis for subject trees is discussed. Its application as a gazetteer is another Web application to which it is put. The range of up to date editions in many languages and the availability of a Web-based version make its use as a switching language increasingly valuable.

1. Subject retrieval on the Web

The challenge of organizing the chaos we call the World Wide Web is still with us. This conference is an excellent example of the problem. We have been hearing of many attempts to address this challenge which is tackled in two different ways. The most favoured is based on words and relies upon matching terms between questions and potential answers. This can be done using a range of different search engines of greater or less sophistication. The second, less popular, more expensive and certainly more time consuming approach is to use a structure of classification. This has the ability to rise above language since its notation can be used in preference to words, provided that all the synonyms and language terms are present in the classification (or the dictionary fed into the data base to match the terms in the classification's index). It also permits searching on more or less specific concepts automatically, provided it has been properly structured.

All the well tried and tested standard classifications and subject heading lists such as DDC, LC and LCSH have been applied to attempts to resolve the dilemma and the UDC is no different. [1] Its appropriateness for the purpose is due to several reasons. Its analytico-synthetic quality has major attractions because it permits concepts to be linked at will, in much the same way as words are linked when searching. It has a notation which not only reflects hierarchies because it is expressive, but also identifies different types of facet clearly, so there is no danger of confusion. It is not language dependent and editions exist in a number of languages all of comparable size, date and development. It is available in a range of formats ranging from small pocket editions in hard copy to the full text in a Web-based format.[2]

2. Theoretical basis and implementation in revision of UDC

Firstly, the theoretical basis of the classification. In recent years the revision process has been well organized and regular, a great change from the period of c. 1960/90. But, because revision was neglected or extremely slow, and not properly co-ordinated for many years, there is a great deal of leeway still to be made up. This we are slowly trying to do, and as well as updating the scheme we are developing revisions that are totally faceted and fully flexible. It is therefore possible to link related concepts as required without spelling out compounds in the text of the classification. Recent examples of such revisions include Environmental Science, Tourism[3] and Theology as well as the long-running revision of the complex Medicine class. The most recent addition to this array is Management.

3. Management as an example

At the end of the year, when *Extensions and corrections* is published, it will include a totally new classification for Management, placing the subject at 005 right at the beginning of the classification. This seems logical since Management is an activity that can be applied to any topic and therefore should be placed early in the scheme, rather than scattered in 33 and several parts of class 65 as has been the case up to the present. As well as being unsatisfactorily located, it was sorely out of date, and had no provision, for example, for the impact of automation. Its new placing, next to Computer science in 004, makes for a happy correlation of this aspect. A virtually new classification has been drafted, which will include Records Management as well as Management proper, and certain elements of accounting, at present in class 33.

The outline is as follows:

005	Management
005.1	Management theory
005.2	Management agents. Mechanisms. Measures
005.3	Management activities. Including: Organizational behaviour. Management psychology
005.4	Processes in management
005.5	Management operations. Direction.
005.6	Quality management. Total quality management (TQM)
005.7	Organizational management (OM)
005.8	Project management.
005.9	Fields of management,. Including: Office management,. Records management. Plant management. Personnel management.Human resources management

The classification provided is fully faceted, and every number can be coloned to one or more as necessary to express compound concepts, e.g.:

005.52:005.33	Swot analysis
005.52:005.334	Risk analysis
005.54:005.31	Use of OR in implementation studies
005.591.4:005.58	Transfer of power
005.591.4:005.743	Departmentalization
005.742:005.72	Corporate control
005.8:005.574	Negotiation tactics
005.922:005.311	Records surveys
005.961:005.914.3	Outsourcing. Subcontracting
005.962:005.56	Staff supervision

Additionally, any of the common auxiliary tables can, of course, be used , e.g.

005.332.1(047.3)	Mission statements
005.7(084.2)	Organization charts
005.42-024.61	Internal relations in the organization
005.742-057.162:005.25	Responsibilities of executives
005.742-057.177.1	Board chairmen

005.745-021.372	Extraordinary meetings
005.921.1"746"	Permanent retention of records. Archiving
005.4-64-024.61	Internal relations in the organization
005.42-021.473	Dissatisfaction at work
005.81-051	Secretaries. Company secretaries
005.825"746"	Permanent retention of records
005.826(0.034.2)	Preservation of digital documents
005.896(085.2)	Sales catalogues
005.898-051	Public relations specialists

including the linking colon, e.g.:

005.311.11:303.62	Operational research using questionaires.
005.32:331.101.32	Job satisfaction
005.322:316.46	Leadership qualities
005.52:330.133.1	Value analysis
005.521:334.7	Business forecasting
005.7:334.722.24	Organizational management in family-owned companies
005.745:81'253	Simultaneous interpreting at meetings
005.922:025.4	Classification and indexing of records
005.922.52:778.14	Microfilming as a method record preservation
005.936.2:72.011.22	Site layouts
005.94:004.9	Automated knowledge management systems
005.954.6:656.03:336.773	Interest-free loans for season tickets

4. Appropriateness and application of faceted theory to Web environment
Because of the flexible nature of the UDC and the increasing use of facet analysis in the development of revisions, this approach is particularly advantageous for application in a Web environment. It enables diverse concepts to be linked at either the input or the search stage. It does, however, mean that class numbers need to be assigned to items so that they are searchable. Recent revisions such as that for Theology which was the subject of a paper at IFLA in Jerusalem in 2000[4], and the Table of Common Properties implemented last year, together with the new Medicine Class when that is eventually completed are all fully faceted. The same is true for several other parts of the classification. The next big project is to devise a Table of Common Activities (i.e. Processes and Operations), comparable to that for properties, which we shall also place alongside the other common auxiliaries, between Materials –03 and Persons –05, using the base notation –04. This is, is a sense, a fulfilment of the Schema Perrault[5] devised for the classification some 40 years ago.

How to capitalize on this synthetic feature of the classification in a Web environment is more of a problem, but that is in terms of making it better known and generating an understanding of how it can be used. There are two approaches and both have been and are being used. The first is to embed UDC notations in the metadata. There is space, for example, in the provision of the Dublin Core to express subject, and a UDC class mark can be inserted here. A fictitious example is the old Guide to the UDC which, if it were mounted on the Web, could include a description embedded in the metadata. Assuming that it was available in HTML at the address http://www.udcc.org/guide.html, from 1 July 2000, it could be described in this way. The element *Subject* states that the scheme used is UDC and that the classification number assigned to this document content is 025.45UDC (Librarianship - Classification and Indexing - UDC)

```
<HTML>
<HEAD>
...[document TITLE here]...
<META NAME="DC.Date" CONTENT="(SCHEME=ISO8601) 2000-07-22">
<META NAME="DC.Title" CONTENT="Guide to the UDC">
<META NAME="DC.Title" CONTENT="An introductory guide to the use and the
application of the Universal Decimal Classification">
<META NAME="DC.Creator" CONTENT="McIlwaine, I. C.">
<META NAME="DC.Subject.Keywords" CONTENT="UDC">
<META NAME="DC.Subject.Classification" SCHEME="UDC"
CONTENT="025.45UDC">
<META NAME="DC.Description" CONTENT="This publication is intended as a
purely practical aid to those who are studying the UDC or who are using it on a day to
day basis for an information system of some kind and does not attempt to give any
general theoretical background to classification. A glossary has been included in the
guide to provide brief definitions of terms used in the course of the text. >
<META NAME="DC.Publisher" CONTENT="UDC Consortium">
<META NAME="DC.Contributor" CONTENT="Buxton, Andrew">
<META NAME="DC.Date.Available" CONTENT="2000-07-01">
<META NAME="DC.Date.Updated" CONTENT="2000-10-12">
<META NAME="DC.Type" CONTENT="book">
<META NAME="DC.Format" CONTENT="HTML">
<META NAME="DC.Identifier" CONTENT="http://www.udcc.org/guide.htm">
<META NAME="DC.Source" CONTENT="Guide to the Use of UDC">
<META NAME="DC.Source" SCHEME="ISBN "CONTENT="926600703X">
<META NAME="DC.Language" CONTENT="en-uk">
<META NAME="DC.Rights" CONTENT="UDC Consortium, FID">
</HEAD>
<BODY>
...[document body begins]...
</HTML>
```

5. GERHARD as example of application of embedded metadata

This method is used, for example, in the GERHARD system.[6] This is a fully automatic indexing and classification system for the World Wide Web which allows integrated searching and browsing. A database-driven robot collects relevant documents. Automatic classification is based on the UDC authority file taken from the library system of Eidgenössischen Technischen Hochschule (ETH) library in Zurich. This authority file contains 60,000 simple and compound UDC numbers used in the actual collection and forms a reliable controlled vocabulary with substantial literary warrant. A notable feature of this system is that it holds index terms attached to classification numbers in German, English and French.

The first step towards a simplified method of automatic classification was to extract the vocabulary called "UDCZ-Lexicon" from the ETH system. Text which has to be classified (in this case German Web pages harvested into a database), has to undergo a text analysis before the words it contains are matched to UDCZ-lexicon and assigned a notation. Notations

assigned to a particular text undergo clustering and the frequency of their occurrence is weighed and statistically compared with the UDCZ database. The quality and specificity are then checked using special algorithms until the average fourteen per document is reduced to the best six to eight notations (secured by the threshold applied). Finally there is a statistical post-processing in which doublets of documents are weeded by matching the title of the document with those already in the database. Titles are analyzed and matched to the exclusion lists produced to stop the classification of pages such as web server statistics or similar non-relevant documents. The notation gathered from the titles, headings and body of the text are matched and their concordance and precision is further checked through special algorithms.
GERHARD offers the facility both to browse and to search the directory. This feature reveals all the advantages of having classification as a backbone. The number of documents assigned to a certain category is clear as is the number of documents in displayed subcategories. It is easy to move through the hierarchy of categories and the system is user-friendly. At each level it is possible to click on the number of documents available. Within each category documents are ranked according to accuracy. It is currently the most sophisticated application of the UDC system for the purposes of web classification.

6. UDC as basis of Subject Trees
The second approach is to use the scheme as a Subject Tree under which items are listed, in a manner not very different in concept from that used for shelving in libraries. Examples of such usage include

- SOSIG - Social Science Information Gateway (http://sosig.ac.uk)

This is part of the UK Resource Discovery Network. It provides quality selection of resources in the social sciences, including business and law. Over 50,000 social sciences web pages are stored in the database and it is updated regularly

- NISS (National Information on Software and Services) Information Gateway (http://www.niss.ac.uk) UK national information services for the education community. This contains thousands of electronic resources descriptions.

7. Area Table as gazetteer
Another way in which we have found that the classification is being used is as a gazetteer. This year's revisions will include a greatly expanded Area Table for Central and South America, so structured as to assist in its use for this purpose. Therefore, instead of giving the instruction to expand alphabetically, the various constituent elements at sub-state level have been included for individual countries. This will permit searching down to municipality, parish, county or whatever subdivision is appropriate, with the names both of the subdivision and the principal town enumerated under the appropriate state. We have likewise expanded the physiographic regions to permit the expression of, for example, the mountain ranges and rivers of the continent in detail comparable to that provided for Europe, which has not been the case formerly. The following demonstrates how this is being done:

(72)	Mexico. United States of Mexico
(721)	Northern states
(721.1)	Tamaulipas. Including: Ciudad Victoria (state capital, municipality and municipal capital). Ocampo (municipality), Ciudad Ocampo (municipal capital). Matamoros (municipality and municipal capital). Nuevo Laredo (municipality and municipal capital). Guerrero (municipality), Nueva Ciudad Guerro (municipal capital). Reynosa (municipality and

municipal capital).Tampico (municipality and municipal capital). Barras Soto la Marina, Los Americanos

(721.2) Nuevo León. Including: Monterrey (state capital, municipality and municipal capital). Agualeguas (municipality and municipal capital). Galeana (municipality and municipal capital). Garza Garcia (municipality and municipal capital). Linares (municipality and municipal capital). Santa Catarina (municipality and municipal capital)

(721.3) Coahuila de Zaragoza. Including: Saltillo (state capital, municipality and municipal capital). Acuña (municipality and municipal capital). Arteaga (municipality and municipal capital). Cuatrocienegas (municipality), Cuatrocienegas de Carranza (municipal capital). Monclova (municipality and municipal capital). Muzquiz (municipality), Cuidad Melchor Muzquiz (municipal capital). Parras (municipality), Parras de la Fuente (municipal capital). Piedras Negras (municipality and municipal capital). Ramos Arizpe (municipality and municipal capital). Sabinas (municipality and municipal capital). Torreon (municipality and municipal capital)

(721.4) Chihuahua. Including: Chihuahua (state capital, municipality and municipal capital). Batopilas (municipality and municipal capital). Cuidad Juarez (municipality and municipal capital). Coyame (municipality), Santiago de Coyame (municipal capital). Cuauhtemoc (municipality and municipal capital). Hidalgo del Parral (municipality and municipal capital). Jimenez (municipality), Jose Mariano Jiminez (municipal capital). Casas Grandes (Paquimé) (ancient site)

Here, each major region is identified individually by its own piece of notation, but the smaller areas within it are listed in alphabetical order, thereby making it very easy to locate a quite small place within its correct region. By spelling out the names, rather than simply providing the instruction to subdivide alphabetically the classifier and the searcher is able to get a precise location for the place being sought, rather than a haphazard guess based on the alphabet.

8. Multilingual availability as basis of switching language

Both this facility and the provision of access to GERHARD via French, English or German, demonstrate the advantage of the UDC as a tool that can be used as a switching device. The production of the classification in a form that enables this facility is something that the UDC has very much to the fore in its planning at the present time. This year the British Standards Institution issued a Web based version of the scheme.[7] Closely linked to this product is the production by the Consortium of a multilingual version of the scheme, again either Web-based or possibly on CD-ROM. There is already a Czech-English CD-ROM and various other publishers, such as Russia, Japan and Spain have produced or are in the process of producing CD-ROM versions. In the first instance, this may well be of a small size, similar to the English Pocket Edition, since there are recent or new editions of a similar size now available in French, German, Spanish, Dutch and English all in machine-readable form, which could be used as a starting point for such a product. If the Consortium were to publish this it would be the first time that they have corporately published the classification in any form or language, since to date they have simply issued the Master File under licence, so it would be a great step forward.

References

[1] The DESIRE project includes a survey of the use of universal classifications and subject headings on the Web. http://www.desire.org/

[2] A list of recent editions and availability can be found on the UDCC website http://www.udcc.org/

[3] McIlwaine, I.C. (2000). Interdisciplinarity: a new retrieval problem? In *Dynamism and stability in knowledge organization: proceedings of the 6th International ISKO Conference, Toronto, Canada, 2000*; ed. by C. Beghtol et al. Würzburg: ERGON. Pp 261-267.

[4] Broughton, V. (2000) . A new classification for the literature of religion, *International cataloguing and bibliographic control* 29, 59-61.

[5]Perrault, J. M. (1965) Categories and relators: a new schema for the replacement of the non-significant symbol, the colon, in the UDC by a letter code, *Revue internationale de la documentation,* 32, 136-144. Reprinted *Knowledge organization,* 21,1994, 189-198.

[6] http://www.gerhard.de

[7] Test version available at http://udc-online.com

Towards DDC-Classified Displays of NetFirst Search Results

Diane Vizine-Goetz and Roger Thompson

Abstract. To determine the potential benefits of providing classified displays of search results, we analyzed the classification features of the OCLC NetFirst database using criteria developed by the Subject Analysis Committee (SAC) subcommittee on Metadata and Classification. We also studied NetFirst search logs to better understand how the classification-based searching and limiting functions implemented in the system are being used. Our findings suggest that to increase the use of classification-based features in systems for general users, classificatory functions must be well integrated with the basic search and display functions.

1. Background

Previous research has shown that users of category displays analyze search results more quickly than users of list displays (Dumais, Cutrell, and Chen, 2000). We will perform users' tests to determine if these findings are also true for the NetFirst database, which contains records that have been assigned one or more Dewey classes. We are developing a prototype to study user preferences and performance for two styles of results display: a list display, the style currently used for NetFirst search results, and an experimental category display, which presents search results ordered by high-level Dewey classes. Prior to developing the prototype, we analyzed the NetFirst service to assess how well classification functions were implemented and used in the existing system. The results of that analysis are presented in this paper.

2. Evaluating classification functions

The ALCTS SAC Subcommittee on Metadata and Classification (1999), charged with studying the application of classificatory frameworks to digital resources, identified seven functions for evaluating the use of classification in the Web environment. These functions are: 1) browsing, 2) hierarchical movement, 3) identification, 4) retrieval, 5) limiting and partitioning, 6) profiling and 7) location. The subcommittee further characterized the functions as core, useful, advanced and outmoded. Browsing by category and hierarchical movement were considered to be core functions that should be present in systems that provide access to substantial collections of classified resources. Display of captions (identification) in metadata records and in browsing structures was considered to be very useful and a highly desirable feature in systems employing classification. Searching and retrieval by class numbers, limiting searches to given classes or categories, and profiling or characterizing search results by class or category were designated as advanced functions that are desirable but not required. The only function considered to be not relevant was the use of classification to locate or "get" a resource. In the Web environment the URL performs this function. Although many of these functions appear to be "common sense" uses of classification, few systems implement all of them.

3. Classification features in the OCLC NetFirst database

To assess the potential benefits of providing classified displays of search results in NetFirst, we performed two evaluations of the existing system. First, we evaluated the OCLC NetFirst service using the criteria identified by the SAC Metadata and Classification subcommittee. Then we studied NetFirst search logs to better understand how the classification-based searching and limiting functions implemented in the system are being used.

We found that the NetFirst service does not employ the core functions of browsing by category and hierarchical navigation of classes; however, several of the other features were present (see Table 1). Dewey Decimal Classification (DDC) numbers are displayed in all records, as are high-level Dewey captions. Searching by class number is supported and searches can be limited to a given DDC main class, division, or section in the advanced and expert search modes. In addition to these classification-oriented features, the service also provides several generic features for sorting and limiting search results.

SAC Classification Features	Feature in NetFirst	Comments
1. Browse	-	-
2. Hierarchical movement	-	-
3. Identification (captions displayed)	+	All records contain class number and captions
4. Retrieval (search on class number)	+	Rarely used feature
5. Limiting (by class)	+	Rarely used feature
6. Profiling (overview by main class, subclass)	-	-
7. Location		All records contain URIs

Table 1. Classification Features in the NetFirst Database

We then analyzed NetFirst search logs to determine how frequently classification-based features are used. To our surprise, we found that they were used very rarely. Only one class number search term was found among 40,000 search terms analyzed. We also found that few searches, 34, were limited by DDC main class and none by subclass. Keyword search terms were the most common type, which is not surprising since keyword searching is the default search type. Title searches were a distant second, followed by subject searches. It is not clear why NetFirst's classification features are used so infrequently, although the corresponding low use of the other search types suggests that users prefer simple Web-like keyword searching and do not want to bother with more complicated search features.

These findings suggest that to increase the use of classification-based features in systems for general users, classificatory functions must be well integrated with the basic search and display functions. In the following example, we show how this might be done in NetFirst using the system's existing indexing and retrieval capabilities. As previously noted, NetFirst records contain high-level DDC captions for the class numbers assigned to the records. For example, a record assigned DDC number 970.00497 (American native peoples) will contain the caption, *General history of North America*, which corresponds to the first three digits of the DDC number. These captions are routinely searched when a keyword search is performed in the system, making it feasible to re-present the results for the keyword search "america" as shown in the proposed display in figure 1.

Current display:

Results for: kw: america. **Records found:** **4999**

Proposed display

Results for : kw: america. **Records found:** **4999**

Results for DDC subjects		
General history of North America	**Records found:**	**1138**
General history of South America	**Records found:**	**160**
Geography of and travel in...	**Records found:**	**76**
Geography of and travel in North America	**Records found:**	**9**
History of Middle America; Mexico	**Records found:**	**265**
General statistics of North America	**Records found:**	**1**
Geography of and travel in South America	**Records found:**	**1**

Figure 1. Current and Proposed Results Set Summary Displays

The proposed display categorizes the results set by grouping records by high-level Dewey classes that contain the search term in the caption field. A user would select one of the categories to view the results set. An alternative would be to present brief records within the context of the category (figure 2). An approach such as this produced the best performance in experiments conducted by Dumais and her colleagues.

Results for : kw: america. **Records found:** **4999**

1. Sukkot
2. Anasazi Theme Page
3. Nomina Insecta Nearctica: A Checklist of the Insects of North America
4. Lesson Plan: Button Blankets: Life in an Eskimo Village
5. Native Americans: Children's Literature

Next>

Results for DDC subjects

General history of North America **Records found:** **1138**

1. Anasazi Theme Page
2. Lesson Plan: Button Blankets: Life in an Eskimo Village
3. Native Americans: Children's Literature
4. Multidisciplinary Lesson Plans: Thanksgiving
5. Omaha Indian Music

Next>

General history of South America **Records found:** **160**

1. Latino/Hispanic Americans: Children's Literature
2. Latin American and South American History and Studies
3. Latino Virtual Gallery
4. Roots of American Culture
5. Selecting Hispanic Books: Hispanic Bibliography: Central and South America: Hispanic Americans

Figure 2. Proposed Results with Titles

4. Search Term Analysis

In addition to analyzing NetFirst system features and search types, we manually searched the NetFirst database for 100 keyword search terms from the log file. Of the 100 search terms analyzed, 43 resulted in zero hits. 39 search terms retrieved from 1 to 16 records and 19 terms retrieved from 30 to 19,267 records. For search terms retrieving from 1 to 16 records, we assumed that users could scan the 1 or 2 pages of search results and would not benefit from additional classificatory features. For the remaining search terms, we again searched the NetFirst database limiting each by the following DDC classes:

- 000 Computers, information, & general reference
- 100 Philosophy & psychology
- 200 Religion
- 300 Social sciences
- 400 Language
- 500 Science
- 600 Technology
- 700 Arts & recreation
- 800 Literature
- 900 History & geography.

The results are shown in Table 2. Because Internet resources described in NetFirst are generally assigned multiple class numbers, the number of records falling into each DDC class is reported in percentages rather than the raw numbers of records. For several of the search terms, a high percentage of the records retrieved cluster in one or two DDC main classes, e.g., 53.8 % of records containing the term "welfare" have been assigned one or more DDC numbers from the 300 *Social sciences* class. Likewise, 55% of the records with the term "volcanoes" contain DDC numbers from the 500 *Science* class. Some of the other terms show a more even distribution across DDC classes, but the intermediate sets can still be quite large, e.g., "aids and resources" limited by the 500 *Science* class still retrieves more than 500 records. Although these findings indicate that deeper level breakdowns are needed to facilitate more effective processing of large results sets, it still may be worthwhile to characterize a set by main class. High-level characterization by main class could be very useful for giving context to the retrieved set and encourage search refinement. In figure 3 we show the results set for the keyword search "wind" characterized by DDC main class.

5. Conclusion

In our effort to determine the potential benefits of providing additional classificatory features for NetFirst records, we analyzed the classification functions of the system, examined search logs, and studied individual queries. We found that NetFirst lacks the core classification functions of browsing and hierarchical navigation, but that the searching and limiting functions are competently implemented although rarely used. The inclusion of class numbers and high-level captions in all records present opportunities for experimenting with classified results displays. Such displays have great potential for improving the analysis of results sets; however, given the low use of existing classification features, new features must be well integrated with the basic search and display functions if they are to be used.

Computers, information, & general reference (not available)
Philosophy & psychology (0)
Religion (2)

1. Inherit the Wind
2. Rainbow Wind

Social sciences (110)

1. Windmills: For Stock and Domestic Water Supplies
2. Historic Brass Society (HBS)
3. Victorian Recorder Guild

Language (Records found 2)
1. Wind in the Willows
2. Anonymous Poetry From the Old English Verse 1900

Science (Records found: 101)
1. Marshall Solar Physics
2. WebQuest: Energy
3. Testing a Windmill Generator

Technology (42 records)
1. Planting Trees
2. Roping the Texas Breezes
3. Renewable Energy Resources for Texas

Arts & recreation (151 records)
1. Canberra Recorder and Early Music Society
2. American Recorder Teachers Association (ARTA)
3. Society of Recorder Players (NZ) Inc

Literature (24 records)
1. George Macdonald
2. Rachel Carson (1907-1964)
3. Wind in the Willows

History & geography (13 records)
1. George Macdonald
2. Kokopelli Flutes
3. High Spirits Flutes

Figure 3. DDC-Classified Results Set

Query	Hits	000	100	200	300	400	500	600	700	800	900
Activities	19267	14.5	1.4	1.1	46.0	2.6	10.9	8.9	5.1	2.7	6.7
Welfare	10889	18.5	2.0	1.2	53.8	0.2	2.9	16.0	2.1	0.9	2.3
America	4999	17.9	0.7	3.2	30.7	1.1	5.4	6.7	6.1	3.5	24.7
AIDS and resources	1495	20.2	1.2	0.6	35.0	4.1	14.7	6.7	2.8	7.1	7.5
wind	320	16.3	0.0	0.4	20.8	0.4	19.1	7.9	28.5	4.3	2.3
water and quality	319	24.1	0.0	0.0	46.4	0.0	14.2	14.3	0.0	0.3	0.7
adoption	246	24.4	6.2	0.2	42.7	0.0	8.1	12.1	3.0	1.5	1.7
African and music	245	13.9	0.0	1.0	25.4	0.2	0.0	1.5	50.4	2.4	5.1
Volcanoes	240	16.5	0.2	0.0	17.4	0.2	55.0	1.9	2.3	0.7	5.8
Yahoo	162	45.1	0.0	0.4	37.4	0.0	1.3	8.5	5.5	0.4	1.3
Whales	147	14.8	2.1	0.0	23.3	1.1	48.4	2.1	3.5	2.8	1.8
1984	145	19.9	1.6	3.3	24.4	0.0	8.5	7.7	11.4	12.2	11.0
working and knowledge	134	40.5	1.4	0.7	32.5	0.7	10.7	10.4	0.3	1.0	1.7
world and trade and organization	84	29.5	0.0	0.0	50.0	0.0	1.2	16.9	1.2	0.6	0.6
Violence and Media	76	45.7	0.0	1.3	45.7	0.7	0.0	2.6	2.0	0.7	1.3
adolf and hitler	69	16.8	1.3	1.9	32.9	0.0	0.0	2.6	1.9	3.9	38.7
working with the and children	62	27.6	1.7	0.0	50.9	0.0	1.7	10.3	4.3	0.9	2.6
volunteer and fire and departments	32	2.8	0.0	0.0	88.9	0.0	0.0	8.3	0.0	0.0	0.0
vision and 21	30	42.9	0.0	0.0	41.4	0.0	1.4	14.3	0.0	0.0	0.0

Table 2. Large results sets by DDC Main Classes

Endnotes

References

Dumais, S. T. et al. (2000). Classified displays of web search results. Invited presentation at ASIS&T SIG/CR Classification Research Workshop, Nov 12, 2000. http://uma.info-science.uiowa.edu/sigcr/papers/sigcr00dumais.doc

ALCTS CCS SAC Metadata and Classification. (1999). SAC Subcommittee on Metadata and Classification, Final Report, ALA Annual Conference 1999. http://www.ala.org/alcts/organization/ccs/sac/metaclassfinal.pdf

LIST OF PARTICIPANTS

Beall, Julianne	Assistant Editor, DDC, Library of Congress, Washington DC, USA beallj@oclc.org
Bean, Carol	Program Officer, NIH, National Library of Medicine, Bethesda, USA beanc@mail.nlm.nih.gov
Beghtol, Clare	Associate Professor, Faculty of Information Studies, University of Toronto, Toronto, Canada beghtol@fis.utoronto.ca
Bresar, Tadeja	Head of Shared Cataloguing, IZUM, Maribor, Slovenia tedaja.bresar@izum.si
Burke, Mary	Professor, Department of Library & Information Studies, University College Dublin, Dublin, Ireland mary.burke@ucd.ie
Chan, Lois May	Professor, School of Library & Information Studies, University of Kentucky, Lexington, USA loischan@uky.edu
Chen, Jiangpeng	Ph.D. Student, Syracuse University, Syracuse, USA jchen06@syr.edu
Chen, Pingyan	Deputy Research Librarian, Tianjin Library, Tianjin, China chenpy@mail.zlnet.com.ca
Chipman, Alison	Editor, Getty Research Institute, Los Angeles, USA achipman@getty.edu
Connell, Tschera	Associate Professor, Serials Coordinator, Ohio State University Libraries, Columbus, USA connell.17@osu.edu
Connolly, Laura	Library Cataloger, Hanford Technical Library, Batelle-Pacific NW National Library, Richland, USA laura.connolly@pnl.gov
Cordeiro, Maria Inez	Information Systems Manager, Biblioteca de Arte, Fundação Calouste Gulbenkian, Lisbon, Portugal ilopes@gulbenkian.pt
Crawford, Josephine	Head of Information Systems, Biomedical Library, University of Minnesota, Minneapolis, USA jocraw@umn.edu
Day, Michael	Research Officer, U.K. Office for Library & Information Networking University of Bath, Bath, UK m.day@ukoln.ac.uk
Dempsey, Lorcan	Vice President, Office of Research, OCLC, Dublin, USA dempseyl@oclc.org

Devadason, Francis — Director, Library, Asian Institute of Technology, Bangkok, Thailand
devdsn@ait.ac.th

Donovan, Maureen — Japanese Studies Librarian, Ohio State University Libraries, Columbus, USA
donovan.1@osu.edu

Dzierba, Judith — Cataloging/Archives Manager, Rush-Presbyterian St. Luke's Medical Center, Rush University, Chicago, USA
jdzierba@rushu.rush.edu

El-Hoshy, Lynn — Senior Cataloging Policy Specialist, Library of Congress, Washington, DC, USA
lelh@loc.gov

Ericson, Edith — Clinton, USA
eericson37@home.com

Evans, Lucy — Cataloguing Manager, British Library, Boston Spa, Wetherby, UK
lucy.evans@bl.uk

Farris, David — Standards Librarian, National Library of Canada, Ottawa, Canada
david.farris@nlc-bnc.ca

Flemming, Christina — Librarian, Vasa Research Library, Finnish-Swedish Library Association, Vasa, Finland
christina.flemming@abo.fi

Fletcher, Jain — Head, Cataloging Division, Special Collections, Young Research Library, UCLA, Los Angeles, USA
jfletchr@library.ucla.edu

Garrison, William — Head, Cataloging Department, University of Colorado at Boulder, Boulder, USA
garrisow@spot.colorado.edu

Geisselmann, Friedrich — Librarian, Universitäts-Bibliothek, Regensburg, Germany
Friedrich.Geisselmann@bibliothek.uni-regensburg.de

Godby, Jean — Senior Research Specialist, Office of Research, OCLC, Dublin, USA
godby@oclc.org

Green, Rebecca — Associate Professor, College of Information Studies, University of Maryland, College Park, USA
rgreen@umd5.umd.edu

Greever, Karen — Technical Services Librarian, Kenyon College, Gambier, USA
greeverk@kenyon.edu

Hedberg, Sten — Associate Director, Library, Uppsala University, Uppsala, Sweden
sten.hedberg@ub.uu.se

Hickey, Thom — Chief Scientist, Office of Research, OCLC, Dublin, USA
hickey@oclc.org

Hjartarson, Fay	Government Information Holdings Officer, National Library of Canada, Ottawa, Canada fay.hjartarson@nlc-bnc.ca
Hoffman, Shannon	Subject Authorities Librarian, Lee Library, Brigham Young University, Provo, USA shannon.hoffman@byu.edu
Holley, Robert	Professor, Library & Information Science Program, Wayne State University, Detroit, USA aa3805@wayne.edu
Holt, Mary	Monographs Librarian, Rudolph Matas Medical Library, Tulane University Health Sciences Center, New Orleans, USA maryholt@tulane.edu
Houghton, Andy	Senior Consulting Systems Analyst, Office of Research, OCLC, Dublin, USA houghton@oclc.org
Hudon, Michele	Assistant Professor, École de bibliothéconomie et des sciences de l'information, University of Montreal, Montreal, Canada michele.hudon@umontreal.ca
Hunt, Stuart	Senior Product Specialist, OCLC Europe, the Middle East & Africa, Birmingham, UK hunts@oclc.org
Jul, Erik	Executive Director, OCLC Institute, Dublin, USA jul@oclc.org
Koch, Traugott	Senior Librarian, Digital Library Specialist, Netlab, Lund University Libraries, Lund, Sweden traugott.koch@ub2.lu.se
Kuhr, Patricia	Editor, H.W. Wilson Company, New York, USA pkuhr@hwwilson.com
Kumbar, Tukaram	Visiting Scholar, Office of Research, OCLC, Dublin, USA kumbart@oclc.org
Landry, Patrice	Head, Subject Indexing, Swiss National Library, Bern, Switzerland patrice.landry@slb.admin.ch
Larsson, Ingrid	Systems Librarian, Stockholm School of Economics, Stockholm, Sweden ingrid.larsson@hhs.se
Lawson, Dawn	Senior Electronic Products Manager, Forest Press, OCLC, Dublin, USA lawsond@oclc.org
Leth, Pia	Senior Librarian, Royal Library, Stockholm, Sweden pia.leth@kb.se
Martin, Giles	Assistant Editor, DDC, Forest Press, OCLC, Dublin, USA marting@oclc.org

McCallum, Sally — Chief, Network Development & MARC Standards, Library of Congress, Washington DC, USA
smcc@loc.gov

McGarry, Dorothy — UCLA, Los Angeles, USA
dmcgarry@library.ucla.edu

McIlwaine, Ia — Professor, School of Library, Archive & Information Studies, University College London, London, UK
i.mcilwaine@ucl.ac.uk

McKiernan, Gerry — Science & Technology Librarian, Parks Library, Iowa State University, Ames, USA
gerrymck@iastate.edu

Mitchell, Joan — Executive Director & Editor-in-Chief, Forest Press, OCLC, Dublin, USA
mitchelj@oclc.org

Moren, Tony — Chief, Information Management, Library & Information Center, Statistics Canada, Ottawa, Canada
moreton@statcan.ca

Naudi, Max — Conservateur, Bibliothèque nationale de France, Paris, France
max.naudi@bnf.fr

Neff, Patricia — Senior Systems Analyst, LexisNexis, Centerville, USA
patricia.neff@lexisnexis.com

Neuroth, Heike — Dep.SSG-FI, Lower Saxony State & University Library, Goettingen, Germany.
neuroth@mail.sub.uni-goettingen.de

Normore, Lorraine — Research Scientist, Office of Research, OCLC, Dublin, USA
normore@oclc.org

Olson, Hope — Associate Professor, School of Library & Information Studies, University of Alberta, Edmonton, Canada
hope.olson@ualberta.ca

Olson, Tony — Head of Technical Services, Galter Health Sciences Library, Northwestern University, Chicago, USA
ajolson@northwestern.edu

O'Neill, Edward — Consulting Research Scientist, OCLC, Dublin, USA
oneill@oclc.org

Orser, Lawan — Associate Librarian, George A. Smathers Library, University of Florida, Gainsville, USA
lvo@ufl.edu

Paradis, Carole — Library Technician, Library & Information Centre, Statistics Canada, Ottawa, Canada
paracar@statcan.ca

Prabha, Chandra	Senior Research Scientist, Office of Research, OCLC, Dublin, USA prabha@oclc.org
Qin, Jian	Assistant Professor, School of Information Studies, Syracuse University, Syracuse, USA jqin@syr.edu
Riesthuis, Gerhard	Leerstoelgroep Archief-, Boek- en Informatiewetenschap, University of Amsterdam, Amsterdam, Netherlands gerhard.riesthuis@hum.uva.nl
Roe, Sandy	Cataloging Librarian, Memorial Library, Minnesota State University, Mankato, USA sandra.roe@mnsu.edu
Seljak, Marta	Assistant Director, IZUM, Maribor, Slovenia marta.seljak@izum.si
Slavic, Aida	Researcher, Library & Information Technology Centre, South Bank University, London, UK slavica@sbu.ac.uk
Spies, Phyllis	Vice President, Worldwide Services, OCLC, Dublin, USA spies@oclc.org
Stapel, Johan	Consultant Electronic User Services, Koninklijke Bibliotheek, The Hague, Netherlands johan.stapel@kb.nl
Sutton, Stuart	Syracuse University, Syracuse, USA sasutton@u.washington.edu
Swanson, Edward	Coordinator, MINITEX, Saint Paul, USA eswanson@qwest.net
Treuernicht, Marcia	Head of Cataloging/Serials, Wallace Library, Rochester Institute of Technology, Rochester, USA mstwml@rit.edu
Vizine-Goetz, Diane	Research Scientist, Office of Research, OCLC, Dublin, USA vizine@oclc.org
Wake, Susannah	HILT Research Assistant, Centre for Digital Library Research, Andersonian Library, University of Strathclyde, Glasgow, UK susannah.wake@strath.ac.uk
Walther, Frederic	Subject Indexing Coordinator, SEBIB, University of Geneva, Geneva, Switzerland frederic.walther@adm.unige.ch
Willey, Kayla	Metadata Cataloger, Lee Library, Brigham Young University, Provo, USA kayla.willey@byu.edu

Williamson, Nancy
Professor, Faculty of Information Studies, University of Toronto, Toronto, Canada
william@fis.utoronto.ca

Witt, Maria
Head of Catalogues, Médiathèque, Cité des Sciences et de l'Industrie, Paris, France
m.witt@cite-sciences.fr

Yarborough, Margaretta
Head, Cataloging Department, Academic Affairs Library, University of North Carolina, Chapel Hill, USA
mjy@unc.edu

Zeng, Marcia
Associate Professor, School of Library & Information Studies, Kent State University, Kent, USA
mzeng@kent.edu

INDEX

Note. Since such terms as Internet, Metadata, Networked environment, World Wide Web are pervasive of virtually all papers, they have not been indexed. Products of OCLC such as WebDewey, CORC, SiteSearch, Scorpion are all indexed directly under acronym, not under OCLC

Printed and bound by CPI Group (UK) Ltd, Croydon, CR0 4YY
13/09/2026
14960852-0002